Objectivity and the Rule of Law

What is objectivity? What is the rule of law? Are the operations of legal systems objective? If so, in what ways and to what degrees are they objective? Does anything of importance depend on the objectivity of law? These are some of the principal questions addressed by Matthew H. Kramer in this lucid and wide-ranging study that introduces readers to vital areas of philosophical enquiry. As Kramer shows, objectivity and the rule of law are complicated phenomena, each comprising a number of distinct but overlapping dimensions. Although the connections between objectivity and the rule of law are intimate, they are also densely multifaceted.

Matthew H. Kramer is Professor of Legal and Political Philosophy at Cambridge University; Fellow of Churchill College, Cambridge; and Director of the Cambridge Forum for Legal and Political Philosophy. He is the author of ten previous books, most recently *The Quality of Freedom* and *Where Law and Morality Meet*, and he is the Legal Philosophy Editor for the *Routledge Encyclopedia of Philosophy* (online edition).

Cambridge Introductions to Philosophy and Law

Series Editor: William Edmundson

This introductory series of books provides concise studies of the philosophical foundations of law, on perennial topics in the philosophy of law, and of important and opposing schools of thought. The series is aimed principally at students in philosophy, law, and political science.

Objectivity and the Rule of Law

MATTHEW H. KRAMER

Cambridge University

CAMBRIDGE
UNIVERSITY PRESS

CAMBRIDGE UNIVERSITY PRESS
Cambridge, New York, Melbourne, Madrid, Cape Town, Singapore, São Paulo

Cambridge University Press
32 Avenue of the Americas, New York, NY 10013-2473, USA

www.cambridge.org
Information on this title: www.cambridge.org/9780521854160

First published 2007

Printed in the United States of America

A catalog record for this publication is available from the British Library.

Library of Congress Cataloging in Publication Data

Kramer, Matthew H., 1959–
Objectivity and the rule of law / Matthew H. Kramer.
p.   cm.
Includes bibliographical references and index.
ISBN 978-0-521-85416-0 (hardback) – ISBN 978-0-521-67010-4 (pbk.)
1. Law and ethics.   2. Objectivity.
3. Rule of law – Moral and ethical aspects.   I. Title
K247.6.K72   2007
340′.11–dc22   2006038560

ISBN   978-0-521-85416-0 hardback
ISBN   978-0-521-67010-4 paperback

To my four brothers: Steven, AJ, Mark, and David

Contents

Preface

While I have endeavored in this book to make an original contribution to the debates surrounding the matters which I discuss, I have likewise striven to provide an accessible overview of those matters. Though I have not altogether eschewed the technical terminology of philosophy – since that terminology is often crucial for the distillation of complex ideas and for the avoidance of cumbersome prose – I have sought to explain each technical term or phrase whenever it first appears (and occasionally also thereafter). Similarly, although I have not dispensed with footnotes completely, I have kept them to a minimum. The ideas presented in this book are sometimes complicated, but I have done my best to articulate them clearly for a wide audience.

As will become apparent in my opening chapter, objectivity is a multifaceted phenomenon. In connection with law, and also in connection with most other domains of human thought and activity, the notion of objectivity gets invoked in quite a few distinct senses. Nonetheless, despite the complex variegatedness of that notion, it partakes of a certain overarching unity. Specifically, each of the dimensions of objectivity is defined in opposition to a corresponding dimension of subjectivity. Legal objectivity, in its manifold aspects, is what marks the divide between the rule of law and the rule of men.

Because of the constraints on the length of each volume in the Introductions to Philosophy and Law series, I have had to forbear from exploring several important topics that would need to be pondered in any full treatment of the objectivity of law. Among the matters left uninvestigated is the fact that most legal systems involve multiple tiers of decision-making; the determinations reached by some officials are subordinate to those reached by higher-ranking officials. That hierarchical structure of adjudicative and administrative authority gives rise to some challenging problems for any analysis that ascribes objectivity to the workings of a legal system. Those problems have not been broached within the confines of the present volume, but I will be addressing them in some of my future writings. (A few of those problems are addressed in the fourth chapter of Kramer 2004a.) Two other important issues omitted from the scope of this book are the fact that many transgressions of legal requirements go undetected and the fact that the perpetrators of many detected transgressions go unidentified and unapprehended. Had I had sufficient space, I would have treated those issues – concerning the limits on the ability of legal-governmental officials to give effect to the mandates of their regime – in the course of my opening chapter's reflections on the discretion exercised by officials in their responses to detected illegalities. (In Kramer 2001, 65–73, I have grappled with some of the theoretical difficulties posed by the occurrence of undescried violations of legal requirements. Several of those difficulties and a number of related problems are illuminatingly discussed in Reiff 2005.)

Still, notwithstanding that the restrictions on the length of this book have obliged me to pass over the topics just mentioned and some other pertinent topics, the present volume provides a compendium of the main elements of the two phenomena encapsulated in its title. It probes many, though inevitably not all, of the intricacies in those elements. In so doing, it aims to reveal the intimacy of the connections between objectivity and the rule of law; and, more broadly, it aims to reveal the depth and fascination of the philosophical cruxes to which those connections give rise.

This book was written during the first year of my Leverhulme Trust Major Research Fellowship. I am very grateful indeed to the Leverhulme Trust for its support of my work. I owe thanks to many people who have supplied extremely helpful comments: Richard Bellamy, Boaz Ben-Amitai, Brian Bix, Gerard Bradley, Alex Brown, Ian Carter, Sean Coyle, Daniel Elstein, John Finnis, Stephen Guest, Kenneth Himma, Brian Leiter, George Letsas, Peter Lipton, Mark McBride, Saladin Meckled-Garcia, Riz Mokal, Michael Otsuka, Stephen Perry, Connie Rosati, Gideon Rosen, Steve Smith, and Emmanuel Voyiakis. Richard Bellamy kindly invited me to present an early version of Chapter 1 as a seminar paper at University College London in November 2005. Laura Donohue and Amalia Kessler kindly invited me to deliver a later version of a portion of Chapter 1 as a paper at Stanford University Law School in October 2006, and Joan Berry and Debra Satz kindly invited me to outline the whole of Chapter 1 for the Stanford University Philosophy Department on the same occasion. Special thanks for very valuable comments are due to William Edmundson – the series editor – and to the anonymous readers of my original proposal, whose perceptive observations were especially valuable in the early stages of my writing.

Cambridge, England
June 2006

1

Dimensions of Objectivity

1.1. Brief Preliminary Remarks

No satisfactory account of the relationships between objectivity and the rule of law can begin with the assumption that the nature of objectivity and the nature of the rule of law are transparent and that the only things to be clarified are the relationships between them. What will become apparent in my opening two chapters is that both objectivity and the rule of law are complicatedly multifaceted. To ponder rewardingly how each of them bears on the other, we need to explore the distinct varieties of each of them.

This first chapter will disentangle multiple aspects or dimensions of objectivity, and the next chapter will then differentiate between the rule of law as a morally neutral mode of governance and the Rule of Law as a moral ideal. The final chapter will mull over some of the relationships between the sundry aspects of objectivity and the moral authority of law. (All three chapters will broach numerous relationships between objectivity and the rule of law or the Rule of Law.) My discussions will aim to provide a general overview, rather than an exhaustive account, of some major issues that have preoccupied legal and moral and political philosophers. Though such an overview will inevitably prescind from countless complexities that would receive attention in any comprehensive treatment of the topic, it should suffice to highlight the most important distinctions by reference to which those complexities are to be fathomed.

1.2. Types of Objectivity

Both in ordinary discourse and in philosophical disputation, people tend to invoke the notion of objectivity in a number of diverse forms. To furnish a map of the terrain, this chapter will recount six chief conceptions of objectivity along with a few ancillary conceptions. Although most of the principal facets of objectivity overlap, and although each of them is fully compatible with the others, none of them is completely reducible to any of the others. Three of them are ontological in their orientation, two are epistemic, and one is semantic. That is, three of them bear on the nature and existence of things; two of them bear on the ways in which rational agents form beliefs about those things; and one of them bears on the relationships between those things and the statements that express the agents' beliefs. An adequate explication of the notion of objectivity has to take account of these differences, and likewise has to take account of crucial divisions within some of the distinct aspects of objectivity.

Types of Objectivity

Genus of Objectivity	Species of Objectivity
Ontological	Mind-Independence
	Determinate Correctness
	Uniform Applicability
Epistemic	Transindividual Discernibility
	Impartiality
Semantic	Truth-Aptitude

The several dimensions of objectivity to be expounded here are of great importance well beyond the domain of law. Some of them, indeed, have been investigated much more searchingly in other areas of philosophy than in the philosophy of law, and a couple of the ancillary dimensions (shunted toward the end of the chapter) are only of extremely limited applicability to the substance of legal norms. Nevertheless, each of the six cardinal aspects of objectivity is not only central to many areas of intellectual endeavor but is also of particular prominence in legal thought and discourse. While we shall be considering a wide range of ways in which any field or enquiry or judgment or requirement might be objective, we shall be doing so precisely in order to ascertain the ways in which law is objective. Moreover, we need to discover the respects in which law does not partake of objectivity as well as the respects in which it does.

1.2.1. Objectivity qua Mind-Independence

Every variety of objectivity is opposed to a corresponding variety of subjectivity. Nowhere is that opposition more evident than in connection with objectivity as mind-independence. This first conception of objectivity is perhaps more commonly invoked than any other, both in everyday discourse and in philosophical argumentation. When this conception informs somebody's remarks, a proclamation of the objectivity of some phenomenon is an assertion that the existence and character of that phenomenon are independent of what anyone might think. Within a domain to which such a proclamation applies generally, the facts concerning any particular entity or occurrence do not hinge on anybody's beliefs or perceptions.

For a proper grasp of this first type of objectivity, we need to take note of some salient distinctions. One such distinction lies between (i) the views of separate individuals and (ii) the shared views of individuals who collaborate in a community or in some other sort of collective enterprise.[1] Sometimes when theorists affirm the mind-independence of certain matters, they are simply indicating that the facts of those matters transcend the beliefs or attitudes of any given individual. They mean to

---

[1] Of course, the shared views to which I refer will often not be merely shared. Frequently, a key reason for the holding of those views by each participant is his knowledge that virtually every other participant holds them and expects him to hold them. That complicated interlocking of outlooks among the participants in a collaborative endeavor is not something on which this chapter needs to dwell.

allow that those facts are derivative of the beliefs and attitudes shared by individuals who interact as a group (such as the judges and other legal officials who together conduct the operations of a legal system). These theorists contend that, although no one individual's views are decisive in ordaining what is actually the case about the matters in question, the understandings which individuals share in their interactions as a group are indeed so decisive. Let us designate as "weak mind-independence" the type of objectivity on which these theorists insist when they ascribe a dispositive fact-constituting role to collectivities while denying any such role to separate individuals. That mild species of objectivity is obviously to be contrasted with *strong* mind-independence, which obtains whenever the existence or nature of some phenomenon is ordained neither by the views of any separate individual(s) nor by the common views and convictions that unite individuals as a group. Insofar as strong mind-independence prevails within a domain, a consensus on the bearings of any particular state of affairs in that domain is neither necessary nor sufficient for the actual bearings of the specified state of affairs. How things are is independent of how they are thought to be.

Before we turn to a second major division between types of mind-independence, a brief clarificatory comment is advisable. When some phenomenon is weakly mind-independent, its existence or nature is ordained by the beliefs and attitudes (and resultant patterns of conduct) that are shared among the members of a group. However, the beliefs and attitudes need not be shared among *all* the members of a group. In any large-scale association or community, very few beliefs and convictions will be shared by absolutely everyone. What is typically present in a state of weak mind-independence – a state that is equally well characterized as "weak mind-dependence" – is not some chimerical situation of unanimity, but instead a situation of convergence among *most* of a group's members. Consider, for example, the loosely knit group of competent users of the English language in Canada. If most of those users regard the employment of "ain't" as improper in any formal speaking or writing (except when the term is deliberately wielded for comical effect), and if most of them accordingly eschew the employment of that slang term in formal contexts, then Canadian English includes a weakly mind-independent rule proscribing the employment of "ain't" in formal discourse. Probably, some competent users of the English language in Canada do not eschew "ain't" in formal contexts. Such a fact, if it is a fact, is perfectly compatible with the existence of the aforementioned rule. Indeed, the exact difference between the status of some entity X as a weakly mind-independent phenomenon and the status of some entity Y as a strongly mind-*dependent* phenomenon is that the existence or nature of X (unlike the existence or nature of Y) is not ordained by the outlook of any particular individual. Instead, it is ordained by outlooks and conduct that prevail among most of the members of some group. Typically, convergence among a preponderance of a group's members – which falls short of convergence among all those members – will be sufficient to ground the existence or to establish the nature of some weakly mind-independent phenomenon. Note furthermore that, when there is very little convergence among a group's members on some particular issue, and when the lack of convergence precludes the existence of some weakly mind-independent entity X (such as a linguistic norm that proscribes "ain't" in formal contexts), the weakly mind-independent character of X is evidenced by the very inexistence of such an entity. Precisely because X is weakly mind-independent rather than strongly mind-independent, the meagerness of the convergence among the outlooks of the group's members is something that matters to X's existence.

Now, before we can come to grips with the question whether legal requirements are strongly mind-independent or weakly mind-independent (or neither), we need to attend to another major dichotomy: the dichotomy between existential mind-independence and observational mind-independence.[2] Something is existentially mind-independent if and only if its occurrence or continued existence does not presuppose the existence of some mind(s) and the occurrence of mental activity. Not only are all natural objects mind-independent in this sense, but so too are countless artefacts such as pens and houses. Although those artefacts would never have materialized as such in the absence of minds and mental activity – that is, although in their origins they were existentially mind-dependent – their continued existence does not similarly presuppose the presence of minds and the occurrence of mental activity. A house would persist for a certain time as the material object that it is,

---

[2] For some good, crisp statements of this distinction – which has been drawn in various terms by many writers – see Moore 1992, 2443–44; Svavarsdóttir 2001, 162.

even if every being with a mind were somehow straightaway whisked out of existence.

Something is observationally mind-independent if and only if its nature (comprising its form and substance and its very existence) does not depend on how any observer takes that nature to be. Whereas everything that is existentially mind-independent is also observationally mind-independent, not everything that is observationally mind-independent is existentially mind-independent. Consider, for example, an intentional action. The occurrence of any such action presupposes the existence of a mind in which there arises the intention that animates the occurrence, yet the nature of the action does not hinge on what any observer(s) – including the person who has performed the action – might believe it to be. Even if every observer thinks that the action is of some type X, it may in fact be of some contrary type Y.

Types of Mind-Independence

	Existential	*Observational*
Weak	The occurrence or continued existence of something is not dependent on the mental activity of any particular individual.	The nature of something is not dependent on what it is taken to be by any particular individual.
Strong	The occurrence or continued existence of something is not dependent on the mental functioning of any members of any group individually or collectively.	The nature of something is not dependent on what it is taken to be by the members of any group individually or collectively.

When pondering the mind-independence of laws, then, we should be attuned to both the strong/weak distinction and the existential/observational distinction. A bit of reflection on the matter should reveal that, if the *existential* status of laws is our focus, some laws (most general legal norms) are weakly mind-independent while some other laws (most individualized directives) are not even weakly mind-independent. That most general legal norms are at least weakly mind-independent is quite evident. The existence of those norms does not stand or fall on the basis of each individual's mental activity; it is not the case that multitudinous different sets of general legal norms emerge and vanish as multitudinous different individuals undergo birth and death, or that no legal norms at all exist for anyone who does not give them any thought. Whereas someone's beliefs and fantasies and attitudes and convictions are existentially dependent on the mind of the particular individual who harbors them, the existence of any general legal norm differs in not being radically subjective. (There can be exceptions in rather unusual circumstances. In a monarchical regime, the officials might adhere to a practice whereby some general laws go out of existence whenever the reigning king's mental activity permanently ceases. Such an arrangement would be peculiar, but it would plainly be possible. Still, in a legal system that is to endure beyond a single person's lifetime, the incidence of any such strongly mind-dependent general laws would have to be highly circumscribed.)

When we move away from general laws and concentrate on individualized directives, we seldom find any existential mind-independence. Typically if not always, an order addressed to a particular person – by a judge or some other legal official – will not remain in effect as such if its addressee's mental activity permanently ceases. Any result sought through the issuance of the individualized order will typically have to be achieved through some other means (perhaps through the issuance of a directive to some alternative individual or set of individuals who will act in lieu of the original addressee). To the utmost, then, an individually addressed legal requirement is existentially mind-dependent; its continued existence as a legal requirement presupposes the occurrence of mental activity in a particular person's mind.

By contrast, the continuation of the sway of general legal norms will almost always transcend the mental functioning of any given individual. Even so, the existential mind-independence of such norms is weak rather than strong. They cannot persist in the absence of all minds and mental activity. They abide as legal norms only so long as certain people (most notably, judges and other legal officials) collectively maintain certain attitudes and beliefs concerning them. Unless legal officials converge in being disposed to treat the prevailing laws as authoritative standards by reference to which the juridical consequences of people's conduct can be gauged, those laws will cease to exist. To be sure, some of the general mandates within a legal system – such as ordinances that prohibit jaywalking – can continue to exist as laws even though they are invariably unenforced. The requirements imposed by such mandates are inoperative practically, but they remain legal obligations. However, the very reason why inoperative legal duties continue to exist as legal duties is that myriad other legal obligations are quite regularly given effect through the activities of legal officials, who converge in being disposed to treat those obligations as binding requirements. Only because those manifold other legal requirements are regularly given effect does a legal regime exist as a functional system. In the absence of the regularized effectuation of most mandates and other norms within a system of law, the system and its sundry norms will have gone by the wayside. In sum, the continued existence of laws (including inoperative laws) as laws will depend on the decisions and endeavors of legal officials. Yet, because those decisions and endeavors inevitably involve the beliefs and attitudes and dispositions of conscious agents, the continued existence of laws as laws is not strongly mind-independent. The existential mind-independence of general legal norms is only weak.

In what manner are legal norms observationally mind-independent? Are they strongly so or only weakly so? We can know straightaway, in regard to their observational status, that general legal norms are at least weakly mind-independent. After all, as has already been remarked, everything that is existentially mind-independent is also observationally mind-independent. The mental states and events presupposed by the existence of a legal system are those shared by many officials interacting with one another. What those mental states and events are is manifestly independent of what any particular individual thinks that they are. Matters become more intricate, however, when we turn from inquiring whether legal norms are observationally mind-independent to inquiring whether their observational mind-independence is strong or weak. A number of legal philosophers, such as Andrei Marmor, have had no doubt that the observational mind-independence of laws is merely weak. Marmor first notes that, when a concept pertains to something that is strongly mind-independent, "it should be possible to envisage a *whole community of speakers* misidentifying [the concept's] real reference, or extension." He then declares: "With respect to concepts constituted by conventional practices [such as the operations of a legal system], however, such comprehensive mistakes about their reference is implausible. If a given concept is constituted by social conventions, it is impossible for the pertinent community to misidentify its reference." He emphatically proclaims: "There is nothing more we can discover about the content of the [norms of our social practices] than what we already know."[3] Actually, however, things are more complicated than Marmor suggests. His comments are not completely wrong, but they are simplistic. (In the following discussion of the strong observational mind-independence of laws, incidentally, there is no need for me to distinguish between general norms and individualized directives. In each case, the observational mind-independence is always strong.)

On any particular point of law, the whole community of legal officials in some jurisdiction can indeed be mistaken. Legal officials can collectively be in error about the attitudes and beliefs (concerning some point of law) which they themselves share. They can collectively be in error about the substance and implications of those shared beliefs and attitudes, and can therefore collectively be in error about the nature of some legal norm which those beliefs and attitudes sustain. To assume otherwise is to fail to differentiate between (i) their harboring of the first-order attitudes and beliefs and (ii) their second-order understanding of the contents of those first-order mental states. The fact that the officials share certain attitudes and beliefs in regard to the existence and content of some legal norm is what establishes the existence and fixes the content of that norm; but the fact that they share those attitudes and beliefs does not exclude the possibility that they themselves will collectively misunderstand what has been established and fixed by that fact. A gap of misapprehension is always possible between people's first-order beliefs and their second-order beliefs about those beliefs.

Indeed, Marmor's elision of the first-order/second-order distinction will land his analysis in incoherence when it is applied to many credible situations. Suppose that the courts in some jurisdiction declare that their previous interpretation of a particular law was incorrect. They now maintain that that law should have been understood and applied (and will henceforth be understood and applied) in some alternative way. If the members of the judiciary are collectively infallible at the current

---

[3] Marmor 2001, 138, emphasis in original. A complicated variant of Marmor's position underlies the famous discussion in Locke 1975 [1689], book IV, chapter IV. Quite close to Marmor's position, but somewhat milder, is the brief discussion in Greenawalt 1992, 48.

juncture when they pronounce on this matter of legal interpretation, then we have to conclude that they were fallible at the earlier juncture when they espoused the now-disowned reading of the particular law. Conversely, if they were collectively infallible at that earlier juncture, then they are currently mistaken when they deem themselves to have been in error. However Marmor might try to analyze such a situation, he will be led to the conclusion that legal officials have collectively erred about a matter of legal interpretation. His insistence on the officials' collective infallibility will have undermined itself.

The observational mind-independence of legal norms is therefore strong rather than weak. Nevertheless, Marmor is not flatly incorrect. If the legal officials in a jurisdiction do collectively err in their understanding of the substance and implications of some legal norm(s) which their own shared beliefs and attitudes have brought into being, and if they do not correct their misunderstanding, that misunderstanding will thenceforth be determinative of the particular point(s) of law to which it pertains. It will in effect have replaced the erstwhile legal norm(s) with some new legal norm(s). Such an upshot will be especially plain in any areas of a jurisdiction's law covered by Anglo-American doctrines of precedent, but it will ensue in other areas of the law as well. The new legal norm(s) might be only slightly different from the previous one(s) – the differences might lie solely in a few narrow implications of the norm(s) – but there will indeed be some differences, brought about by the legal officials' mistaken construal of the substance and implications of the superseded norm(s). Subsequent judgments by the officials in accordance with the new legal standard(s) will not themselves be erroneous, since they will tally with the law as it exists in the aftermath of the officials' collective misstep. The officials go astray in perceiving the new standard(s) as identical to the former standard(s), but, once their error has brought the new standard(s) into being, they do not thereafter go astray by treating the new standard(s) as binding. (There can be limited exceptions to this general point. If the officials in some legal system adhere to a norm requiring them to undo any mistaken judgment whenever they come to recognize their mistake within a certain period of time, and if they comply with that norm in most circumstances to which it is applicable, then their nonconformity with it in some such set of circumstances would temporarily vitiate the new legal standard that has been engendered by their original misstep.

However, the additional error of nonconformity – if left uncorrected – will itself quickly be absorbed into the workings of the legal system, along with the original misstep, as something that is binding on the officials.)

Of course, a new legal norm engendered by the officials' collective misunderstanding of a preexistent legal norm may itself become subject to misapplication in the future. If it does indeed undergo distortion in that manner, it will have been displaced by some further legal norm that is the product of the distortion. The process through which a collective error on the part of officials will have led to the supersession of some legal standard(s) by some other legal standard(s) is a process that can recur indefinitely. Legal change can occur by many routes, but a succession of errors is one of them.

Thus, although Marmor is incorrect in contending that the observational mind-independence of legal norms is weak rather than strong, his remarks can serve to alert us to the fact that the *existential* mind-independence of those norms is never strong. Legal officials can collectively be wrong about the implications of the laws which their own shared beliefs and attitudes sustain, but their errors (unless subsequently corrected) quickly enter into the contents of those laws and thereby become some of the prevailing standards. Moreover, we should note that – in the remarks quoted above – Marmor does not initially assert that community-wide mistakes about the referential extensions of conventional concepts are impossible. He initially asserts merely that they are implausible. Such an assertion is overstated, but it is not entirely misguided. There is some merit to the thesis that our epistemic access to the products of our own practices is more intimate than our epistemic access to the phenomena of the natural world. Though that thesis should never obscure the possibility of disaccord between people's first-order beliefs and their second-order beliefs about the contents and implications of those first-order beliefs, it aptly suggests that we can sometimes feel greater confidence in our grasp of our own ideas than in our grasp of entities which we have not fashioned. Within limits that prevent it from hardening into a dogma about the incorrigibility of our apprehension of our own practices, a tenet about relative levels of confidence is pertinent. That tenet is particularly cogent in connection with very narrowly and precisely delimited conventions such as the rules of chess, but it also has some force in connection with more diffuse conventions such as those that make up a large legal system.

In short, when we ponder whether the general norms of a legal system are objective in the sense of being mind-independent, we should arrive at a complex conclusion. Such norms are both existentially and observationally mind-independent, but their existential mind-independence is weak, whereas their observational mind-independence is strong. The weakness of the existential mind-independence minimizes any gaps between perception and actuality that have arisen because of the strong observational mind-independence. It does so not by averting errors on the part of legal officials collectively, but by ensuring that any of their uncorrected errors will quickly be incorporated into the law of the relevant jurisdiction. In other words, any gaps between the officials' collective perceptions and the actualities of the law are quite rapidly removed through the recurrent reshaping of the actualities in accordance with the perceptions. Furthermore, because legal officials are intimately familiar with their own practices and the products of those practices, the gaps between what is collectively perceived and what is actual should be relatively uncommon.

Before we leave this discussion, one potential objection should be allayed. My comments on objectivity qua existential mind-independence have presupposed that legal systems and the norms within them are conventional in character. Those comments might thus seem additionally to presuppose that legal positivism is correct as a theory of law. Some readers may feel disquiet. They may argue that, whether or not positivism is true, an account of legal objectivity should not take its truth as given. They would complain that my own account has not been neutral in the debates between legal positivists and natural-law theorists. Any such query would be misdirected. Although legal positivists do insist on the conventionality of law, so does every minimally credible natural-law theory. Legal positivists and most natural-law theorists disagree not over the question whether law is conventional, but over the question whether law is exclusively conventional. Many natural-law theorists maintain that the norms of every legal system encompass basic moral principles whose status as legal norms does not depend on the conventional practices of officials. A number of natural-law theorists further submit that some of the norms classified as laws by the officials within certain legal systems are not genuinely laws; appallingly heinous norms are excluded from such a status, or so we are told. Natural-law theorists are at odds with positivists on these points, but not on the question whether most of the laws in any legal system are conventional in origin. Everyone or virtually everyone recognizes that the answer to that latter question is affirmative.[4] Hence, in application to all the legal norms that would be classified as such by jurisprudential positivists and natural-law theorists alike – and therefore in application to the vast majority of legal norms that would be classified as such by jurisprudential positivists and the vast majority of legal norms that would be classified as such by natural-law theorists – my account of the existential mind-independence of such norms is neutral between positivism and natural-law doctrines. Moreover, the account can easily be amplified to accommodate the distinctive contentions of natural-law theorists. Such theorists should accept the account and add to it the claim that the existential mind-independence, as well as the observational mind-independence, of some general legal norms is strong rather than weak. More specifically, strong rather than weak is the existential mind-independence of the basic moral principles that are characterized by natural-law theorists as legal norms irrespective of any conventional practices. (Of course, the natural-law theorists would not contend that the status of those moral principles as laws *of some particular jurisdiction* is strongly mind-independent existentially. No legal system can endure if the minds of all the people within it have permanently ceased to function; hence, the natural-law theorists would accept that moral principles qua laws of some particular jurisdiction are only weakly mind-independent existentially. However, they would ascribe strong existential mind-independence – rather than weak existential

---

4 Ronald Dworkin, perhaps in a moment of polemical hyperbole, comes close to denying that the answer to the latter question is affirmative. See Dworkin 1986, 136–39. For a critical rejoinder to Dworkin, see Kramer 1999a, 146–51. Whatever may be the merits of Dworkin's position with specific reference to American constitutional law, it is wildly implausible as a general jurisprudential thesis applicable to all the main components of every legal system. At any rate, even if I were to accept Dworkin's view that a legal system operates not through conventions but through arrays of independent moral convictions that converge with one another, I would not need to modify anything said here about the weak existential mind-independence of legal norms. Dworkin clearly accepts that law is only weakly mind-independent existentially. What would need to be modified is simply my suggestion that law's weak existential mind-independence consists in its conventionality. A follower of Dworkin would insist that the weak existential mind-independence consists instead in law's nature as a product of overlapping medleys of moral convictions harbored by officials and citizens.

mind-independence – to those principles qua laws *tout court*. Even in the absence of any minds and consequently even in the absence of any legal systems, those principles will timelessly abide as laws that would belong to every such system if there were any. So, at least, the natural-law theorists believe.)

1.2.2. Objectivity qua Determinate Correctness

When the objectivity of law is at issue, the dimension of objectivity that is perhaps most commonly at the center of attention is that of determinate correctness. Philosophers and ordinary people who mull over these matters are often especially interested in ascertaining whether the legal consequences of people's actions, in any particular jurisdiction, are determinately settled by the terms of the prevailing legal norms. The extent to which there are determinately correct answers to legal questions is inversely proportional to the extent of the leeway left to legal officials in arriving at concrete decisions. That leeway is effectively eliminated in connection with any legal question to which there is a uniquely correct answer (although any legal official will still of course have to exercise his or her judgment in seeking to descry what the uniquely correct answer is, and although any such official will typically have some latitude in pondering how to give effect to the correct answer). Even when there is more than one correct answer to a legal question, the range of the correct answers may be small. If so, then the leeway left to legal officials is severely limited. More generally, as has just been suggested, the extent of that leeway is directly proportional to the breadth of the aforementioned range.

When none of the possible answers to some legal question would be incorrect, every answer is correct in the sense of not being incorrect. In such circumstances, the leeway of legal officials is unrestricted; every answer to the particular legal question is as good (or as bad) as any other answer. Indeterminacy, which is the negation of legal objectivity qua determinate correctness, prevails in such a situation. Either the regnant norms of the legal system do not address at all the matter covered by the particular legal question, or – for whatever reason – they are completely open-ended in their handling of that matter. In either case, there is no objective answer to the specified legal question. Every answer is correct (in the sense of not being incorrect), but no answer is determinately correct.

Claims about the existence of objective answers to legal questions can be unsustainable even when the indeterminacy surrounding those questions is expansive rather than thoroughgoing. Indeterminacy is a scalar property; that is, it obtains in varying degrees. A given legal matter can be utterly indeterminate – if every answer to a question about that matter is genuinely no better than any other answer – but usually the indeterminacy surrounding a problematic legal question is less than exhaustive. Though multiple contrary answers to such a question will each be correct, many other answers are incorrect. Suppose, for example, that the question whether some specified set of actions can appropriately be classified as an instance of the crime of murder is an indeterminate matter. An affirmative answer is no better or worse than a negative answer, for the balance between the applicability and the inapplicability of the legal prohibition on murder is even. All the same, some answers to the question will patently be wrong. For example, should anyone reply that the specified set of actions can appropriately be classified as an instance of the crime of murder if and only if the actions took place on a Tuesday, his or her answer would manifestly be incorrect. Nonetheless, although the reply focused on Tuesdays and any similarly misguided replies can be rejected as erroneous, there is no basis for deciding with minimal determinacy between an affirmative answer and a negative answer to the question whether a murder has been committed. In such circumstances, neither of those answers to that question is objectively correct. Objectivity qua determinate correctness is missing, even though the indeterminacy engendered by the question is less than exhaustive. The degree of indeterminacy is sufficiently large – encompassing both "yes" and "no" – to undermine an ascription of objective correctness to any answer.

1.2.2.1. Indeterminacy Overestimated

An obvious inquiry poses itself, then. To what extent can law partake of objectivity qua determinate correctness? That is, to what extent can legal norms ordain the legal consequences of people's conduct? To what extent can there be determinately correct answers to legal questions? Some writers have responded to this inquiry (or set of inquiries) with skeptical pessimism. Such pessimism has most conspicuously surfaced from time to time in the United States, where some of the Legal Realists in the

1920s and 1930s and most of the Critical Legal Scholars in the 1970s and 1980s notoriously trumpeted the notion that laws do not ever genuinely constrain the discretion of legal officials. Deeply skeptical about the very coherence and meaningfulness of legal norms, they insisted on the presence of rampant indeterminacy in any system of law. Although some theorists very loosely associated with Legal Realism were philosophically sophisticated, the members of that movement who wrote about legal indeterminacy were not; even more shallow and philosophically naive were many of the proclamations of indeterminacy that later emanated from the Critical Legal Scholars. Each of those schools of thought sparked controversy and won followers for a short period, but each of them rather quickly buckled under the weight of its own dogmatism and hyperbole. To be sure, the best writings in each of those movements (especially in Legal Realism) were salutarily piquant, and they have left an imprint on subsequent jurisprudential thinking. Nonetheless, the sterile and philosophically uninformed skepticism that tarnished each of those schools of thought is something that has fortunately receded.

1.2.2.1.1. Unwarranted Generalizations from Appellate Cases. Why have jurisprudential scholars intermittently fallen prey to the idea that legal systems are riven by sweeping indeterminacy? The first and most obvious factor behind their confusion lies in their tendency to extrapolate unwisely from the appellate cases on which they typically concentrate in their legal pedagogy and research. Cases that get appealed from lower courts are usually marked by difficult issues with quite evenly balanced countervailing considerations. Law students and legal theorists alike often succumb to the temptation to think that those interestingly thorny cases – to which they generally devote far more attention than to boringly routine cases – are representative of the innumerable situations addressed by a legal system's workings. In fact, however, such cases are as anomalous as they are engaging. What are really representative of the situations that confront a legal system are the humdrum cases that never appear in the casebooks studied in law schools, and the untold sets of circumstances in which the legal consequences of people's conduct are so clear-cut that they never give rise to any litigation. Most of the operations of a legal system are unexcitingly straightforward, and are therefore largely overlooked by legal academics who train their attention on controversial appellate cases. The fixation of those academics on such cases can foster in them a greatly exaggerated sense of the indeterminacy that afflicts a legal system.

1.2.2.1.2. Indemonstrability versus Indeterminacy. A second reason for that exaggerated sense is the failure of many theorists to distinguish adequately between determinacy and demonstrability.[5] An answer to a legal question can be determinately correct – that is, either uniquely correct or within a small range of answers that differ from all other answers in being correct – even though its correctness cannot be demonstrated to the satisfaction of virtually every reasonable person who reflects carefully on the matter. If some way of resolving a legal dispute is determinately correct, it is so regardless of whether anyone discerns as much. By contrast, a resolution of a dispute is demonstrably correct only if its singular appropriateness can be perceived and endorsed by virtually every sensible person who competently ponders the arguments in favor of it. As should be apparent, determinate correctness does not entail demonstrable correctness. The latter involves more than the former. As should likewise be apparent, the best answers to the principal legal questions in difficult appellate cases are very seldom demonstrably correct. Yet, because of the lack of entailment between determinate correctness and demonstrable correctness, the absence of the latter property does not entail the absence of the former; there may be some determinately correct answer(s) to the principal legal question(s) in any particular appellate case, even though the answer(s) will very likely not be demonstrably correct.

This elementary point, which we shall explore further in a later subsection of this chapter, is frequently missed by writers who declare that law is inevitably plagued by indeterminacy. Too often such writers simply point to the intractability of the disagreements that erupt in hard cases, and they then assert that there are no determinately correct answers to the pivotal questions in those cases. From there, they arrive at their conclusion that law is racked by indeterminacy. Now, even if we put aside the fact that these writers should not be drawing general conclusions about law from the peculiarities of difficult appellate cases, we should resist their prior inference about the absence of determinately correct answers in such cases. Though there might not be any determinately

---

[5] This distinction is damagingly elided in Tamanaha 2004, 103–05.

correct answers in some of those cases, the sheer fact that legal officials (or other people) differ fiercely with one another about the suitable outcome in any particular case is far from sufficient to establish that no outcome is determinately appropriate. The tenacity of the disagreement does not in itself have any bearing on the existence of a uniquely correct resolution of the crux to which the disagreement pertains. Only an elision of the distinction between determinacy and demonstrability could impel anyone to think otherwise. A theorist who wishes to justify claims about indeterminacy by adverting to the persistence of divergences among officials in hard cases will have to back up her position with pertinent arguments. Such a theorist will have to show, for example, that there are solid reasons for attributing the persistence of the divergences to the absence of determinately correct answers rather than to the temperamental or intellectual or ideological limitations of the people involved.

Very closely related to the division between determinate correctness and demonstrable correctness is the nonequivalence of determinacy and predictability, along with the nonequivalence of indeterminacy and unpredictability. In many difficult cases, the outcomes will be unpredictable because of the knottiness of the issues in dispute and the consequent discordances among people's views of those issues. It may be exceedingly difficult to pin down beforehand exactly how judges or other legal officials will deal with heatedly controversial matters. Still, because the unpredictability of the official decisions in such circumstances is due to the lack of any demonstrably correct answers, and because the lack of any demonstrably correct answers does not entail the lack of any determinately correct answers, unpredictability and indeterminacy are not equivalent or even coextensive. They sometimes go together, of course, but not invariably. Much the same is true of determinacy and predictability. As is evident from what has just been argued, determinacy does not entail predictability. Nor is there any entailment in the other direction. When judges or other legal-governmental officials confront some question of law to which there is no determinately correct answer, their handling of the question may be amply predictable because of a palpable predilection on the part of each official for a particular outcome. (Perhaps the relevant officials will predictably share a predilection for a particular outcome, or perhaps their divergent predilections will be well known and will render predictable their fractionated handling of the matter.) Thus, just as we cannot validly draw inferences about indeterminacy from unpredictability, so we cannot validly draw inferences about determinacy from predictability.[6]

1.2.2.1.3. Oversimplifications of Indeterminacy. A third factor behind the overemphasis on legal indeterminacy in some quarters is a simplistic understanding of indeterminacy itself. Some theorists appear to think that a legal question is beset by indeterminacy if they can reveal that there are credible points in favor of each main potential response to that question. Having shown that a plausible case can be made for each of the principal competing answers to the question (such as "yes" and "no"), these theorists conclude forthwith that there is no determinately correct answer. Whether or not such a conclusion is true in any particular case, it is unacceptably facile when advanced on the basis of the argument just outlined. What that line of argument neglects is that indeterminacy consists in more than a clash of conflicting considerations. Indeterminacy consists in a clash of conflicting considerations that are equally strong or incommensurably strong. That is, indeterminacy obtains only when the competing claims on each side of an issue are evenly balanced or are insusceptible to any comparisons that would rank their strength. None of the competing claims is better than any other, in a situation of equal counterpoises or incommensurably strong counterpoises. The existence of any such situation involves genuine indeterminacy, but it is far rarer than the existence of a situation wherein countervailing considerations (which may or may not be evenly balanced) are present. Hence, to advert starkly to the existence of considerations on each side of an issue as a ground for inferring the absence of any determinately correct way of resolving that issue is to commit a flagrant non sequitur. Proclamations of the prevalence of indeterminacy in systems of law too often rest on non sequiturs of that sort.

1.2.2.1.4. Indeterminacy versus Uncertainty. Overlapping with some of the factors already adduced is a fourth reason for the tendency of many legal theorists to exaggerate the extent of legal indeterminacy: their failure to

---

[6] For an apt recognition of this latter point, see Greenawalt 1992, 39. This point is also ultimately recognized in Tamanaha 2004, 87–90, after an initial effacement of the distinction between indeterminacy and unpredictability.

distinguish between indeterminacy and uncertainty.[7] Uncertainty is a state of inadequate beliefs (an epistemic state), whereas indeterminacy is a state of equipollent justifications (an ontological state). When somebody is uncertain about the correct answer to some legal question and is furthermore uncertain whether there is any determinately correct answer to that question, he or she is hardly in a position to deny the existence of any such determinately correct answer. He or she should be withholding judgment on that matter, just as much as on the specific content of the correct answer. His or her beliefs are insufficient for any verdict on either of those points. Contrariwise, if someone announces that there is no determinately correct answer to some legal question, he or she is not giving voice to uncertainty. He or she is instead maintaining that neither an affirmative reply nor a negative reply to the question is superior to the other. (If the question is not such as to lend itself to being pertinently answered "yes" or "no" – for example, a question about the appropriate level of the minimum wage – then the denial of determinate correctness amounts to the claim that none of the principal competing answers to the question is superior to any others.) To substantiate one's insistence that each answer is no better than the rival answer(s), one has to show that the counterpoised considerations are evenly balanced or that they are insusceptible to being ranked. Far from being a product of uncertainty, any such substantiation will have to be grounded on at least as much solid argumentation as will any satisfactory effort to demonstrate that some particular answer is better than every other. Uncertainty is no basis at all for the substantiative arguments.

In any context where the main matters in contention are of gnarled complexity and where there are significant justificatory grounds on each side of a case, many knowledgeable observers may be inclined to feel uncertainty not only about the correct disposition of the case but also about the very idea that a determinately correct disposition is attainable even in principle. Yet, as has just been indicated, any observers who do feel considerable uncertainty about those points are not in a position to deny that a determinately correct resolution of the case is possible. Until their uncertainty has been overcome, they should be refraining from either affirming or gainsaying the existence of a determinately correct

---

[7] This distinction is pertinently highlighted in Dworkin 1996, 129–39.

answer to the question of how the case should be handled. Their verdict should instead be a verdict of indecision. All too often, however, when legal theorists examine difficult cases and report their own uncertainty or the uncertainty of other knowledgeable observers about the possibility of determinately correct outcomes for those cases, they then deem the law in those cases to be indeterminate. Such slippage from uncertainty to declarations of indeterminacy is to be resisted. It is manifestly a non sequitur, and it leads jurisprudential theorists to overestimate the scale of the indeterminacy to which the legal regulation of people's conduct is subject. The distortive effects of that non sequitur are exacerbated, of course, when theorists commit the further misstep of generalizing from the law in difficult cases to the law as a whole. (On some occasions, the slippage from uncertainty to indeterminacy is an offshoot of a failure to comprehend that the weak existential mind-independence of legal norms is conjoined with their strong observational mind-independence. Many writers appear to assume that, if all or most of the legal officials in a given jurisdiction are themselves uncertain about the content and very existence of a determinately correct answer to some legal question, there cannot be any such answer to that question. An assumption along those lines would be well-founded if the observational mind-independence of legal norms were like the existential mind-independence thereof in being only weak. In fact, however, although legal norms as legal norms are constitutively underlain by the shared first-order beliefs and attitudes of legal officials, they are endowed with contents and implications that can exceed the officials' own second-order grasp. Think, for example, of a constitutional provision or some other legal norm that prohibits the infliction of severely cruel punishments. Legal officials will need to reflect on the substance of that norm in order to ascertain how it bears on various punitive measures. In so doing, all or most of the officials might feel uncertain about the legitimacy of this or that type of punishment. All the same, there may well be a uniquely correct answer to each question about which they feel uncertain. Their perplexity over some of the implications of a legal norm that exists because of their law-creating activities is not a bar to the determinacy of those implications.)

1.2.2.1.5. Indeterminacy versus Ultimacy. Another factor behind the overestimation of legal indeterminacy – the fifth and philosophically most

far-reaching factor to be expounded here – is the tendency of some
jurisprudential theorists (especially the Critical Legal Scholars) to become
bedazzled by certain deep philosophical cruxes. Such theorists note, for
example, that Ludwig Wittgenstein and several other eminent modern
philosophers have highlighted some formidable obstacles in the path
of any attempt to specify the facts that constitute the following of a
rule.[8] Summarized with the utmost terseness, the fundamental problem unearthed by those philosophers is that any specified set of facts will
be consistent with a limitless abundance of rules rather than only with
some rule R which the facts are supposed to instantiate or constitute.
We are hard pressed indeed to say why the specified facts instantiate or
constitute R rather than any of the countless other rules with which they
are consistent. Now, while jurisprudential theorists are plainly warranted
in regarding this problem as important and profound, they go astray
insofar as they regard it as a basis for alleging that massive indeterminacy
engulfs the workings of legal systems. Indeed, it is not a basis for any valid
inferences about indeterminacy whatsoever.

For one thing, the Wittgensteinian problem is applicable not only to
the following of rules in law but also to the following of rules in every
other domain. It is applicable, for example, to the following of rules in
mathematics and logic and ordinary language. Hence, if that problem
somehow undermined the determinate correctness of all answers to legal
questions, it would likewise undermine determinacy in the domains just
mentioned and in all other domains. Jurisprudential theorists who preen
themselves on their skepticism about the determinacy of legal regulation
should hesitate before committing themselves to the notion that the sum
of 2 plus 2 is indeterminate.

What is more important, the Wittgensteinian problem does not really
have anything to do with the determinate correctness of answers to legal
questions (or of answers to questions in other domains). The conundrums which it exposes are not any snags in the actual following of
rules within various activities, but snags in philosophical efforts to provide a comprehensive analysis of the following of rules. Exactly what

---

[8] For a good recent account of some of these obstacles and their implications (or lack of
implications) for jurisprudential theorizing, see Green 2003, 1932–46. See also Landers 1990;
Schauer 1991, 64–68; Greenawalt 1992, 71–73; Coleman and Leiter 1995, 219–23; Endicott 2000,
22–29; Bix 2005; Patterson 2006.

Wittgenstein aimed to establish with his reflections on the following of rules is a matter for intense debate among specialists in his work; however, no one or virtually no one among those specialists would maintain that he was even remotely seeking to reveal that the following of rules in myriad activities is untenable or illusive. He was hardly seeking to discredit those activities or the apposite judgments that are reached within them. On the contrary, his work in this area is best read as a challenge to certain philosophical thinking about those activities and judgments. More specifically, it is a challenge to the idea that the task of philosophy is to come up with the foundations for those activities and judgments, which rest instead on themselves as their own foundations.

When Wittgenstein is understood in the way favored here, we can perceive that his central objective was to show that the notion of following a rule is basic. That notion, in other words, is not subject to being elucidatively analyzed by reference to anything deeper and more perspicuous. A couple of brief analogies may be helpful here. Suppose that someone were to endeavor to supply a noncircular philosophical foundation for the Law of Noncontradiction (a law of logic under which it can never be the case that some proposition and the negation of that proposition are both true). Any such project would be futile and pointless, for its theses would have to presuppose the truth of the Law of Noncontradiction at every stage; the very coherence of those theses would depend on such a presupposition. There is no deeper ground for the truth of the Law of Noncontradiction than the fact that everything at odds with that law is self-contradictory. Any other ground that might be adduced in support of that law would inevitably rest on the ultimate ground just stated. Entirely and unproblematically circular, that ultimate ground is the only foundation which the Law of Noncontradiction has ever needed, and it is the only foundation that could be fully adequate (since any other ostensible foundation would itself be derivative of that ultimate ground). The Law of Noncontradiction is basic, in that it is not susceptible to being justified or elucidated by reference to anything more profound than itself.

Consider also, in this connection, David Hume's critique of induction (the inferring of future regularities from past regularities).[9] Exactly what Hume aspired to achieve with his critique of induction is as much

---

[9] For some of the issues raised by Hume's critique, see Stroud 1977, 51–67.

a matter of controversy among specialists as are Wittgenstein's precise aims in his critique of the following of rules; however, one thing surely shown by Hume's arguments is that any full justification of induction will be circular. Any putative foundations for a thesis which upholds the inferability of future regularities from past regularities will themselves have to presuppose the truth of that thesis, and will therefore be ersatz foundations. Like the Law of Noncontradiction, a general tenet affirming the propriety of induction (within limits indicated by the observed regularities themselves) is its own ground. It is not susceptible to being underpinned by anything deeper or more solid than itself.

We can best understand Wittgenstein as revealing that the notion of following a rule is similar to the Law of Noncontradiction and to a general tenet affirming the propriety of induction, in that it is basic. Any attempt to explain how some specified facts instantiate or constitute some particular rule will have to presuppose what it is purporting to demonstrate. Construed in this manner, the Wittgensteinian critique of the notion of following a rule does imply the futility of philosophical efforts to analyze that notion by reference to anything deeper than itself. Such a notion is opaque to noncircular philosophical analyses. Wittgenstein's critique hardly implies, however, that the following of rules is itself futile or problematic in any fashion. No inferences about indeterminacy can validly be derived from his critique. Questions about the applicability or inapplicability of rules in various domains will continue to be answerable in determinately correct ways, just as will questions about the conformity or nonconformity of various propositions with the Law of Noncontradiction. The facts that constitute or instantiate any particular rule will continue to be present, even though their status as such does not lend itself to being illuminated through further philosophical explication. Those facts will continue to require certain decisions, and to disallow contrary decisions, by people whose behavior is subject to the rules which the facts constitute or instantiate. The insusceptibility of those facts to philosophical analysis does not detract one whit from their decision-prescribing force. Far from disclosing that everything is unsettled in activities such as the operations of a legal system, Wittgenstein's critique leaves everything in those activities as it is. To believe otherwise is to fail to grasp that the unanalyzable fundamentals of some practice are indeed fundamentals of that practice. Though their unanalyzable character thwarts philosophical elucidation, it does not even slightly impair their operativeness within the practice. That operativeness scarcely depends on our being able to provide a noncircular philosophical account of it.

1.2.2.1.6. Executive Discretion. Whereas the last several paragraphs have examined a philosophically momentous factor behind some jurisprudential theorists' overblown claims about indeterminacy, a final factor to be explored briefly here is peculiar to law (and to other domains with closely similar institutional structures). Virtually any advanced system of law will include institutional features that complicate the implementation of the system's norms. My present discussion will concentrate on one feature that has induced some Critical Legal Scholars and other jurisprudential theorists to presume that there is pervasive indeterminacy in the workings of legal systems. Such theorists may grant that legal norms in themselves are determinately applicable or inapplicable to any number of situations, but they then point out that the actual implementation or effectuation of those norms is often subject to quite a large degree of discretion on the part of certain officials (most notably the officials responsible for policing and monitoring, and the officials such as prosecutors who are responsible for initiating and sustaining any procedures of enforcement that are undertaken on the basis of the policing and monitoring). These theorists conclude that the discretionary element in the effectuation of legal norms is sufficient to support their pronouncements about the prevalence of legal indeterminacy.[10]

Any legal discretion exercisable by the aforementioned officials is held by them within the sway of general principles of political morality. In any particular case, those moral principles may well require some definite course of action by the relevant officials. *Pro tanto*, the officials' legal discretion is not accompanied by moral discretion. However, this point about moral discretion is not enough for a successful riposte to the Critical Legal Scholars, since their pronouncements are about legal indeterminacy rather than about general normative indeterminacy. Unless the principles of political morality have been incorporated into the law of a jurisdiction as legal requirements that will be transgressed by officials whose effectuation of the law is morally inapposite, the officials' lack of

---

[10] For a rejoinder to arguments of this sort, see Greenawalt 1992, 53–56. My own rejoinder is different from Greenawalt's, but the two are complementary.

moral discretion does not in itself curtail their legal discretion. Hence, if their being possessed of legal discretion is somehow problematic for the objectivity of the operations of their legal system, an insistence on their lack of moral discretion will not per se redeem that objectivity. Instead of focusing on the moral restrictedness of the officials, then, we need to ask directly whether their legal discretion undermines the determinate correctness of answers to legal questions within their system of law.

Let us concentrate (at a very abstract level) on the exercise of official discretion within the criminal-justice system of some jurisdiction. What the skeptical jurisprudential theorists would need to show is that the presence of such discretion renders indeterminate the occurrence of the legal consequences that are ordained by the applicable criminal-law mandates. Those skeptics point to the fact that, because of the exercise of legal discretion on the part of police officers or prosecutors or other legal officials, many people who detectedly commit crimes are not convicted or not punished. The quite frequent absence of punitive consequences – or, more precisely, the fact that the absence of such consequences is due to legally permissible exercises of official discretion – is regarded by skeptics as sufficient to vindicate their view that jural officials are authorized to pretermit any of the legal consequences ordained by criminal-law mandates. Answers to questions about the legal consequences of people's conduct are therefore said to be devoid of determinate correctness. Once we move from the contents of legal norms in the abstract to the contents of legal norms as they are given effect in processes of implementation, we find that legal consequences are up in the air. Or so the skeptics maintain.

Before considering why this skeptical argument is unsound, we should note that it does not perforce run together indeterminacy and unpredictability (two properties whose distinctness has already been discussed in this chapter). Skeptics are not asserting that the presence and exercise of official discretion in the implementation of legal norms will inevitably have made that implementation erratic. They can allow that legal officials might exercise their discretion in predictably regularized ways in most contexts. Such predictability is hardly guaranteed, but it is perfectly possible. Nonetheless – the skeptic would go on to argue – the foreseeability of the officials' handling of various matters will be due to extralegal factors such as shared psychological inclinations, rather than to the terms of legal requirements and entitlements. Those terms do not correspond to the ways in which the requirements and entitlements are actually brought to bear on people's conduct, even if the departures from those terms are regularized and predictable. Most important, the aforementioned departures are all legally permissible exercises of discretion, and any decisions by officials against engaging in such departures (and thus in favor of effectuating the terms of the relevant laws) would likewise have been legally permissible. The law as it actually gets applied to people's conduct is therefore indeterminate, for any application could have gone either way. Since a decision either way would have been correct, neither a decision in favor of enforcement nor a decision against enforcement is *determinately* correct. Such is the conclusion of the skeptical argument.

Though that skeptical argument does not conflate indeterminacy and unpredictability, it rests on a simplistic understanding of legal mandates and legal systems. Specifically, it rests on a simplistic understanding of the legal consequences that attach to people's conduct under the mandates and other norms of a legal system. We are concentrating here on criminal-law prohibitions. Skeptics advert to the fact that some people who detectedly transgress those prohibitions are unpunished as a result of legally permissible exercises of discretion by officials such as policemen and prosecutors. Skeptics think that the withholding of punishment is at odds with what is ordained by the terms of the prohibitions. In fact, however, what is ordained under those terms is more subtle than the skeptics realize.

Integral to the terms of any criminal-law mandate is not that every violator will have undergone some punishment, but that every violator will have incurred a legal liability to be subjected to punishment. The term "liability" is used here in the sense assigned to that term by the American jurist Wesley Hohfeld. That is, it designates a susceptibility to a change in one's legal position (Kramer 1998, 20–21). Such a change can be brought about through the exercise of some legal power(s) by oneself or by somebody else. In the case at hand, the relevant powers will be held by the legal officials responsible for pursuing sanctions against malefactors. (Those powers will typically be exercisable through a complex sequence of steps such as an arrest, a set of pretrial proceedings, a trial, and a process of sentencing.) If the appropriate officials exercise their powers to undertake punitive measures against some person P who has criminally flouted a legal requirement, then P will have incurred a legal duty to submit to those measures. His legal situation will have changed – through the imposition of a new legal duty – in precisely the respect to which he makes himself liable when he breaches a legal mandate. However, the essential effect of his breach of the mandate is not the occurrence of that subsequent change (which depends on exercises of powers of enforcement by appropriate officials), but his incurring of a liability to undergo such a change. That liability will have been incurred even if the subsequent imposition of a duty never in fact takes place. If a police officer or some other relevant legal official exercises her discretion and declines to initiate punitive proceedings, then *P* will not acquire a duty to submit to any sanctions that might have ensued from such proceedings. All the same, *P* through his violation of the law will have placed himself under a liability to acquire just such a duty. His placing of himself under that liability is what ineluctably follows from his having criminally transgressed a legal requirement, and is something that occurs irrespective of whether he is ever subjected to punitive measures.

By contrast, the subjection of *P* to punitive measures is not something that ineluctably follows from his having criminally transgressed a legal requirement, even if we leave aside the fact that punitive proceedings might go awry for any number of reasons such as a lack of clinching evidence. His subjection to punitive measures does not *ineluctably* follow, because the norms of the legal system that govern the handling of his liability-to-be-subjected-to-sanctions are such that they endow the relevant officials with discretion. Vested with that discretion, the officials are both legally empowered and legally permitted to choose between pursuing and waiving the application of punitive measures against *P*. If they opt to waive those measures, they will not thereby have done anything that clashes with the terms of the norms in their legal system. They will obviously not thereby have done anything that clashes with the terms of the norms which confer their discretion upon them. Less obviously, they will also not have done anything that clashes with the terms of the mandate which *P* has breached. After all, as has just been remarked, the only essential effect of a breach of that mandate by *P* is his incurring of a liability-to-be-subjected-to-punishment. That liability does indeed descend upon him in the aftermath of his breach, even though he is not subsequently subjected to any punishment. In other words, far from being at variance with the terms of the applicable laws, the legal situation involving the officials' discretionary waiver of punitive measures against *P* is fully in accordance with those terms. *P* incurs a liability just as is ordained under the mandate which he has violated, and the officials reach a decision (a decision to forgo punitive measures) which they are permitted and empowered to reach under the norms that invest them with discretion in such matters.

When a skeptic argues that legal requirements as they actually get applied to people's conduct are indeterminate because of the existence of official discretion in the implementation of those requirements, he or she is failing to heed the chief distinction highlighted in the two preceding paragraphs: the distinction between a liability-to-undergo-punitive-measures and the actual undergoing of punitive measures. Once we take account of that distinction, we can see that the existence of official discretion in the implementation of legal requirements does not unsettle the immediate legal consequences of people's conduct. Those consequences will be as they are ordained by the legal directives that impose the requirements. That is, everyone who disobeys any of those directives will incur a liability to be subjected to punitive measures. Such a consequence occurs immediately regardless of the existence and exercise of discretion on the part of the officials who give effect to the directives. Thus, quite simplistic is the notion that the legal consequences of unlawful conduct are up in the air.

Skeptics, then, go astray by disregarding the distinction highlighted in the last few paragraphs. Their inattentiveness to that distinction blinds them to the ways in which the determinacy of legal directives as they exist *in abstracto* is paralleled by the determinacy of such directives as they actually impinge on people's legal positions. The sheer fact that the officials responsible for enforcing legal requirements are vested with discretion in carrying out their task is not sufficient to undermine the objectivity of the workings of their legal regime. Still, although the skeptical argument is facile, there is plainly an element of truth in it. Everything hinges here on the nature of the discretion with which the officials are endowed.

Suppose that there is some system of governance in which the officials are empowered and permitted to do whatever they please in their implementation of the system's dictates. Whenever a transgression of those dictates has occurred, the officials are fully empowered and permitted to pursue or waive a procedure of punitive enforcement. Any decision either for or against the pursuit of such a procedure, reached for any reason or for no reason at all, will be both efficacious and permissible within the norms of the system of governance. The caprice of any official is a sufficient basis for every such decision, and no official is required to make any effort to treat like cases alike or to differentiate between distinguishable cases. No official has to take account of any other official's decisions or of his own past decisions. Now, in any system of governance along these lines, most of the legal consequences of people's transgressive conduct will indeed be up in the air – and, as my later chapters will suggest, they will therefore probably not be genuinely legal consequences. Although the immediate legal consequence of each instance of transgressive conduct (namely, the incurring of a liability-to-undergo-sanctions) will be determinate, any further legal consequences of each such instance will be radically unsettled. Whether a malefactor will actually be subjected to penalties or not is a matter to be determined by the whim of any relevant official. Under the norms of the system, before such penalties are officially sought or waived, there is no determinately correct answer to the question whether they should be sought or waived. Even if the officials in fact exercise their thoroughgoing discretion in ways that are highly regularized and coordinated, their being endowed with such blanket discretion is sufficient to render indeterminate most of the legal consequences of people's transgressive conduct. (Note that an even stronger version of the point made in this paragraph would be pertinent with regard to an iniquitous system of governance in which the officials are also sweepingly empowered and permitted to undertake sanctions against people who have not violated any norms of the system. I have not focused on such a situation here, simply because it is not invoked by the skeptics to whom I am retorting. They endeavor to substantiate their claims about legal indeterminacy by adverting to the existence of official discretion in the enforcement of laws that have indeed been breached.)

With reference to a system of governance like the one sketched in the preceding paragraph, the skeptical argument is still simplistic – because of its elision of the distinction between the liability of a person to be subjected to punitive measures and the actual subjection of the person to punitive measures – but it is largely correct. When the discretion of officials in enforcing the law is completely untrammeled, most of the legal consequences of people's unlawful conduct will be up in the air. The workings of the system that comprises those consequences will partake of only meager determinacy. Nonetheless, there are good grounds for querying whether the skeptical argument has any troublesome purchase on the legal systems of Western liberal democracies (the legal systems about which the skeptics profess to be writing). To show that the argument does troublingly bear on those legal systems, the skeptic will have to establish that the official discretion operative therein is wholly or largely untrammeled. As is evident, discretion can exist in many forms and with varying degrees of restrictedness. If the official discretion that exists in some or all of the legal systems of Western liberal democracies were approximately as extensive as the official discretion recounted in my last paragraph, then the skeptic could warrantedly claim to have thrown into doubt the objectivity of the operations of those systems. If contrariwise the official discretion in those legal systems is far more modest and is hemmed in by quite stringent restrictions concerning the attainment of consistency in the handling of myriad situations, then the skeptical argument is undamaging. Any indeterminacy exposed by that argument in the workings of liberal-democratic legal systems will be circumscribed rather than pervasive.

Do we, then, have any strong reasons for presuming that officials' discretion in the implementation of legal mandates within liberal-democratic systems of governance is virtually untrammeled? Or do we instead have solid reasons for presuming that that discretion is much more modest? Any informed answers to these questions would have to stem from a wide-ranging empirical study undertaken on a scale far beyond any study that has ever been carried out by skeptics. No such study is possible here, of course, but we can reflect briefly on some reasons for thinking that any survey would go against the skeptics. For one thing, it is manifest that no legal official in a liberal-democratic regime (or in many an autocratic regime) would be legally empowered and permitted to base decisions about law-enforcement on sheer caprices. If there is no credible rationale for some such decision(s) reached by an official, and if the matter is suitably brought to the attention of higher-level authorities, then the official will very likely be upbraided or the decision(s) will very likely be set aside. More generally, there are numerous broad legal restrictions – within any liberal democracy – on the sorts of considerations that can permissibly underlie the decisions of officials to pursue or waive punitive proceedings against lawbreakers. For example, such decisions cannot permissibly be based on the religion or race or gender or ethnicity or political allegiance or socioeconomic status of any lawbreaker or of any victims of lawbreaking, except in extremely unusual circumstances. Furthermore, past and present decisions constrain what can permissibly be decided in the future. Requirements of consistency, such as the American constitutional principle of equal protection of the laws or the hoary procedural-justice principle that like cases are to be treated alike, impose limits on the validity or permissibility of any law-enforcement decisions within a context of other law-enforcement decisions. Similarly, rules about desuetude divest officials of the legal power to enforce legal requirements that have long gone unenforced despite the occurrence of infractions. These restrictions on the discretion involved in the implementation of legal mandates do not eliminate that discretion entirely, of course, but they do cabin it much more tightly than is envisaged in skeptical pronouncements about the operations of liberal-democratic systems of law.

In several respects, then, skeptical arguments that concentrate on the role of official discretion in the effectuation of legal directives are glib. Such arguments do not show (and do not purport to show) that legal directives as they obtain in the abstract are without determinate implications for most circumstances. Moreover, by failing to distinguish between one's liability to be subjected to punishments and one's actual undergoing of punishments, the skeptics overlook the determinacy of the immediate legal consequences of illicit conduct. In addition, by paying inadequate attention to the curbs on officials' discretion in the effectuation of legal directives within liberal-democratic systems of law, skeptics markedly overestimate the extent of that discretion. In these various ways, the conclusions drawn by skeptics from their observations of official discretion in law-enforcement are overblown. To be sure, more can and should be said on these matters. (For example, a thorough investigation would need to ponder the fact that many contraventions of legal requirements go undetected – and the further fact that the identities of the perpetrators of many detected contraventions go undiscovered.) Already, however, we have strong grounds for believing that the discretionary aspect of law-application in Western liberal democracies cannot soundly be adduced by the Critical Legal Scholars and other skeptics in vindication of their hyperbolic proclamations of legal indeterminacy.

The preceding paragraph's antiskeptical verdict would be reinforced if we were to take account of the ways in which the procedural devices of a legal system can curtail the discretion that might be left by the system's substantive norms. For instance, various rules of closure – such as the rule that the defendant should win whenever there is no determinately correct answer to the pivotal point of contention in a private-law case before a court – can remove some of the gaps of indeterminacy that would otherwise exist in a society's law. Of course, not all such devices are desirable. What is more, none of them can ever eliminate indeterminacy completely; for example, there might be no determinately correct answer to the question whether there is a determinately correct answer to the pivotal point of contention in some particular case before a court. (A crux of this kind would involve second-order indeterminacy.) Nevertheless, rules of closure and other procedural measures can expand the range of situations in which there are uniquely correct outcomes to be reached by legal decision-makers. Skeptics have concentrated on the ways in which the administrative and adjudicative workings of a legal system reduce the determinacy of the system's requirements and authorizations. Were they also to notice the ways in which those workings can augment the determinacy of such a system, they would be less inclined to overstate their skeptical findings.

1.2.2.2. Indeterminacy Underestimated

If the Critical Legal Scholars have significantly exaggerated the degree of the indeterminacy in functional legal systems, a key inquiry to be addressed is how far one should go in rejecting their skeptical claims. Should one follow Ronald Dworkin in maintaining that there is a uniquely correct answer to every legal question or virtually every legal question that might arise in some particular jurisdiction (Dworkin 1977; 1978, 279–90; 1985, 119–45; 1991)? On the one hand, his position is by no means as outlandish as it might initially seem. He contends that – at least in any legal system relevantly similar to that of the United States – the answers to legal questions are determined not only by the familiar materials of law such as statutes and judicial rulings and administrative regulations and constitutional provisions, but also by the most attractive moral principles that are immanent in those materials. Even when the explicit formulations in the ordinary materials of the law do not by themselves yield a uniquely correct answer to some difficult legal question, the most appealing moral principles that underlie those materials can do so. Such principles can close up any juridical open-endedness, for the uniquely correct moral answer to each difficult question will likewise be the uniquely correct legal answer.

By insisting that major principles of morality are incorporated into the law of any particular jurisdiction, Dworkin in effect submits that the range of legally dispositive standards is much more expansive than might be thought by somebody who concentrates only on the overt formulations of statutes and regulations and ordinances and adjudicative doctrines and contractual clauses and constitutional provisions. Because the repertory of decisional bases within a legal system as understood by Dworkin is so ample, an affirmation of the existence of a uniquely correct answer to every legal question within such a system is not wildly implausible. Furthermore, Dworkin's point about the importance of supplementary legal standards can be generalized. In some legal systems, the supplementary role will be filled by correct principles of morality, which serve as legally binding bases for official decision-making; but, even in a legal system that cannot credibly be characterized as having incorporated many correct principles of morality into its law, some supplementary standards will be operative. Those standards might be the precepts of the conventional moral code that prevails in the society over which the legal regime presides. Or, in a flagrantly evil legal regime, the supplementary standards might be shameless principles centered on the exploitatively power-hungry interests of the officials who draw upon them. Moreover, in any functional legal system – whether benign or malign – the officials will have recourse to countless assumptions about the typical desires and intentions and inclinations of human beings, and also to assumptions about the typical meanings associated with ordinary language. Although the contents of those common-sense assumptions are not themselves standards that are the normative bases for juridical decision-making, they greatly strengthen the determinacy of the standards that are those normative bases. That is, they contribute greatly to settling whether the statutes and regulations and ordinances and judicial doctrines and other legal standards in some jurisdiction are applicable or inapplicable to any particular sets of circumstances. Like the moral principles or other principles that have been incorporated into a jurisdiction's law as dispositive touchstones for gauging the legal consequences of people's behavior, the contents of the common-sense assumptions mentioned above will help to close any gaps of indeterminacy left open by the language of explicitly formulated legal norms. Very much the same can be said about the technical interpretive techniques employed by judges and other legal officials to construe the bearings of complicated legal language. We should keep these points in mind whenever we are assessing the plausibility of Dworkin's insistence that there is a uniquely correct answer to every legal question.

One additional point in Dworkin's favor is the distinction between indeterminacy and indemonstrability, to which we have already devoted some scrutiny. When Dworkin insists on the existence of uniquely correct answers to legal questions, he is hardly implying that judges and other legal officials (to say nothing of members of the general public) will invariably concur on what those answers are. On the contrary, he has repeatedly emphasized the intractability of the disagreements that surround difficult legal cruxes. The distinction between determinate correctness and demonstrable correctness is especially salient in his jurisprudential theorizing because of his contention that correct principles of morality will be among the legal norms in any morally authoritative regime of law. Given that the correct principles of morality are strongly mind-independent not only observationally but also existentially, his claims about uniquely correct answers to knotty legal questions plainly do not entail any claims about widely agreed-upon answers to those questions. Hence, the preposterousness of claims of the latter sort should not be attributed to claims of the former sort.

On the other hand, although Dworkin's insistence on the existence of a uniquely correct answer to every legal question is far from risible, it is excessively bold. Notwithstanding all that has been said in the last three paragraphs, there are no compelling grounds for going as far as Dworkin. He is right to challenge the orthodox (and rather complacent) view that there are no determinately correct answers to quite a few difficult legal questions, but his challenge does not altogether succeed. Though the presence of moral principles in the law as legally binding bases for decisions will close up many of the gaps of indeterminacy that would otherwise yawn, the notion that those principles remove all or virtually all such gaps is implausible. There undoubtedly remain a number of issues in connection with which the competing considerations are either evenly balanced or incommensurably pitted against each other. Dworkin's position on this matter is closely bound up with his resistance to the idea of the incommensurability of countervailing moral factors, and with his concomitant rejection of value-pluralism in morality (the thesis that basic moral values collide with one another in certain respects and that they therefore sometimes have to be traded off against each other). To be sure, his doubts about incommensurability and value-pluralism in the domain of morality are salutary to a certain degree; people are too ready at times to presume that the trickiness of reconciling certain desiderata is due to the sheer impossibility of doing so. Nevertheless, his stance is overweening insofar as it is meant to apply in a blanket fashion. There are no solid moral reasons for thinking that moral principles will have yielded a uniquely correct answer to *every* problem that comes to be addressed by a legal system. In his efforts to show that moral and political values do all mesh in ways that overcome incommensurability and value-pluralism, Dworkin has to resort to some far-fetched lines of argument (Williams 2001, 13–14). The matter deserves much more attention than can be bestowed on it here, of course, but we are well advised to conclude – *pace* Dworkin – that any functional systems of law, including systems that have taken on board the correct principles of morality among their norms, will be confronted by situations that occasion legal questions to which there are no determinately correct answers.

This conclusion is reinforced by a recognition of the ineliminable vagueness of many legal concepts (Endicott 2000, 63–72, 159–67). Though we shall briefly return to the topic of vagueness in Section 1.2.6, a full-scale treatment of the matter is beyond the scope of this book; a laconic sketch of one mundane instance of the problem will suffice for my present purposes. Suppose that six months would be an unreasonably long period of time for the marking of an examination, and that three days would be a reasonably short period of time for such a task. Yet, if a period of six months is unreasonably long, then so is a period of six months minus one second. Any basis for deeming the former to be unreasonable in length would apply as well to the latter. Conversely, if a span of three days is reasonably short, then a span of three days plus one second is likewise reasonable. Any reasonableness/unreasonableness distinction between those lengths of time would be without foundation. In this context, much the same can be said about such a distinction between any span of length L and a span of L-plus-one-second or a span of L-minus-one-second. Whatever may be the numerical value of the "L" variable, a reasonableness/unreasonableness distinction between L and L-plus-one-second or between L and L-minus-one-second would be untenably arbitrary. Given as much, however, someone who ventures to pin down the distinction between the reasonably short and the unreasonably long will proceed indefinitely in contemplating the addition of seconds to the length of three days, and will likewise proceed indefinitely – until reaching zero – in contemplating the subtraction of seconds from the length of six months. There is no point at which we can stop and draw a nonarbitrary line marking the end of the reasonableness of the former length or marking the beginning of the unreasonableness of the latter length. We therefore seem impelled toward the verdict that a period of six months (or even longer) is reasonably brief, and that a period of three days (or even shorter) is unreasonably protracted.

To resolve this paradox, which has been known since ancient times and which bears *mutatis mutandis* on many dichotomies rather than only on the reasonable/unreasonable distinction (Sainsbury 1988, 25–48), we should acknowledge that each such dichotomy is associated with a gray area of borderline cases. Within that gray area – the boundaries of which are themselves vague – there is no determinate answer to the question whether any particular borderline phenomenon falls on one side or the other of the relevant dichotomy. Now, among the vague concepts that give rise to such gray areas are many of the major concepts that figure in legal systems. Those juridical concepts differ among one another in the extent of their vagueness (and in the degree of its practical importance), but each of them can generate questions to which there are no determinately correct answers. The potential for some such questions is ineliminable, since any means of closing off vagueness in one or more of its manifestations will rely on concepts that are themselves not impervious to lines of reasoning broadly parallel to the argument sketched in my preceding paragraph. Although vagueness within a legal system can usually be reduced, and although it can always be shifted from one focal point to another, it can never be overcome completely.

Indeterminacy does exist in legal systems, then, albeit on a far more limited scale than is imagined by the Critical Legal Scholars. It extends to legal norms even at the level at which they obtain as abstract standards; *a fortiori*, it extends to those norms at the level at which they actually get invoked and effectuated by legal officials. Still, the precise extent of the indeterminacy – and the specific types of problems that give rise to it – will of course vary from legal system to legal system. Objectivity qua determinacy is a scalar property, rather than an all-or-nothing property, of each legal system as a whole.

1.2.3. *Objectivity qua Uniform Applicability*

Another prominent aspect or dimension of objectivity is that of uniform applicability, which overlaps with some of objectivity's other aspects or dimensions. If laws are uniformly applicable to people within a jurisdiction, they apply alike to everyone there. The uniform applicability of legal norms is to be understood in contrast with several kinds of differentiated applicability. In the first place, it consists in categorical imperativeness; that is, it consists in the mandatoriness of legal requirements for everyone irrespective of his or her preferences and inclinations. A legal prohibition on acts of murder, for example, applies with equal force to people naturally inclined toward pacifism and people naturally inclined toward violent sadism. Although compliance with such a prohibition will be effortless for the former people and frustratingly irksome for the latter, the former are just as strictly forbidden to commit murders as are the latter. Similarly, the prohibition applies alike to people who are desperately afraid of being imprisoned and people who are largely unafraid because of their brazen indifference toward their surroundings and prospects. Penalties await anyone who has been convicted of the crime of murder, whether or not those penalties are perceived as daunting.

A few important qualifications should be appended to the proposition that legal norms are categorically imperative. One caveat is that the categorical imperativeness of a legal norm such as the prohibition on murder does not mean that all the legal consequences of a person's breach of such a norm will perforce be the same as those of a breach by anybody else. Some of the consequences, such as the immediate consequence of incurring a liability-to-undergo-punishment, will indeed be the same for everyone. Other legal consequences may well differ, however, and the differences may be partly or wholly due to differences among people in their propensities and desires. A person of depraved desires who commits a murder for nefarious reasons will typically receive a heavier sentence for the crime than will someone of a generally good character who commits a murder for much less ignoble reasons. Many aggravating or mitigating factors of this sort – relating directly to people's predilections and temperaments – may call for lesser or greater leniency in the punitive responses to some murders than in the punitive responses to others. These variations are perfectly consistent with the categorical imperativeness of a legal norm that forbids murder. Such a norm partakes of categorical imperativeness because it establishes that a certain mode of conduct is a legal wrong regardless of whether anyone is attracted or repelled by that mode of conduct. The requirement imposed by the norm is a requirement for everyone; its status as a requirement does not depend on anyone's objectives or desires. In that key respect, a legal mandate is categorically imperative. Its disallowance of some specified type of behavior renders that type of behavior legally impermissible for everyone alike, even though the severity of the legal consequences of acting athwart the mandate might not be similarly uniform for everyone.

Another crucial caveat that qualifies any attribution of categorical imperativeness to law is centered on the heterogeneity of legal norms. Some legal norms, such as the norm that proscribes murder, clearly do partake of categorical imperativeness. Each such norm requires everyone to act in a certain way or to abstain from acting in a certain way, without regard to what anyone's aims might be. Other legal norms, however, do not in themselves produce any such effect. The most important distinction in this context is between duty-imposing norms and power-conferring norms (Hart 1961, 27–41). As jurisprudential theorists have emphasized for many decades, power-conferring laws – for example, laws vesting people with legal powers to form contracts or to bequeath property – differ from duty-imposing laws in that they do not categorically require people to adopt any particular modes of conduct. Instead, they provide people with opportunities to achieve certain aspirations. People are able to take advantage of those opportunities or to decline to take advantage of them, in accordance with their objectives. Of course, anyone who wishes to bring about an outcome made possible by a power-conferring law will have to comply with the conditions or procedures prescribed for the exercise of the power in question. However, the power-conferring law itself does not obligate anyone to endeavor to bring about any outcome which it enables. One's having to conform to the prescribed conditions or procedures for the exercise of a legal power is contingent on one's seeking to exercise that power. (To be sure, people are sometimes legally obligated to exercise legal powers with which they are endowed. Such obligations are especially common in relation to the public powers of legal-governmental officials. Nonetheless, any such obligations are established by duty-imposing norms that accompany the power-conferring norms under which the officials hold their powers. The power-conferring norms themselves do not render mandatory the performance of any particular action or function.)

A further caveat concerning the categorical imperativeness of law is that, although categorical imperativeness is one species of uniform applicability, those two properties are by no means simply equivalent. For instance, although power-conferring laws are not categorically imperative, they typically are uniformly applicable (at least in Western liberal democracies) in that typically they apply alike to everyone within a jurisdiction. Normally, any such law lays down procedures that have to be followed by everyone who wishes to exercise the power(s) which the law bestows. Specifications of such procedures are not categorical imperatives – because they do not require anyone to act in the prescribed ways unless he or she desires certain outcomes – but they are conditional imperatives that obtain as such for everyone within a jurisdiction.

Conversely, just as a lack of categorical imperativeness does not entail a lack of uniform applicability in other respects, so too a lack of uniform applicability in other respects does not entail a lack of categorical imperativeness. Suppose for example that the laws of some deeply racist nation in Africa include mandates which forbid Caucasian people to murder anyone but which do not impose any cognate prohibition on black people; instead, black people are forbidden to slay other black people but are permitted to slay Caucasians. In two major respects, the mandates in question are not uniformly applicable. They differentiate among people, on the basis of skin color, both with regard to the limitations imposed on what anybody can permissibly do and with regard to the protection afforded against the misconduct of others. Notwithstanding, those mandates are categorically imperative. The requirements established thereunder do not differentiate among people at all on the basis of their desires and aims. A person's attitude toward the act of committing a murder or toward the prospect of being punished is irrelevant to the question whether the person is legally forbidden or permitted to carry out such an act. Every Caucasian person in the jurisdiction is legally prohibited from murdering anyone, and every black person in the jurisdiction is legally prohibited from murdering any black person. Thus, although the imagined mandates are far from uniformly applicable in some conspicuous respects, they are uniformly applicable in the sense of being categorically imperative.

1.2.3.1. Uniformity versus Individualization

As is apparent from the last couple of paragraphs, uniform applicability goes well beyond categorical imperativeness. It stands in contrast with countless kinds of disparate applicability, indeed. Some of those types of disparate applicability (such as racial or religious discrimination) are pernicious in most contexts, whereas other types – which are especially often broached in discussions of legal objectivity – are somewhat more equivocal in their moral bearings.[11] Perhaps most notable among these is differentiation on the basis of abilities or intelligence. Within Anglo-American law, such differentiation is quite frequently eschewed. For instance, the standard of negligence in Anglo-American tort law is generally defined by reference to the level of care that would be taken by a reasonable person, and is applied to people who lack the intelligence or the physical dexterity to exercise such a degree of care. Jurists frequently designate that standard as "objective," and thereby distinguish it from an approach that would take the peculiar shortcomings of individual defendants into account. Admittedly, some exceptions are made for young children and for lunatics and for people with severe physical handicaps. Nevertheless, the normal practice in Anglo-American tort law is to hold people legally answerable for the harmful effects of their negligence irrespective of anyone's ability or inability to satisfy the standard of reasonable care. A number of other areas of Anglo-American law are broadly similar in favoring

---

[11] For a nuanced discussion of some of these matters, with a focus principally on criminal law, see Greenawalt 1992, 100–19.

objectivity-qua-uniform-applicability over any accommodatingly sub-jective way of proceeding that would cater to individual weaknesses.

Whether any areas of the law *should* maintain a posture of uniform applicability by disregarding individuals' physical and mental deficien-cies is a moot question. On the one hand, a practice of differentiating among people by adverting to such deficiencies would not be glaringly invidious in the manner of racial or religious or ethnic bigotry. Applying a more lenient standard of legal wrongdoing to people whose physical or mental inadequacies prevent them from abiding by a more demand-ing standard is fairer to such people in some palpable respects. Even though the principle that "ought" implies "can" is not always correct as a moral precept (Kramer 2004a, 249–94; 2005), it is often correct. There is something unpleasant about marshaling the coercive force of legal-governmental institutions against somebody for having brought about an untoward event which he or she was incapable of avoiding in the circumstances. On the other hand, there are several considerations that militate in favor of the current position in Anglo-American tort law (and in other relevantly similar areas of the law).

One such consideration centers on the very issue of fairness. Although an award of damages against a hapless defendant is undoubtedly quite a harsh burden for that person, a failure to award compensation to an inno-cent victim of the defendant's substandard conduct is – *ceteris paribus* – even more harshly unfair. Perhaps an alternative to the private-law system of compensation would be appropriate in such a situation. Perhaps, for example, the compensation for the victim should come from a publicly maintained fund. It is not overwhelmingly obvious, however, why tax-payers should bear the burden of remedying the injurious consequences of somebody's slipshod conduct. A critic of private-law compensation might respond by invoking familiar arguments about the ostensible com-passionateness of spreading the costs of mishaps among large numbers of people. Such arguments, however, are more than offset by lines of reasoning about the disadvantages of impairing the financial incentives for people to refrain from participating in activities which they are inca-pable of performing safely. At any rate, even less appealing than a public compensatory fund would be a system in which the victims of others' carelessness have to rely on first-party insurance (that is, insurance poli-cies purchased by potential victims to indemnify them for any harm suffered as a result of other people's actions). Any sustainable scheme of first-party insurance that is not itself heavily funded through public subventions will be marked by either of two undesirable features: either people who suffer more frequently from the remissness of others will have to pay higher premiums for their coverage, or else all the purchasers of the insurance will be paying higher premiums to defray the costs of the remissness-induced accidents. Thus, imperfect though a system of private-law compensation admittedly is, it is probably less unattractive as a mechanism for remedying the effects of negligence than any arrangements that might be substituted for it. Given as much, and given the unfairness to innocent victims if they receive no redress for the damage which they incur through the maladroitness of their fellows, the reluctance of jurists within Anglo-American tort law to indulge the shortcomings of dim-witted people is well-founded.

Another consideration that supports such reluctance has been fleetingly broached above. Many of the accidents caused by anybody's characteristic clumsiness or oafishness are quite easily avoidable through the forgoing of certain activities. For example, if someone is physically not able to drive a car in an acceptably safe manner – maybe because of poor eyesight or maybe because of a lack of physical dexterity – she commits an error of judgment by driving at all. If her substandard driving eventuates in a mishap, then the attribution of negligence to her is a censorious reflection on her initial judgment as much as on the inept bit of driving that immediately preceded the collision. Because she could have averted the harmful incident by refraining from driving, she will be in a weak position to request leniency when she has declined to avail herself of that option. (Of course, in the unlikely event that her driving has been prompted by the occurrence of a dire emergency, this particular point against indulgence will lack its usual force. In such circumstances, her bad driving might be deemed nonnegligent.)

Another factor in support of the current position within Anglo-American tort law is that a practice of differentiating among people by reference to their physical and mental inadequacies could be a slippery slope. After all, an inveterately malign disposition is likewise an inadequacy or inability. Somebody unfortunate enough to be possessed of such a disposition is unable to conform to ordinary standards of decency and sociability. Quite unconscionable, however, is the notion that tort-law proceedings or even criminal-law proceedings should treat such a person in a notably favorable fashion by exonerating him whenever his wrong-doing is due to his ingrained disposition. To be sure, the provenance of his depraved character – its origin in a troubled childhood, for example – might be taken into account by a criminal-justice system at the stage of sentencing. Still, the idea that he should be absolved of all penalties sim-ply because of his profoundly evil temperament is ridiculous. Yet, if the longstanding unintelligence or physical clumsiness of a defendant in a negligence case were to be treated as a ground for deeming her slipshod conduct to have satisfied the standard of reasonable care, there might be no strong reason for refusing to treat a defendant's perdurably evil out-look in a broadly parallel manner. Any inept defendant in a negligence case would be shielding herself by highlighting her inability to live up to an ordinary requirement of reasonableness. Correspondingly, then, a deeply depraved defendant who is sued for committing an intentional tort might shield himself by highlighting his inability to abstain from forming and pursuing the evil intention on which he has acted. Such a defendant would argue that he should not have to pay damages for giving effect to intentions of which the formation has lain wholly beyond his control; he should not have to pay damages for acting on intentions that flow irresistibly from his inveterate character, just as a maladroit defen-dant should not have to pay damages for instances of slapdash conduct which she was incapable of improving upon. If we wish to reject the con-clusion reached by this nefarious intentional wrongdoer about his own situation, we ought *pari passu* to reject the chief premise of his argument. That is, we should reject the thesis that the standard of reasonable care in tort law is to be adjusted downward for people whose obtuseness or physical uncoordination prevents them from satisfying that standard at its normal level.

An additional reason for querying the thesis just mentioned is that, although special treatment for people with paltry mental or physical endowments would not be repellently invidious, it would very likely stigmatize such people. They would be classified not as full adults who are to be answerable for their conduct on a par with everyone else, but as degraded specimens of humanity to whom condescending indulgence is to be extended by the courts. Though some or all of them might feel that the demeaningness of such treatment would be outweighed by the benefits of escaping the imposition of compensatory obligations, the demeaningness would be a genuine drawback both for them and for the society in which they interact with everyone else. So long as the normal standard of reasonable care is itself set at an appropriate level by the courts, a person's being held to that standard is one of the indicia of her dignity as a full member of her society.

Also militating in favor of the uniform applicability of the test for negligence within Anglo-American tort law is the lowering of the administrative costs in the implementation of that test. If judges and other legal officials had to investigate the physical or mental shortcomings of defendants in order to gauge how stringent the test for negligence should be in application to each individual, the costs of administering the doctrine of negligence would significantly rise. Moreover, such an increase in administrative costs would be accompanied by an increase in the likelihood of fraud on the part of defendants. Admittedly, these concerns about greater costs and more frequent dishonesty are not in themselves dispositive. In combination with the factors discussed in the last several paragraphs, however, they are enough to warrant the retention of the unaccommodating objectivity of the negligence standard. Though differential applicability on the basis of physical and mental inadequacies is doubtless desirable in many criminal cases at the stage of sentencing and maybe at earlier stages, it would be more detrimental than beneficial if it were introduced into the law of negligence.

1.2.3.2. Uniform Applicability versus Neutrality

Before we move on from this topic, we should note that these remarks on the objectivity-qua-uniform-applicability of the test for negligence in Anglo-American tort law can alert us to an important distinction. Uniform applicability, at least as explicated throughout this subsection, is not equivalent to neutrality. A situation of uniform applicability is a situation in which everyone is judged by reference to the same criteria. When everyone's conduct is so judged, some people will clearly tend to fare better than others. Uniform applicability will generate disparate outcomes. For instance, a criterion of reasonable care that is applied to thick-witted people and percipient people alike will naturally tend to favor the latter.

Neutrality is quite different. It consists not in uniform applicability but in uniformity of impact. If some law *L* were thoroughly neutral, it would leave all benefits and burdens distributed exactly as they would be if *L* did not exist. Obviously, then, no law is thoroughly neutral – unless it is purely nominal and of no practical effect whatsoever. In regard to any law that is not purely nominal, the most that can be attained is neutrality in this or that particular respect. A revenue-neutral change in the law of taxation, for example, will yield the same amount of revenue for the government as was received before the occurrence of the change. While keeping the total revenue unmodified, however, it will alter the distribution of the burdens of taxation among various taxpayers.

Neutrality in some particular respect(s) can be achieved through departures from uniform applicability in some particular respect(s). For instance, the revenue-neutrality of an alteration in the law of taxation can come about through the augmentation of existing levies for some taxpayers and the elimination of those levies for other taxpayers. A charge previously applicable to all taxpayers is henceforth applicable only to some, and at a more onerous level.

Now, although uniform applicability and neutrality are decidedly not equivalent, any uniformly applicable laws will be neutral in some respects while being nonneutral in sundry other respects. As has already been observed, no law that is of any practical effect will leave everything in the existing distribution of benefits and burdens unaltered; what should now be added, conversely, is that no law or set of laws can ever alter everything. The ways in which a law is uniformly applicable may well be salient, and the ways in which it is neutral may be much less interesting and important and evident, but there are bound to be ways in which it is indeed neutral. Hence, our attentiveness to the distinction between uniform applicability and neutrality should hardly induce us to think that those two properties never coincide. Inevitably, each of those properties in *some* form will coincide with the other in *some* form. We should recognize as much, while also recognizing the significant difference between judging everyone by the same criteria and bringing about an equal upshot for everyone.

1.2.4. *Objectivity qua Transindividual Discernibility*

Having pondered some of the respects in which law is ontologically objective, we shall now turn to some epistemic aspects of objectivity. That is, we shall now probe the relationships between legal phenomena and the minds of the people (both legal officials and ordinary citizens) who ascertain or seek to ascertain what those phenomena are. For any domain of enquiry, the central hallmark of its epistemic objectivity is the transindividual discernibility of the bearings of the things within it. In other words, a domain of enquiry is epistemically objective insofar as people who competently investigate the entities within the domain are able to concur on the nature or specifics of each of them. If all or nearly all competent enquirers agree about those entities, then – within the domain comprising them – the tastes and peculiarities of individuals are not dispositive touchstones for what can warrantedly be affirmed. If any field of enquiry is such that individuals' tastes and peculiarities are indeed epistemically dispositive touchstones within it, then the field is highly subjective (as an epistemic matter); contrariwise, if a field of enquiry is such that those tastes and peculiarities are subordinate to very widely shared perceptions which sustain virtual unanimity on the matters to which the perceptions pertain, then those matters are epistemically objective. In sum, the epistemic objectivity of any phenomena consists in the pronounced tendency of individuals to converge in their beliefs about those phenomena.

As should be apparent, epistemic objectivity in the sense just expounded is a scalar property rather than an all-or-nothing property. Things partake of it to varying degrees. An area of enquiry can be epistemically more objective or less objective than any number of other areas of enquiry, and the issues covered within such an area will themselves almost certainly differ from one another in the extent to which they elicit agreement. Furthermore, the epistemic objectivity of some or all of those issues can evolve over time. Topics formerly controversial can eventually evoke consentaneous views among people, and topics formerly agreed upon widely can become heatedly unsettled. Thus, in its epistemic standing, an issue can become more objective or less objective than it used to be.

What has just been said about changes over time in the epistemic objectivity of certain areas of enquiry does not imply that the epistemic objectivity of a matter will always hinge on the existence of a current consensus concerning that matter. If there is widespread agreement on appropriate methods for arriving at a consensus on the answer to some question, and if the employment of those methods will indeed ultimately eventuate in approximate unanimity on some answer, then the question is currently classifiable as epistemically objective even if the state

of approximate unanimity will not be reached for quite a while. Epistemic objectivity is lacking – or is significantly diminished – only if there
is neither broad agreement on the answer to some question nor broad
agreement on techniques by which the disagreements over that question
can in due time be resolved.

Objectivity qua transindividual discernibility does not entail objectivity qua strong existential mind-independence, nor does the latter entail
the former. Similarly, objectivity qua determinate correctness does not
entail objectivity qua transindividual discernibility, nor does the latter
entail the former. These points are crucial for an understanding of the
epistemic objectivity of law. Hence, although some of them overlap with
points made in previous subsections of this chapter, we should mull over
each of them carefully.

Let us begin, then, with the lack of entailment between epistemic
objectivity – transindividual discernibility – and strong existential mind-
independence. On the one hand, to be sure, epistemic objectivity is perhaps most conspicuous in some domains whose entities are strongly
mind-independent existentially as well as observationally. The physical
entities of the natural world, studied by the natural sciences, are epistemically objective and are also strongly mind-independent (existentially as
well as observationally). Though experimentation and theorizing at the
frontiers of the natural sciences are inevitably attended by controversy,
the correct answers to untold other questions about natural entities are
recognized by everyone or virtually everyone who addresses those questions. Countless elementary matters concerning the size and substance of
natural objects do not provoke any disputation whatsoever, and a myriad
of scientifically more sophisticated matters are likewise wholly uncontroversial among all the people who are competent to understand them. Even
in regard to the contentious questions at the edges of the natural sciences,
there is often very widespread agreement (among people with relevant
expertise) on the appropriate methods for coming up with firm answers
to those questions. In the domains of enquiry that are the precincts of
the natural sciences, in short, the strong existential mind-independence
of the phenomena is accompanied by a very high degree of epistemic
objectivity.

On the other hand, we should not leap to the conclusion that epistemic objectivity presupposes strong existential mind-independence. As

was argued earlier, the existential mind-independence of the general mandates and other general norms of a legal system is only weak rather than strong. Those mandates and other legal norms are operative as such in any particular legal regime only because the regime's officials share certain beliefs and attitudes that impel them to treat the aforementioned norms as authoritative. Yet, although the existential mind-independence of general laws is only weak, those laws and the system which they compose are characterized by a high degree of epistemic objectivity. Under any functional legal regime, the jural consequences of people's conduct will be clear-cut in a vast range of circumstances. In fact, those consequences most of the time go unmentioned precisely because they are so obvious to everyone who is competent to discuss them. Only in a small proportion of circumstances do significant disagreements arise (among people with relevant expertise) over the legal implications of various instances of conduct. Admittedly, there is not frequently very widespread agreement on the appropriate methods for resolving disagreements among experts when they do occur. Disagreements among jurists on problematic points of law quite often prove to be intractable. In that respect, the epistemic objectivity of law may be more tenuous than the epistemic objectivity of mathematics and the natural sciences. Nonetheless, the epistemic objectivity of law in most situations is robust. Convergence (at least among experts) is typical, and serious disaccord is exceptional. Given as much, and given that the existential mind-independence of general legal norms is weak rather than strong, the epistemic objectivity of some phenomenon plainly does not per se presuppose the strong existential mind-independence of that phenomenon. Things dependent on human minds for their occurrence or continued existence can be things on whose bearings there is generally a consensus. Indeed, as was suggested in Section 1.2.1, our epistemic access to such things may in quite a few contexts be singularly reliable. Accordingly, there should be a very high degree of epistemic objectivity in those contexts.

Let us now briefly turn to the lack of any entailment between strong existential mind-independence and transindividual discernibility. Some of the questions investigated by the discipline of cosmology – a branch of science dealing with the origin and dynamics of the universe as a whole – well exemplify that lack of entailment. Although the answers to some cosmological questions are now widely agreed upon (among experts), and although the answers to many of the remaining questions are pursued with great mathematical rigor, cosmologists are far from approaching a consensus on what the answers to those remaining questions are. They have devised multiple sophisticated models, each of which generates answers that are largely inconsistent with those generated by the other models. Some of the models have attracted more adherents than others, but there is not at present anything close to unanimity on any of them; nor is there anything close to unanimity on appropriate methods for adjudicating among them. Across many questions of cosmology, then, the epistemic objectivity of the discipline is currently quite low. All the same, the existential mind-independence of the facts and occurrences to which the moot questions of cosmology pertain is paradigmatically strong rather than weak. Those unresolved questions of cosmology therefore strikingly illustrate a general point. When expert enquirers plumb phenomena whose occurrence or continued existence is completely independent of the enquirers' minds and everyone else's mind, there are no guarantees against the emergence of intractable disagreements among them. The experts will undoubtedly converge with one another in many of their judgments, but persistent divergences are abidingly possible and sometimes actual.

We should next contemplate the relationship of nonentailment between determinate correctness and transindividual discernibility. *Mutatis mutandis*, the preceding paragraph has made clear that the existence of uniquely correct answers to various questions does not entail the existence of a consensus (even among experts) on what those answers are. After all, to each of the unsettled questions of cosmology there is a uniquely correct answer – even if we might never know what the answer in each case is. Given that there is currently nothing close to unanimity (even among experts) on what the uniquely correct answer to each of those unsettled questions is, we can infer quite readily that determinate correctness does not entail epistemic objectivity. However, this point is applicable not only to phenomena whose existential mind-independence is strong, but also to phenomena (such as legal norms) whose existential mind-independence is merely weak. We have seen as much in this chapter's earlier discussion of the distinction between determinacy and demonstrability.

Determinately correct answers to legal questions in multitudinous easy cases are very widely agreed upon, but difficult cases in appellate courts are typically much more controversial. Still, especially within a legal system where the officials have incorporated the correct principles of morality into the law to fill in where the ordinary sources of law run out, there will be determinately correct answers to the questions in some difficult cases. Suppose for example that such a legal system exists in a society in which racial relations are at a stage similar to that reached in the United States by the early 1950s. Suppose that the system's highest court must decide whether racial segregation in public schools is consistent with constitutional provisions requiring equal protection of the laws. Given the specified state of racial relations in the imagined society, the legal question of the constitutionality of segregated public schools will be intensely controversial (as it was when the U.S. Supreme Court arrived at a unanimous but circumspect decision on the matter in 1954). Legal experts will disagree with one another, and numerous lines of reasoning will be advanced on each side of the question. Some of the arguments affirming the constitutionality of segregation in public schools may evince racial prejudice, but many of them will focus quite reasonably on factors such as the proper role of courts in a liberal-democratic society. Nevertheless, despite the vigorous disaccord among experts on the issue, there is a uniquely correct answer to the legal question whether the sustainment of racial segregation in public schools is consistent with constitutional provisions requiring equal protection of the laws. Notwithstanding the genuineness of some countervailing considerations, the uniquely correct answer to that question is negative. For the court addressing the question, then, only a decision that disallows the segregation is appropriate. To say as much, however, is hardly to say that that decision will be commended by all or nearly all legal experts at the time when it is rendered. Determinate correctness does not entail transindividual discernibility.

Let us finally turn to the absence of any entailment between transindividual discernibility and determinate correctness. That absence of any entailment sometimes manifests itself across a whole body of ostensible knowledge. Suppose that the wise men and magicians of ancient Egypt fully concurred with one another about the most effective incantations and ceremonies for various occasions. They all agreed, we may assume, that a spell or ritual of such and such a type would propitiate the gods in such and such a context, and that a spell or ritual of some other type would propitiate the gods in some other context. Their wisdom consisted in a host of answers to a host of questions about the optimal means of currying favor with the gods. In fact, however, there was no determinately correct answer to any of those questions – except an "answer" that would brand each question itself as utterly misconceived because of the wildly false assumptions underlying it. Whenever the Egyptians posed one of their questions, such as an inquiry whether the gods would look more favorably upon the sacrifice of a goat at a funeral than upon the sacrifice of a sheep, every nondismissive reply was wrong and was therefore no worse and no better than every other nondismissive reply. There was, in short, no determinately correct answer to any of the Egyptians' questions; a wholesale rejection of each such question was the uniquely correct response. Hence, although the Egyptian wise men and magicians themselves converged with one another in their views of the gods' wishes, the epistemic objectivity of the topics covered by their body of putative knowledge was not matched by the determinate correctness of any of their claims. Those claims were baseless, in spite of the transindividual discernibility of their apparent pertinence.

More often, the absence of any entailment between transindividual discernibility and determinate correctness manifests itself not in relation to a whole practice or a whole body of thought, but in relation to certain theses that are advanced within some practice or some body of thought. Consider, for instance, a legal system in which a question arises to which there is not any determinately correct answer. (Perhaps the question is whether a skateboard falls under the scope of a ban on any vehicles in a public park. Or perhaps it is a loftier issue revolving around a constitutional provision that guarantees equality or liberty or justice. We need not concern ourselves here with the specifics of the matter or of the case that raises it.) Now, although there is not genuinely any determinately correct answer to the question that has arisen, all or most of the legal officials and other legal experts who address the problem may incline toward one view. To be sure, insofar as the legal officials' decisions on the matter carry precedential force, their shared view will henceforth constitute the uniquely correct answer to the legal question that has been posed. Their shared view will become the binding law on that question. At the time when the officials articulate that view authoritatively, however, there is (*ex hypothesi*) not yet any determinately correct position. The transindividual discernibility of a certain position does not entail its determinate correctness.

Although I have here emphasized that transindividual discernibility is separable from strong existential mind-independence and from determinate correctness, I obviously do not mean to suggest that those types of objectivity will invariably or typically diverge. They will frequently coincide. What these remarks have sought to highlight, rather, is simply the persistent possibility that epistemic objectivity will not coincide in this or that particular context with some major kinds of ontological objectivity. Ontological objectivity pertains to how things actually are, whereas epistemic objectivity pertains to how things are collectively believed to be. Thus, although there are solid reasons for expecting epistemic objectivity and ontological objectivity to be frequently concurrent in many domains of enquiry – reasons centered on the evolutionary pressures that have formed human minds to be similar to one another and to be generally responsive to the actualities of the world – there is never a guarantee of such concurrence. There always abides the potential for incongruity between how things actually are and how things are collectively believed to be.

1.2.5. Objectivity qua Impartiality

Another epistemic variety of objectivity is impartiality,[12] which consists of disinterestedness and open-mindedness, and which can also be designated as "detachedness" or "impersonality." It is to be contrasted with bias and partisanship, but also with impetuousness and whimsicalness (though sometimes not with genuine randomness). In legal contexts, this dimension of objectivity can apply to the stage at which laws are created and to the stage at which they are administered. Like some other aspects of objectivity, it is a scalar property rather than an all-or-nothing property; it is realized to varying degrees.

1.2.5.1. Impartiality Distinguished from Neutrality

This chapter has already distinguished between uniform applicability and neutrality. A broadly similar distinction is advisable here between impartiality and neutrality. Admittedly, as some commentators have observed

---

[12] For a good recent discussion of impartiality in legal contexts, see Lucy 2005. See also Marmor 2001, 147–52.

(Lucy 2005, 13), "impartiality" and "neutrality" are quite often used inter-
changeably in ordinary discourse. Each of those terms can denote the
detachedness of someone whose decisions are not inflected by any peculiar predilections or by any direct personal stake in the matters to which
the decisions pertain. All the same, the two terms are differentiated in
ordinary discourse as readily as they are assimilated. Whereas "impartiality" ordinarily denotes a property that relates to the conditions under
which decisions are made, "neutrality" frequently denotes a property that
relates to the consequences of decisions. The latter property, as has been
indicated in my earlier discussion of it, consists in the retention of the
existing distribution of benefits and burdens among the people in a society. No law and no process of law-enforcement can ever be neutral in all
respects, but every law or process of law-enforcement is neutral in some
respects (though its lack of neutrality in other respects may be far more
conspicuous and important).

Impartiality is different. Usually, when somebody asks whether the
workings of a legal system are impartial, she is not inquiring about their
effects. Instead, she is inquiring about the processes through which the
decisions of legal officials are reached and implemented. A rigorously
impartial decision can be strikingly nonneutral.

1.2.5.2. Disinterestedness

Impartiality is, obviously, a lack of partiality. Among the things essential
to it is either the absence of any perceived personal stake in one's decision
or an ability to let one's decision be unaffected by one's awareness that one
has a stake therein. Somebody usually has a personal stake in a decision
if he himself or a close relative or friend stands to benefit significantly
in the event that the decision goes in some direction(s) rather than in
some contrary direction(s). To be sure, such a stake is not present if
a person has a close relative or friend on each side of the issue under
consideration. For example, when a parent has to decide which of her
two children should be allowed to play with a certain toy, her impartiality
is not undermined by the fact that she has two close relatives who will
each stand to benefit significantly if her decision goes in one direction
rather than the other. Precisely because the personal stake of each of
those relatives is offset by that of the other, the parent's impartiality is

unimpaired. When there is not an even balance of this sort on each side of an issue, however, a decision-maker's impartiality is tarnished by her knowing that the fortunes of a close relative or friend will be significantly affected by the upshot of her deliberations.

Impartiality is strongest when there is no personal stake on the part of anyone who renders a judgment on some matter. However, especially in connection with the creation of laws but even sometimes in connection with the administration of them, the avoidance of a personal stake for each decision-maker is not altogether possible. Consider, for example, the legislators who have to vote on a bill that will affect the distribution of the burdens of taxation among people with differing levels of income. If the proposed bill will be quite sweeping in its effects, then every legislator will to some degree have a personal stake in the outcome of the vote. Much the same can be said about judges and administrators who have to interpret central provisions of the bill or who have to arrive at other determinations that will significantly bear on the distribution of the burdens of taxation. If the absence of any personal stakes in these legislative and judicial and administrative decisions were prerequisite to the impartiality of the processes through which the decisions are reached, then those processes could not be impartial. Every legislator or judge or administrator will have a personal stake in the aforementioned decisions (and in a number of other determinations that will have to be rendered in the course of the fulfillment of legislative or judicial or administrative responsibilities). We should not conclude, however, that impartiality concerning these matters is impossible. In regard to any decision for which the avoidance of a direct personal stake on the part of the decision-maker(s) is not feasible – because every legal official will have such a stake – each official involved should strive for impartiality by seeking to prescind from his personal prospects as he arrives at the decision in question. There are no grounds for thinking that people are incapable of mentally stepping back from their personal fortunes in order to assume a disinterested perspective on matters with which they have to deal. Efforts to step back may fail in particular instances, but they are not inevitably doomed to failure.

Nevertheless, although impartiality is possible even in circumstances in which the personal interests of a decision-maker will be substantially affected by a decision that has to be made, it is obviously less likely in such circumstances. An endeavor by a decision-maker to prescind from his personal prospects may fail in either of two respects: he might remain prejudiced in favor of his own interests, despite his sincere attempt to ascend to a disinterested stance; or, more subtly, he might overcompensate for his personal stake in the matter by showing more sympathy for the position opposed to his own well-being than is really due. All in all, then, a quest for impartiality in legal decision-making is best advanced when each official responsible for dealing authoritatively with some issue is genuinely disinterested. Insofar as decisions can be assigned to legal officials whose own fortunes are not tied up with them, they should be so assigned.

This point about genuine disinterestedness is particularly weighty when the issue on which a legal-governmental official has to pass judgment is not some broad matter of public policy such as taxation, but a matter that impinges on his own interests far more than on those of all or most other people. For example, a paradigmatic deviation from impartiality would be a judge's presiding over a trial of someone accused of having murdered the judge's daughter, or a public regulatory administrator's presiding over a hearing of allegations against a company of which the administrator is a director. Even in circumstances in which a legal official's interests are not at stake to a far greater degree than those of most other people, moreover, genuine disinterestedness should be sought if it is reasonably attainable. Suppose, for instance, that a public regulatory administrator is to preside over a hearing of allegations against a company in which he holds a large number of shares. Suppose further that virtually everyone else in the community holds a similar quantity of shares in the company. Nonetheless, despite the fact that the administrator does not stand to lose or gain much more from his judgment on the company's dealings than does anyone else, he should be required to take measures to achieve a posture of genuine disinterestedness. He should at least be required to place his shares in a blind trust that can be managed by an independent third party; perhaps, more robustly, he should even be required to divest himself of his shares altogether before undertaking the investigative hearing. When a legal-governmental official confronts a serious problem that obliges him to decide between competing claims and interests, and when he can deprive himself of any personal stake in the matter by taking steps that are not unreasonably onerous, his taking those steps should be mandatory. Impartiality would not be impossible without those steps, but it would be far more difficult and precarious.

Ideally, these remarks about disinterestedness would be applicable to the legislative branch of a legal-governmental system as well as to the judicial and executive branches. Legislators passing judgment on matters of public policy should be doing so from a perspective focused on the common weal rather than on personal gain. However, in Western liberal democracies – to say nothing of tyrannical regimes in other parts of the world – the requirement of disinterestedness is typically much less stringent for legislators than for adjudicators and administrators. On the one hand, undoubtedly countenanceable or at any rate tolerable is the fact that most legislators quite routinely vote in ways that are calculated to gratify their constituents. A legislator who very frequently goes against the wishes and interests of her constituents will not usually fare well in subsequent elections. Besides, in addition to furthering her own aspiration to remain in power, a legislator who endeavors to please her constituents is actually performing one of the principal roles of her office. In a liberal democracy, each member of a legislature is called upon to fulfill a representative function as well as the function of promoting the general public good. Hence, when a legislator advances her own interests as a future candidate for reelection by heeding the views of her constituents, she is not really straying from what she ought to be doing (at least if fundamental rights are not under consideration). On the other hand, although a legislator does not really act improperly when she abandons strict impartiality by following the inclinations of her constituents on matters of public policy (as opposed to matters of fundamental rights), legislators' departures from strict impartiality in the major liberal democracies – especially in the United States – frequently go well beyond the fulfillment of any representative function. Large and well-funded organizations, many of them devoted principally to lobbying legislators on various issues, exert enviable influence in the areas of public policy that concern them. Such organizations, which hail from sundry points on the political spectrum, attain their influence by offering financial support and other electoral assistance to friendly politicians and by threatening to resist fiercely any politicians who are not sympathetic to their aims.

Faced with these carrots and sticks, many legislators vote (on certain issues) in compliance with the organizations' behests rather than on the basis of any disinterested assessments.

It is debatable whether these marked deviations from the ideal of disinterestedness on the part of legislators should be sharply curtailed through more stringent regulation. As James Madison recognized in his classic discussion of the role of factions in politics (Madison 1961 [1788], 78), the suppression of factions is a cure worse than the disease. What is more, the coalescence of citizens into a high-profile lobbying group may be the sole effective means by which they can garner support and respect for their possibly worthy cause. Thus, although legislators would act optimally if they were to take the general public weal rather than their own political fortunes as their lodestar when arriving at decisions on key matters of public policy, the electoral pressures that divert them from doing so are by no means unequivocally deplorable. Of course, certain types of departures from disinterestedness (involving corruption, for example) should be proscribed for legislators as much as for other legal-governmental officials. However, a severe requirement of disinterestedness for legislators – involving, for instance, harsh limits on the spending and the political activities of organizations devoted to lobbying – would not be unalloyedly beneficial for the workings of a liberal-democratic system of politics.

Whatever may be the desirability of a greater degree of disinterestedness on the part of legislators, the importance of a very high degree of disinterestedness on the part of judges and administrators is virtually undisputed. We shall ponder the reasons for that importance shortly (and in the next chapter), but we should first consider the other main element of objectivity qua impartiality. An impartial perspective for decision-making is not only disinterested but also open-minded.

1.2.5.3. Open-Mindedness

One evident component of open-mindedness is the absence of prejudice and favoritism. If some person P harbors special animosity or special fondness toward certain people – particularly on grounds such as race and religion and ethnicity, which are unrelated to people's merits and probity – then P lacks the open-mindedness that is essential for reaching impartial decisions on matters that pit such people against other people. To be sure, P might still be able to render impartial judgments on matters that involve only the sorts of people toward whom he feels peculiar antipathy or affection. If P is biased in favor of Hispanic people, for instance, he might nevertheless be suitably impartial when passing judgment on a contract-law dispute between two Hispanic businessmen. However, insofar as his prejudices do bear on an issue which he is called upon to decide – and, thus, insofar as those prejudices are likely to inflect his stance on that issue – his perspective on the issue is not open-minded and is therefore not impartial.

Of course, biases vary in intensity. If P is only mildly prejudiced (favorably or unfavorably) toward people of a certain kind, then his open-mindedness when dealing with such people is not very materially compromised. Moreover, just as somebody may be able to prescind from her personal stake in some matter in order to deliver an impartial judgment thereon, P might be able to put aside his prejudicial attitudes in order to reach decisions fair-mindedly. All the same, the likelihood of a genuinely impartial stance in such circumstances is far lower than in circumstances in which P does not harbor any invidious biases. Even less likely, if P's attitudes have become known, is that his decisions will be perceived as impartial. Consequently, both for the actual objectivity of a legal system's operations and for their perceived objectivity, a lack of bigotry on the part of legal officials is crucial.

Another central component of open-mindedness (and thus of impartiality) is the absence of whimsicalness and impetuosity. Someone who plunges ahead without attending to the actualities of a situation is failing to display open-mindedness, just as dramatically as someone whose prejudices blind him to those actualities. To be open-minded in addressing some problem is in part to be scrupulously ready to learn of the sundry facts from which the problem arises. Albeit somebody who proceeds on the basis of caprices and conjectures might fortuitously arrive at a correct decision in any particular context – as might somebody who proceeds on the basis of prejudices – the outcome will not have been reached through a process that is designed to avoid favoring or disfavoring anyone arbitrarily. A process that is appositely designed will ensure that decision-makers become apprised of all relevant facts to which they can reasonably gain access.

1.2.5.4. Open-Mindedness in a Juridical Setting

In a system of law, judges and other legal officials will need to make use of techniques through which they can become acquainted with all the reasonably ascertainable facts that bear upon the legal questions to which they have to come up with answers. This requirement of official open-mindedness can of course be satisfied through more than one set of techniques for the gathering of information. While the adversarial structure of disputes and prosecutions in Anglo-American law involves one such set of techniques, the very different structure of disputes and prosecutions in many civil-law countries involves a different set of information-gathering techniques that can be just as suitable. Whatever may be the exact procedures that are employed, legal officials will not be performing their roles in an open-minded manner unless they do their best to attune themselves to the specificities of the situations on which they are passing judgment. For that purpose, the participation of each party to a legal dispute in the information-gathering processes is essential, whether those processes be adversarial or inquisitorial. Since some key aspects of the relevant facts may be missed if the parties do not have opportunities to express their views, the provision of such opportunities is indispensable for the impartiality of a legal system's workings. In the absence of such opportunities, those workings may be placing certain parties at a disadvantage simply because the legal officials are being kept ignorant of vital information. Also indispensable, clearly, are opportunities for participation by witnesses or by other people who are in possession of germane information. If such sources of information are excluded from the processes by which legal officials determine the jural consequences of people's conduct, those processes will be conjectural rather than open-mindedly sensitive to complexities. Officials who rely on surmises are hardly doing their best to avoid arbitrariness.

Precisely what should count as the adequate participation of parties and witnesses in legal decision-making is something that can vary quite considerably from jurisdiction to jurisdiction. In most circumstances, the parties should be free to avail themselves of expert legal advice and assistance (which may have to be supplied for them if they are indigent). However, the delivery of the advice and assistance can take many different paths, which will be affected by factors such as the adversarial or inquisitorial character of the legal system in any particular jurisdiction. Linguistic assistance for parties or witnesses, if needed, is plainly unforgoable (Lucy 2005, 11). Any inputs from such people will be of little value if they are completely nonplussed because of linguistic barriers. Further prerequisites of the ability of parties and witnesses to contribute satisfactorily to the processes of legal decision-making will loom larger in some societies than in others, but they should be accommodated wherever they are important.

A caveat should be entered here. Notwithstanding the general invaluableness of the receipt of accurate and relevant information in a quest for impartiality, the success of such a quest will sometimes depend on the exclusion of certain information that is both relevant and accurate. As has long been familiar in Anglo-American criminal law, some truths have to be left unstated if the trial of a defendant is to be impartial and fair. Those truths, though they are indeed truths, can be unacceptably prejudicial. That is, the disclosure of such a truth engenders a high probability that the jurors will become fixated on it and will fail to assess the other evidence dispassionately. In many jurisdictions, for example, the commission of past crimes by a defendant is not something that can be divulged to a jury in most circumstances before the stage of sentencing. Information about those previous misdeeds would be accurate and relevant (since people who have perpetrated crimes in the past are much more likely than other people to commit crimes in the present and the future), but the presentation of it to the jurors might well induce some of them to pay scant attention to the other evidence. Thus, in order to maintain the impartiality of a trial as a whole, the withholding of information about a defendant's past convictions can be warranted.

This point about the nondisclosure of accurate and relevant information is singularly pressing in some cases where the information is of a general statistical nature. Suppose for example that 70 percent of the drive-by shootings in some country are committed by young black men, who make up only 2 percent of the country's population (and only 12 percent of the total number of young men in the country). Were those statistics to be imparted to a jury in a trial involving a young black man accused of having engaged in a drive-by shooting, some jurors would probably be led to focus unduly on the color of the defendant's skin and insufficiently on the particulars of any exculpatory evidence. Hence, although those data might be fully reliable, and although they are not entirely irrelevant to the question of the defendant's guilt or innocence, the admission of them as evidence would detract from the impartiality and fairness of the trial as a whole. In order to keep the jurors' attention trained on the specificities of the case, the presiding judge should deem the aforementioned data to be inadmissible. (Of course, even given the average person's ineptitude in drawing valid inferences from statistics, one scarcely ought to conclude that all statistical data should be excluded as evidence. When such data are accurate and relevant and not prejudicial, the adducing of them as evidence is unobjectionable and pertinent. Even when they may be prejudicial, the adducing of them as evidence will be appropriate if their relevance to the question of a defendant's guilt or innocence is far more direct and weighty than in the case hypothesized here.)

A second caveat should be entered. Although whimsicalness and impulsiveness are to be eschewed in any serious process of decision-making, there can occasionally be a place for aleatory procedures (Duxbury 1999). Aleatoriness, in a limited range of settings, can be compatible with seriousness. Consider, for instance, the allocation of scarce resources for medical treatment in a country with a nationalized health-care system. Among a group of ailing people who are not distinguishable on the basis of the sundry touchstones that are normally determinative of medical priorities – the gravity of one's malady, the length of time spent waiting for treatment, the remediability or alleviability of one's malady, one's age and general health, the costs of a suitable course of treatment, and so forth – perhaps the best way of assigning resources for treatment is the adoption of an aleatory procedure such as a lottery. A procedure of that sort with effect among such people would not be arbitrary in any pejorative sense, since it would not supplant any conclusive principled basis for selecting among them. It would be strictly impartial, as it would amount to an acknowledgment of the absence of any clinching grounds for prioritization (grounds such as desert or need or social cost). Still, although impartiality would be upheld rather than undermined through the introduction of a random mechanism for prioritizing among the people in the situation envisaged, my description of that situation has presumably made clear that there will seldom be a role for randomness in the decision-making activities of administrative officials and other legal officials. Rarely will there be no conclusive principled grounds for selecting between people's competing claims, and even more rarely will there be no principled grounds at all for selecting between those claims. Yet, since aleatory procedures are impartiality-preserving only where there are indeed no such conclusive grounds, circumstances calling for those procedures will be uncommon. Such circumstances will arise from time to time, especially when only two or three people are involved; but they will not arise frequently. As has been contended earlier in this chapter, genuine indeterminacy in the law is exceptional rather than typical. What is more, the adoption of a random procedure will be improper in some settings even when there is no clinching basis for a decision. In a typical adjudicative setting, where the task is to ascertain the legal consequences of people's conduct, and where (in common-law countries) an outcome and its rationale will be endowed with precedential force until it is overruled, the use of aleatory devices such as the flipping of coins will be inappropriate even in the few difficult cases that hinge on legal questions to which there are no determinately correct answers. A court should have to explain why its ruling is correct, even if there are no grounds for maintaining that that ruling is uniquely correct. Nevertheless, there can be a limited range of other situations – such as the medical-care situation broached in this paragraph – in which administrators might permissibly and impartially resort to aleatory devices. The potential occurrence of such situations is especially plain when we turn our attention from the apportionment of benefits and reflect instead on the apportionment of certain burdens. Aleatory procedures for distributing some burdensome responsibilities such as jury service are generally fair.

One further caveat should be registered. Although impartiality does consist in detachedness, it does not in any way entail a lack of empathetic understanding of human actions and intentions. Legal-governmental officials who have to pass judgment on countless instances of the conduct of others will frequently not be able to perform their functions adequately unless they grasp the typical mainsprings of human behavior and the specific mainsprings of particular individuals' behavior. They have to be able to identify themselves with other people sufficiently to fathom why those people have acted in certain ways. Such identification does not in itself constitute approval, and therefore does not constitute a departure from impartiality. Though officials may well countenance some of the motivational patterns which they encounter, they may well deplore other such patterns; the sheer feat of gaining an empathetic understanding of those patterns, a feat that can take place in response to evil conduct as well as in response to laudable conduct, is per se neither a condonation nor a condemnation. It is fully consistent with impartiality. It is indeed often essential for impartiality, since officials cannot guard against arbitrariness unless they base their decisions on all reasonably accessible information that is both accurate and relevant. In many contexts, that information squarely includes what can be gleaned through empathetic understanding.

1.2.5.5. Why Impartiality?

Before we leave this exposition of impartiality, we should return to a key question that was deferred earlier. Why is it so important that processes of decision-making by public officials should partake of objectivity qua impartiality? In other words, what is the justification for requiring such processes to be free of any significant biases and to be based on all reasonably obtainable information rather than on guesswork and caprices? Why should legal officials (especially in the judicial and executive branches of government) be disinterested when making their decisions? This general justificatory matter will receive more sustained attention in Chapter 2, but a few remarks here will aptly round off the present discussion.[13]

Impartiality is important partly because of its epistemic reliability. That is, insofar as decision-making is not swayed by self-interested motivations or skewed by prejudices or clouded by ignorance, it is considerably more likely to yield determinately correct results. When legal officials are called upon to arrive at decisions and to answer legal questions, they are endeavoring – or should be endeavoring, at least in a liberal-democratic system of law – to reach the decisions and answers prescribed by the applicable legal norms. They are seeking to construe and effectuate those norms in accordance with the terms thereof. For that end, a posture of impartiality is crucial. If legal officials allow their deliberations to be inflected by their own selfish interests or by invidious biases or by uninformed impulses, they are substantially reducing the probability that

---

[13] For some illuminating comments on this justificatory matter, see Coleman and Leiter 1995, 242–45.

those deliberations will culminate in correct decisions. They are thereby shirking their legal responsibility to give effect to the laws of their system and to foster the values embodied in those laws. Unless the laws in question are iniquitous, the officials are likewise shirking their moral responsibilities.

Note that these observations about the epistemic reliability of impartial decision-making do not overlook a fact already discussed in this chapter: the fact that the officials in virtually any system of law will be legally empowered and permitted to exercise discretion in some of their law-effectuating activities. Whether the norms of the system which confer the discretionary authority on the officials are explicitly formulated or not, they exist as second-order norms with legally dispositive force. As such, they themselves have to be construed and applied by the officials along with the other laws of the system. If the approach of the officials to those norms is marred by departures from impartiality, then the likelihood of incorrect applications of the norms is greatly increased. Engaging in such departures, the officials are heightening the risk that the manner or the occasion of some exercise of discretion will not be in keeping with what they have been authorized to do. Impartiality, in short, is as important for the epistemic reliability of officials' discretionary decisions as it is for the epistemic reliability of their other legal decisions.

One major reason for insisting on legal officials' impartiality, then, is focused on the outcomes of their processes of decision-making. Impartiality markedly increases the probability that those outcomes will be correct. Another major consideration in favor of impartiality is focused on the processes of decision-making themselves. While helping to ensure that legal norms take effect in accordance with their terms, the impartiality of officials additionally helps to ensure that the operations of a legal system are fair and are perceived as fair. When a decision-making procedure lacks impartiality, it is doubly injurious to every person *D* who is disadvantaged by the upshot of the procedure. It is injurious because the upshot itself is of course detrimental to *D*'s interests, but also because the whole procedure bespeaks contempt – or, at the very least, a dearth of respect – for *D*. That second type of harm would have been present even if the outcome of the procedure had fortuitously gone in *D*'s favor. If the absence of impartiality stems from the dominance of self-seeking motivations on the part of the officials involved, then their pursuit of their own interests at the expense of D is a cavalier devaluation of him. That devaluation is a baneful slight quite apart from the disadvantageousness of the officials' ultimate decision. If the absence of impartiality is due to prejudice against D, then the indignity inflicted upon him is even more noxious and palpable. If the absence of impartiality resides in a state of uninformedness that could have been overcome without unreasonable difficulty, then the officials are displaying the meagerness of their concern to do justice to D.

The harms just enumerated will have occurred whether or not D is aware of their occurrence. In many contexts, moreover, the people disadvantaged by officials' deviations from impartiality will possess at least a general awareness of what has been done to them. They will sense, in outline if not in detail, that they have been treated disdainfully. Thus, a credible stance of impartiality adopted by legal-governmental officials is vital not only for the actual fairness and legitimacy of their proceedings but also for the perceived fairness and legitimacy thereof. Admittedly, the officials' strict adherence to impartiality in their judgments does not guarantee that the people affected will accept that they have been treated fairly. Even if we leave aside the possibility that the legal norms applied by the judgments are themselves odious, we should recognize that people who do not fare well at the hands of legal officials will quite often feel aggrieved irrespective of the actual reasonableness of the ways in which their situations have been handled. Nonetheless, although the actual impartiality of officials' law-ascertaining and law-applying endeavors does not ensure that those endeavors will be perceived as impartial and legitimate by citizens, it is the best means of cultivating such a perception. In a liberal-democratic society, in which there is no totalitarian conditioning of people's thoughts, officials will usually be most effective in conveying an impression of impartiality if they and their proceedings are in fact impartial. Insofar as such a state of affairs does obtain, justice is done, and justice is seen to be done.

Whenever officials stray from the ideal of impartiality, they derogate from the objectivity of their legal system by overweeningly infusing its operations with elements of their own outlooks. They skew those operations as they let their decisions be shaped by their selfish interests or their prejudices and predilections or their impulses and conjectures. They thereby deviate from their responsibility to gauge the legal consequences of people's conduct by reference to the terms of the applicable legal norms. They gauge those consequences instead by reference to aspects of themselves. In so doing, they increase the likelihood of their arriving at morally inappropriate outcomes, and they diminish the procedural fairness of their legal system's workings. They evince disrespect for the people who are subject to their rule, and they hazard the risk that those people will develop a commensurate sense of disrespect for them. Furthermore, as will become clearer in the next chapter, they impair the very functionality of their legal system as a legal system. They thus impair the realization of any values that can be secured by such a system.

Let us note, finally, that some strands of this discussion of impartiality bear upon the functions of legislators in a liberal democracy as much as on the functions of judges and administrators. On the one hand, as has been observed, the representative role of elected legislators is to some degree in tension with any firm expectation or strict requirement concerning the absence of self-interested promptings for their decisions. Most legislators will be sensitive to electoral pressures, and, when fundamental rights and liberties are not at stake, their sensitivity is morally legitimate. On the other hand, the representative role of legislators does not similarly warrant departures from impartiality in the direction of uninformedness or bigotry. Arbitrariness arising from ignorance and prejudice is as objectionable for legislators who are reaching decisions on matters of public policy as for judges and administrators who are reaching decisions on particular cases. Of course, because the legislators are addressing general problems rather than concrete circumstances in which those problems surface, their responsibility to apprise themselves of relevant facts is different from that of judges and administrators. Legislators are focused on the broad consequences that are likely to follow from various public-policy choices – consequences very often expressible in statistical formulations. They are not focused more narrowly on the details of particular disputes between specifiable individuals. All the same, although legislators will not normally be expected to train their attention on any of those narrowly circumscribed details, they will be obligated and expected to acquaint themselves with the general advantages and disadvantages of different public-policy options. Their decisions on such options will be arbitrary if they do not equip themselves with that general information (insofar as it is reasonably available). To ascend to a posture of impartiality that averts arbitrariness, legislators have to eschew guesswork. They should strive to know what they are doing.

In so striving, the legislators will maximize the epistemic reliability of their proceedings. That is, they will maximize the likelihood of their arriving at the determinately correct answers to the questions which they are addressing. Of course, unlike the problems addressed by judges and administrators who are seeking to give effect to legal norms, the questions confronting legislators are typically not legal questions. In other words, those questions are not about the implications of already existent laws. Rather, the legislators are addressing (or should be addressing) moral issues concerning the virtues and drawbacks of laws which they propose to bring into existence. Their chances of resolving those moral issues in determinately correct ways will be slim indeed unless they approach their task without prejudices and without rectifiable ignorance. The arbitrariness introduced by such prejudices and ignorance would not only be inimical to procedural fairness – in that some people's interests would be discounted on the basis of bigotry or capricious speculation – but would also undermine the reliability of the legislators' deliberations as a means for coming up with correct answers to major questions of political morality. Both from a perspective that concentrates on the legitimacy of processes and from a perspective that concentrates on the correctness of outcomes, we can grasp that impartiality is a regulative ideal for legislative deliberations as well as for adjudicative and administrative deliberations. Its requirements are not precisely the same for legislators as for adjudicators and administrators, but legislative responsibilities in a liberal democracy cannot genuinely be fulfilled without it.

1.2.6. Objectivity qua Truth-Aptitude

Having explored some ontological and epistemic conceptions of objectivity, we now turn to the chief semantic conception. As was mentioned near the outset of this chapter, semantic objectivity concerns the relationships between people's assertions and the things about which those assertions are propounded. Such objectivity, as expounded here, consists in statements' being endowed with truth-values (that is, values of "true" or "false"). If meaningful declarative statements can be made in a certain domain, and if many of those statements are each true or false, then the domain is semantically objective to a greater or a lesser extent. Contrariwise, if no meaningful declarative statements are assertible in some domain, or if all such statements that can be asserted therein are not possessed of any truth-values, then the domain lacks semantic objectivity.

This account of semantic objectivity stands in need of some elucidation before we can ponder it in connection with law. Why, specifically, does the account confine itself to meaningful declarative statements? Meaningfulness is attached as a condition in order to exclude nonsensical utterances such as "Green ideas sleep furiously" or "The eyelashes of the number seven become triangular more rarely than a nonexistent baseball game." Because such utterances are devoid of any intelligible meaning, they are likewise devoid of truth-values. The possibility of such utterances should not count against the semantic objectivity of a body of discourse in which they might occur. Much the same can be said about nondeclarative sentences. Such sentences, most notably imperatives (such as "Shut the door") and interrogatives (such as "On which day of the week were you born?") and interjections (such as "Hello" or "Good grief!"), do not possess any truth-values. The evident possibility of the utterance of such sentences in some domain of enquiry is hardly a factor that should count against the semantic objectivity of that domain. If all or some of the meaningful declarative statements in a body of discourse are evaluable as true or false, then that discourse is semantically objective regardless of how many questions might be asked and how many imperatives might be issued within it.

In any domain of enquiry that is not artificially restricted, some of the meaningful declarative statements assertible within the domain will lack determinate truth-values. For example, every paradoxical statement – such as "The present statement is not true" – will lack any coherent truth-value, since the truth of any such statement entails its falsity, while its falsity entails its truth. Some other examples of meaningful declarative statements without determinate truth-values are statements involving presuppositional failures, of which the most striking instances are statements that involve radical reference failures. The assertion "There is at present a King of France" is importantly different from the assertion "The present King of France has run a one-mile race in under four minutes." Whereas the former assertion directly *affirms* the current existence of a King of France, the latter assertion merely *presupposes* the current existence of such a person. Consequently, the former statement is possessed of a determinate truth-value – it is false – whereas the latter statement is not possessed of any such truth-value.

Of considerable interest to jurisprudential theorists is another class of meaningful declarative statements without determinate truth-values: a class comprising some statements that apply vague predicates (Endicott 2000). Here we return to a theme explored from a slightly different angle near the end of Section 1.2.2. A vague predicate, such as "tall" or "short" or "thin" or "bald" or "being a heap," is not fully precise across the full range of the phenomena to which it might be applied. Across that range there is an unsettled region of borderline cases, an unsettled region whose beginning and end are themselves only vaguely specifiable. Within that area of indeterminate application, we can neither correctly affirm nor correctly deny that some entity partakes of the property denoted by the vague predicate in question. For example, a certain man may be of such a height that we can neither correctly affirm nor correctly deny that he is tall. Likewise, an accumulation of grains of sand may be of such a size that we can neither correctly affirm nor correctly deny that it is a heap. (In each case, we might not know or even be capable of knowing that we can neither correctly affirm nor correctly deny the relevant proposition.) Juridical examples of this phenomenon are abundant. We have indeed already encountered one such example, in my earlier discussion of vagueness. Insofar as the legal predicate "reasonable" is vague in the sense indicated, some possible instances of conduct are such that we can neither correctly affirm nor correctly deny that they are reasonable. In that event, a statement asserting or gainsaying the reasonableness of any such borderline instance of conduct is not possessed of a determinate truth-value.

Thus, when we seek to ascertain whether the statements advanced in some discourse or practice are semantically objective, we need to keep in mind that many statements are to be excluded from our investigation. We are putting aside statements that are unintelligible or nondeclarative,[14]

---

[14] The exclusion of nondeclarative utterances is especially important for an enquiry into the semantic objectivity of legal discourse, since some general laws and many situation-specific legal directives are correctly construable as imperatives.

and we are likewise putting aside meaningful declarative statements that lack determinate truth-values because of paradoxicalness or presuppositional failures or vagueness. We are concentrating on the other meaningful declarative statements (if any) that can be articulated in the discourse or practice under examination. Can each of them be assigned a value of truth or falsity? Anyone who aspires to answer this question with reference to any domain will plainly need to draw upon a conception of truth. For jurisprudential purposes, and perhaps for any purposes, the best theory of truth is what is often labeled as "minimalism."[15] That label covers a number of cognate approaches to truth, but the variant favored here is the so-called disquotational account. Under that account, the nature of truth is given by the following equivalence schema:

> The proposition "p" is true if and only if p.

Here "p" stands for any proposition, expressible through a meaningful declarative statement. Thus, one of the countless potential instantiations of the equivalence schema for truth is as follows:

> The proposition "Abraham Lincoln was assassinated in 1865" is true if and only if Abraham Lincoln was assassinated in 1865.

From the domain of legal propositions, potential instantiations of the equivalence schema for truth are legion. Consider, for example, the following:

> The proposition "Murder is a legally forbidden mode of conduct throughout the United States" is true if and only if murder is a legally forbidden mode of conduct throughout the United States.

According to the disquotational theory, the nature of falsity is given by the following equivalence schema:

> The proposition "p" is false if and only if not-p.

Given the restrictions on the scope of my discussion, the expression "not-p" can here be understood as "it is not the case that p." Hence, one

---

[15] The most prominent elaboration of the minimalist approach to truth is Horwich 1998, though I disagree with Horwich's sophisticated arguments on some important points. For an excellent recent discussion of minimalism, see Holton 2000.

of the innumerable potential instantiations of the equivalence schema for falsity is the following:

> The proposition "Abraham Lincoln was assassinated in 1864" is false if and only if it is not the case that Abraham Lincoln was assassinated in 1864.

This instantiation can equally well be formulated as follows:

> The proposition "Abraham Lincoln was assassinated in 1864" is false if and only if Abraham Lincoln was not assassinated in 1864.

From the domain of legal propositions, one of the multitudinous potential instantiations of the equivalence schema for falsity is the following:

> The proposition "Whistling on public streets is a legally forbidden mode of conduct in New Jersey" is false if and only if whistling on public streets is not a legally forbidden mode of conduct in New Jersey.

Now, on one's first encounter, the disquotational approach to truth can seem so obvious and jejune as to be trivial. It can seem utterly uncontroversial simply because there might appear to be nothing about it that is worth controverting. In fact, however, the approach brims with technical difficulties and has given rise to some protracted and illuminating debates over its sustainability. Although the aims of its proponents are indeed deflationary – that is, although they rightly present its message as "attractively demystifying" (Horwich 1998, 5) – the disquotational theory itself is hardly uncomplicated. It leads straightaway into deep waters of philosophical logic and the philosophy of language. We cannot enter into those technicalities here. Suffice it to say that the disquotational approach has been cogently defended by its ablest champions, and that in any event I have dodged a lot of the arcane difficulties that surround it. My circumvention of those difficulties is a happy consequence of the restrictions deliberately imposed on this discussion. Some of the most formidable and recondite problems confronting the minimalist theory of truth concern its ability to handle the sorts of meaningful declarative statements that have been put aside here: namely, paradoxical statements, statements involving radical failures of reference, and statements that apply vague predicates to borderline cases. We can skirt those problems by concentrating solely on other meaningful declarative statements. (Two brief caveats are advisable here. First, my remarks on the absence of determinate truth-values for some meaningful declarative statements are not entirely uncontroversial. From Bertrand Russell onward, some philosophers have presented analyses – such as that in Horwich 1998, 78 – which maintain that statements involving radical reference failures are determinately false. Second, if I were to tackle the problems that are being pretermitted here, my own defense of the minimalist account of truth would differ on a few significant points from some of the most prominent defenses that have been mounted by other philosophers.)

Under the minimalist account of truth, then, the semantic objectivity of legal statements will hinge on the applicability of the disquotational technique to them. For example, the statement "Murder is a legally forbidden mode of conduct throughout the United States" is true if and only if murder is a legally forbidden mode of conduct throughout the United States, and it is false if and only if murder is not a legally forbidden mode of conduct throughout the United States. Murder is in fact a legally forbidden mode of conduct throughout the United States. We can ascertain as much through a combination of empirical investigations and elementary legal interpretation. Thus, the specified legal statement about murder is true, and we can straightforwardly know that it is true. Conversely, the statement "Whistling on public streets is a legally forbidden mode of conduct in New Jersey" is false because whistling is in fact not a legally forbidden mode of conduct in New Jersey. Once again, we can ascertain as much through a combination of empirical investigations and elementary legal construction. Hence, the statement about whistling has a determinate truth-value, and we can straightforwardly know what that truth-value is. Countless other legal statements will likewise be possessed of determinate truth-values, though in many cases the requisite methods for ascertaining those truth-values will be much more complicated than the methods for ascertaining the truth-values of the statements singled out here. In short, we can conclude that – subject to the restrictions within which this discussion of semantic objectivity is unfolding – legal discourse is semantically objective.

1.2.6.1. Correspondence Theories of Truth Deflated

Correspondence theories of truth, which maintain that statements are true if and only if they correspond to the reality of the world, are usually put forward as rivals to minimalist theories. However, the minimalist account is perfectly consistent with a deflationary version of the correspondence account. Whether a correspondence theory can be sustained in a noncircular form in application to any domain (such as the realm of scientific investigation) is not something on which we need to dwell. What is clear is that a deflationary rendering of the theory is apposite in application to the domain of legal discourse. Such a rendering, in application to that domain, can be presented as two theses:

(1) A statement articulating the legal consequences of a pattern of conduct is true if and only if its content follows from the legal standards – expressed in statutes, constitutional provisions, judicial doctrines and practices, contracts, administrative regulations, and the like – that are actually operative and applicable to such conduct within the relevant jurisdiction.

(2) A statement affirming the existence of some legal standard is true if and only if the conditions that would underlie or constitute such a standard are actual.

As was to be expected, these two theses do not make any easier the task of discerning whether any particular legal statement is true. To judge the truth or falsity of a statement that recounts the legal consequences of a pattern of conduct, we shall have to find out what the operative and applicable legal standards are, and we shall have to engage in any legal interpretation and legal reasoning that may be necessary to pin down the implications of those standards for the conduct in question. To judge the truth or falsity of a statement that affirms the existence of some legal standard in a jurisdiction, we shall have to find out what the conditions are for the existence of a standard of that sort, and we shall have to ascertain whether those conditions are satisfied. In other words, if we let "S" stand for a legal statement, the processes required for verifying or disconfirming "The statement 'S' is true" are the same as those required for verifying or disconfirming "S" itself. For example, the processes required for verifying or disconfirming "The statement 'Murder is forbidden in New Jersey' is true" are exactly the same as those required for verifying or disconfirming "Murder is forbidden in New Jersey." Quite predictably, the epistemic upshot associated with the deflationary version of the correspondence theory of truth is the same as that associated with the disquotational version of the minimalist theory.

Each theory highlights the indistinguishability of pondering whether "*S*" is true and pondering whether *S*.

1.2.6.2. Does Anyone Doubt the Semantic Objectivity of Legal Discourse?

Faced with the foregoing vindication of the semantic objectivity of legal discourse, some readers may wonder whether such a vindication has really been necessary. How could anyone doubt that meaningful declarative statements within legal discourse are endowed with determinate truth-values? In fact, what has been doubted by some of the zanily extreme Legal Realists – especially by some of the early thinkers in the Scandinavian school of Legal Realism[16] – is the occurrence of any genuinely meaningful declarative statements within legal discourse. Theorists adopting this extreme position have contended that we need to look beyond the superficial grammar of legal statements in order to descry their real substance and functions. We are told that, although those statements may appear to be meaningful and declarative, they are in fact interjections (akin to "Ouch!" and "Boo!" and "Hurray!" and "Oh no!" and "Wow!"). Their function is to express or elicit emotions rather than to convey truths. All legal mandates and other legal norms are themselves construed by these theorists as interjections or as sheer imperatives (akin to "Stay off the grass!"), whose function is to induce attitudes of submissiveness; such theorists leave no room for any legal mandates or other legal norms that are correctly construable as declarative prescriptions. Now, as has already been noted, interjections and stark imperatives are devoid of truth-values. Utterances such as "Boo!" and "Sit down!" are never either true or false. Accordingly, if the most zealous Scandinavian Realists' analyses of all legal norms and legal statements were correct, then juridical discourse would completely lack semantic objectivity. A vindication of that objectivity has therefore not been a pointlessly superfluous enterprise – though, admittedly, Scandinavian Legal Realism has been out of favor for quite some time.

What led the most fervent Scandinavian Legal Realists astray was a faulty assumption to which the best antidote is the minimalist account of truth. According to that assumption, any nontautological and non-self-contradictory statement to which a truth-value can be assigned is about

[16] For some introductory-level discussions of Scandinavian Legal Realism, see Harris 1997, 103–08; Freeman 2001, 855–72.

some entity or event whose existence or occurrence (if any) is in the world explored by the natural sciences. If something is such that it could not ever exist as a component of the natural world of matter and energy, then any statement about it is not genuinely meaningful and declarative. Such a statement, if it is performing any role at all, must be performing something other than an informational role. In sum, what underlies the extreme Realist approach is a crude version of the correspondence theory of truth coupled with a severely naturalistic ontology (that is, the doctrine that the only entities which do or can exist are those in the physical world investigated by the natural sciences).

A proponent of the minimalist approach to truth will forswear the assumptions of the extreme Scandinavian Realists not by becoming embroiled in metaphysical disputation with them, but by showing that such disputation is utterly beside the point. Minimalism does not involve either an endorsement or a repudiation of the metaphysical theses derided by the Scandinavian Realists. Instead, it reveals that those theses never have to be broached in a perfectly satisfactory vindication of the semantic objectivity of legal discourse. It reveals as much because it indicates that the questions to be answered about the truth or falsity of a legal statement within any particular society are juristic and moral and empirical rather than metaphysical. By collapsing the distinction between discovering whether some legal statement "S" is true and discovering whether S, the minimalist approach (along with the deflationary version of the correspondence theory of truth) makes clear that assignments of truth-values to legal statements do not depend on metaphysical buttressing. Assignments of those values require juristic expertise and moral perspicacity and empirical knowledge rather than philosophical acumen.

1.2.6.3. Two Caveats

This discussion should close with two cautionary observations. First, although I have looked askance at the Scandinavian Legal Realists' suggestions that legal statements are nothing more than vehicles for the expression or evocation of emotions, no one should deny that legal statements frequently do play expressive or evocative roles. Furthermore, some formulations of general legal mandates and many formulations of individualized legal directives are correctly construable as imperatives. My point has certainly not been to discount those expressive and evocative and imperative functions. I have sought, instead, to emphasize that one's recognition of those functions should be conjoined with one's firm awareness that the central role of meaningful declarative statements about the law in this or that jurisdiction is to articulate beliefs about facts. Although that central role is very often in the service of a justificatory purpose on the part of legal officials who wish to present the grounds for their actions or decisions, it is indeed a fact-reporting role. Meaningful declarative statements about the law are not other than what they appear to be; they are meaningful declarative statements in their substance as well as in their grammatical form. (Note that, when I attribute to legal statements the role of articulating beliefs about facts, I am not introducing some new mysterious type of entity known as "facts." Facts, like truth, are understood here along minimalist lines. If and only if unprovoked assaults are a legally forbidden mode of conduct in New Jersey, it is a fact that unprovoked assaults are a legally forbidden mode of conduct in New Jersey. Note also that, in my present discussion, facts are not understood as being in contrast with norms. The beliefs articulated and facts reported by legal statements are typically normative in their content.)

Second, some readers may worry that this subsection's minimalist vindication of the semantic objectivity of juridical discourse will have opened the floodgates to other discourses that are far less reputable. After all, when the minimalist account of truth is brought to bear on juridical discourse, a key element of its message is that evaluations of legal statements as true or false are to be determined by reference to the legal standards that prevail in a particular jurisdiction. Should not the same be said, then, about the statements in myriad other discourses? Should not the same be said, for example, about Scientology and Creationism and Druidism and Maoism and Nazism? That is, when people hoodwink themselves and others with such creeds, are they somehow entitled to insist that the standards which they formulate and sustain in their preposterous discourses are determinative of the truth or falsity of the sundry claims advanced in those discourses?

Such a complaint seriously misunderstands the point of this discussion, not least by overlooking the fact that semantic objectivity is only a single type of objectivity. On the one hand, let us suppose that many of the utterances that occur in Scientological and Creationist and Maoist and Druidistic activities are meaningful declarative statements. Let us

suppose further that some of those statements are not marred by incoherent paradoxicalness or vagueness-induced indeterminacy or presuppositional failures such as radical reference failures. If so, then the discourses respectively associated with those activities are each semantically
objective to a greater or a lesser extent. Each such discourse includes
statements to which truth-values can be correctly assigned. On the other
hand, our ascription of semantic objectivity to each of those discourses
is perfectly compatible with – and indeed presupposed by – the view
that every one or virtually every one of the aforementioned statements
to which truth-values can be assigned is false. We cannot consistently
denounce the central theses of Scientology and of the other pernicious
creeds as false unless we assume that they are semantically objective.

1.2.6.4. The Internal Standards Doctrine

Once we properly keep in mind the distinctions between semantic objectivity and other dimensions of objectivity such as mind-independence
and determinate correctness, we can see that an imputation of semantic
objectivity to some discourse is hardly in itself a commendation. However, the complaint posited in the penultimate paragraph above is not
focused solely on such an imputation. Rather, it is focused primarily on
the notion that the truth-values of the statements uttered in some practice are to be ascribed on the basis of the practice's own standards. That
notion about the ascribing of the truth-values can be designated here
as the "Internal Standards Doctrine." Insofar as that doctrine is construed as objectionable, it is at odds with much of what has been said in
this discussion; but it can more generously be reconstrued as a wholly
unobjectionable corollary of what has been said.

The gravamen of the posited complaint is that, according to my minimalist account of the semantic objectivity of legal discourse, the participants in any particular practice are collectively infallible judges of the
truth or falsity of the assertions that are made in the practice. Any such
criticism of my arguments is doubly mistaken. The lesser of the two major
errors in the criticism should be apparent from my discussion of observational mind-independence in Section 1.2.1. Although the procedural and
substantive standards in any regime of law are conventional, and although
their existential mind-independence as such standards is therefore only

weak, the observational mind-independence of their contents and implications is strong. Those standards are engendered and sustained by the
shared beliefs and attitudes of officials, but the officials' second-order
beliefs about those first-order beliefs and attitudes are not guaranteed
to be correct on any given occasion. Admittedly, we do not have any
grounds for thinking that their second-order beliefs will be frequently
and markedly inaccurate; but we certainly do not have any grounds for
thinking that those beliefs will never be inaccurate. Legal officials can collectively misunderstand the bearings of the norms which they themselves
have collectively fashioned as legally binding standards. Such misappre-
hensions might have precedential force, and they might be final – in
other words, they might not be appealable to any higher authority within
the legal system in which they occur – but they are indeed misappre-
hensions. A parallel point applies, of course, to other institutions and
activities. The people centrally involved in carrying on any institution
or activity can collectively err when construing the norms that structure
it. Hence, even if my minimalist approach to semantic objectivity were
committed to the thesis that the truth-values of statements within any
practice are determined only by reference to the practice's own criteria, no
additional problematic commitment would follow. That is, there would
be no additional commitment to the ridiculous thesis that the participants within any practice are individually or collectively infallible when
they assign truth-values to the statements which they have made as such
participants.

Even more important in the present context is another mistake that
undermines the complaint hypothesized above. That complaint, centered
on the Internal Standards Doctrine, grossly underestimates the diversity
of the criteria for correctness that are operative in any complex practice
such as a system of law. Within the workings of any legal regime, many
of the authoritative utterances of officials concern empirical matters. In
order to attach legal consequences to people's conduct, adjudicators and
administrators have to apprise themselves of the nature of the conduct
(including its main causes and effects). In so doing, they will have to
make numerous empirical judgments that will get expressed in many
of their official statements. Some of their empirical findings will relate
to simple details of events and transactions, whereas others will relate to
more complex matters such as causal influences that are inferred through

statistical analyses. In connection with all such findings, the truth-values of the statements that express them are determined by the facts of the world – and, where applicable, by the laws of mathematics and statistics. Legal officials who engage in these empirical enquiries are subject to the same requirements of accuracy and adequacy to which anyone in the natural and social sciences is subject. (They are subject to those requirements as well, of course, when they engage in the partly empirical task of ascertaining what the laws in their jurisdiction are.) If officials blunder in their empirical findings, and if their missteps vitiate their applications of legal norms to the situations with which they are dealing, the verdicts which express those applications are rendered false by the officials' unwitting distortions of empirically discernible facts. Those applications are misapplications, even though the officials' interpretations of the relevant legal norms themselves may well be impeccable.

Each of the motley schools of charlatanry mentioned earlier is likewise subject to requirements of empirical accuracy and adequacy, for each of them encompasses a throng of empirical assertions. For example, when Nazis make claims about human biology, the truth-values of those claims are determined by the actualities of human genetics and anatomy and physiology rather than by the Nazis' anserine beliefs about those actualities. Likewise, when Creationists articulate the cosmological tenets of their creed, the truth-values of those tenets are determined by the actualities of the physical world rather than by anything internal to Creationism. On the myriad occasions when Creationists or Nazis or Maoists or other mountebanks resort to empirical assertions, the truth or falsity of each such assertion is to be gauged by reference to the same basic considerations that govern one's appraisal of the truth or falsity of any empirical assertion by an ordinary scientist. Assessed against such a yardstick, the ludicrous theses of the aforementioned moutebanks do not fare well.

Not only do the officials in any legal system utter innumerable empirical claims; in most legal systems, the officials also frequently utter moral claims. Such utterances are especially salient in any legal regime in which the officials have incorporated the correct principles of morality into the law for difficult cases. So incorporated, those principles are some of the legally binding (as well as morally binding) standards by recourse to which the officials attach legal consequences to people's conduct. When the officials in such a regime of law invoke and apply moral principles, their moral assertions are subject to exactly the same criteria for truth and falsity that are applicable to moral assertions generally. The fact that the officials' moral judgments are also legal judgments is something that does not alter one whit the standards of moral correctness by which the truth-values of those judgments are determined. Moreover, even in a legal system in which the officials have not incorporated the correct principles of morality into the law for hard cases, they will usually be inclined to engage in many moral pronouncements. They will, for example, usually be inclined to characterize crimes deploringly not only as legally impermissible but also as morally unacceptable. Though such pronouncements about the moral obligatoriness of the law do not amount to invocations of the legal bases for adjudicative and administrative decisions, they are far from merely incidental to those decisions. They are rightly classifiable as juridical statements. Yet their truth-values, like those of juridical statements wherein officials do invoke moral precepts as the bases for their decisions in difficult cases, are determined by the correct principles of morality rather than by the shared beliefs of the officials. Given that this point is so easily recognized within my account of the semantic objectivity of legal discourse, any suggestion that that account has somehow attributed infallibility to legal officials is utterly without foundation.

Moral claims, albeit often hideously misguided moral claims, are central to each of the outlandish creeds that have been mentioned above. Nazis and Maoists, for instance, espouse repulsive moral-political doctrines that have led them to call for the slaughter of millions of human beings. Creationists and Scientologists and Druidists are far less bloodthirsty and vile, but they too give voice to medleys of moral injunctions for their followers and for humanity generally. The truth-values of their moral prescriptions, like the truth-values of the rebarbative moral prescriptions advanced by Nazis and Maoists, depend solely on the conformity or nonconformity of those prescriptions with what morality actually enjoins. In no way are the truth-values dependent on the criteria for correctness that are endorsed by the advocates of those benighted credos.

In sum, an ascription of semantic objectivity to some discourse is scarcely in itself a tribute to the discourse's intellectual solidity. Such objectivity may be a necessary condition, but is hardly a sufficient condition, for the intellectual respectability of a field of enquiry. Although a minimalist approach to legal statements can readily establish that a host of such statements are endowed with truth-values, and although it reveals that their being possessed of those truth-values does not presuppose the existence of any abstruse entities, it does not per se show that the workings of legal systems are objective in any more richly ambitious sense. It does not per se enable us to distinguish between legal discourse and Scientology (or Creationism or the other deranged schools of thought that have here been touched upon). To draw such distinctions, we would have to advert to some of the other dimensions of objectivity that have been plumbed in this chapter.

1.2.7. Objectivity: Some Further Types?

We have heretofore examined six main types of objectivity: three ontological, two epistemic, and one semantic. In the philosophical literature on objectivity, further conceptions quite frequently surface. This chapter will present each of those remaining conceptions only cursorily. In most cases, the brevity of the exposition is due to the subsumability of the additional facets of objectivity under the facets that have already been expounded. We shall begin, however, with two aspects of objectivity that are discussed only tersely because their relevance to the substance of law is meager.

1.2.7.1. Objectivity qua Rational Requisiteness

Within several traditions in moral philosophy, especially within the very broad Kantian tradition, the objectivity of morality has often been understood as the rational compellingness of moral requirements. That is, those requirements are viewed as objective because they cannot be violated by any moral agent except at the cost of outright irrationality. To transgress a moral principle is to land oneself in a logical contradiction. Such a pattern of behavior is not only wrong but also incoherent. Moral obligations, then, are objective in much the same way as the Law of Noncontradiction; compliance with them is indispensable for the sustainment of one's practical rationality, just as compliance with the Law of Noncontradiction is indispensable for the sustainment of one's rationality generally.

I have argued elsewhere against this assimilation of the force of moral duties to the rational compellingness of logic (Kramer 1999b, 174–99). Breaches of such duties are moral failings rather than logical lapses (Hills 2004). To be sure, the commission of logical errors in moral discourse is always possible. If someone maintains that the perpetration of unprovoked assaults is invariably forbidden, and if she simultaneously maintains that the perpetration of unprovoked assaults is permissible on Tuesdays, then she is adopting two logically inconsistent positions. Likewise, if she asserts that Joe is morally obligated to visit some sick friends and morally at liberty not to visit them, then she is contradicting herself. Instances of sheer irrationality of this sort in the moral domain are certainly possible. However, they are far from common. Most contraventions of moral requirements do not involve such logical missteps; and the efforts by some philosophers to disclose subtler logical missteps in those contraventions have been quite unavailing.

Thus, although the conception of objectivity as rational compellingness is not by any means to be dismissed – in other words, although it specifies "an intelligible and adequate sense of objectivity" (Williams 1985, 206) – it is a conception that does not illuminate the nature of morality. Morality is objective in many senses, but not in the sense that everyone acting athwart its demands is guilty of a self-contradiction. In the domain of law, the relevance of objectivity qua rational compellingness is even more limited. The operations of legal systems are objective in many senses, but not in the sense that everyone who misconstrues or transgresses a legal mandate is displaying arrant irrationality. On the one hand, logical errors can occur in the domain of law just as they can occur in the domain of moral deliberation. People sometimes commit outright paralogisms while reasoning about the law, just as they sometimes do while reasoning about nonlegal matters. On the other hand, most misapplications or violations of legal norms do not involve such logical lapses. When a jurist or layperson goes astray in his understanding of the contents and implications of legal norms, or when he elects to disregard those norms in order to behave unlawfully, he is not usually contradicting himself in some fashion; instead, he is exhibiting insufficient sensitivity to the balance of considerations on which his interpretation or decision should hinge. A stumble of that sort is hardly a failure to respect the basic laws of logic. Hence, when we ask whether the workings of a legal system are objective, we are not asking – or should not be asking – whether its mandates are such that everyone who flouts or misapprehends them is mired in incoherence. No legal system is objective in that respect.

Admittedly, the term "irrational" in everyday discourse is often used quite expansively (as are the terms "illogical" and "insane" and "senseless," for that matter). For example, people sometimes apply that epithet to particularly horrific misdeeds or to egregiously silly misjudgments or to dismayingly mulish bouts of obstinacy. Very seldom indeed, however, is this pattern of usage intended to suggest that the people responsible for the misdeeds or misjudgments or obstinacy have contradicted themselves. Rather, the term "irrational" in application to heinous misdeeds is meant to indicate that the unrestrained savagery which has impelled those misdeeds is far outside the range of motivations that can be comprehended (in a minimally empathetic manner) by any decently civilized person. In application to stupid misjudgments, the term is meant to indicate that the level of obtuseness evidenced by those misjudgments is far greater than would normally be expected from anyone who possesses even moderate intelligence. And in application to somebody's severe obstinacy, the epithet "irrational" is meant to indicate that the degree of unyieldingness displayed by the obdurate person is so extravagant or unwarranted as to be detrimental to the person's own interests. That epithet is likewise tellingly wielded against fields of enquiry – such as astrology and sorcery – that have been discredited by modern science. In my present discussion, the notion of irrationality is invoked more narrowly and precisely to refer to instances of logical incoherence. When I contend here that breaches or misconstruals of legal requirements are very seldom irrational, I am simply contending that they very rarely consist in commitments to logically inconsistent theses. Whether they are typically irrational in some looser sense is not a matter on which my present discussion takes any position.

Given the conception of irrationality on which my remarks here are centered, any investigation of this aspect of objectivity stands to benefit from a distinction between irrationality and unreasonableness.[17] Whereas irrationality resides in self-contradictoriness, unreasonableness resides

---

[17] My distinction between irrationality and unreasonableness is quite different from a distinction drawn in similar terms by Paske 1989. Closer to my distinction is the dichotomy between simple rationality and basic reasonableness in Greenawalt 1992, 176–79, though the first couple of pages of Greenawalt's discussion are puzzling.

in moral or intellectual blameworthiness. If some action or judgment is unreasonable, it falls below a threshold of moral extenuability or intellectual credibility. A designation of "unreasonableness" in such a situation is singularly appropriate because the person undertaking the action or judgment is blind or indifferent to the preponderant reasons that militate in favor of a contrary course. Inadequate sensitivity to those reasons, stemming either from one's unawareness of them or from one's depreciation of them, is what marks one's conduct or outlook as unreasonable.

What makes the distinction between irrationality and unreasonableness noteworthy here is that, whereas very few transgressions of moral or legal requirements are *irrational,* most transgressions of moral requirements and many transgressions of legal requirements are *unreasonable* (to a greater or a lesser degree). When a person is under a moral duty to perform some action X and is not under an equally stringent or more stringent moral duty to eschew X, and when no extraordinarily weighty prudential factor militates against his performing X, there is a conclusive reason for him to perform it.[18] A failure to perform X is therefore unreasonable; such a failure betrays insufficient sensitivity to the considerations on the basis of which he should be conducting himself. Of course, the severity of the unreasonableness will vary in proportion to the weightiness of the duty and to the consequent gravity of the wrong committed through the nonperformance of the obligatory action. Any breach of a moral duty, however, is unreasonable to some degree unless the duty has been offset by an equally important or more important moral obligation or by an extraordinarily weighty prudential factor. In regard to legal duties, the situation is more complicated but broadly similar. Even in a liberal democracy, not every legal obligation gives rise to moral reasons for compliance therewith (Kramer 1999a, 204–09, 254–308). Hence, not every breach of a legal obligation is unreasonable at all. Indeed, in some contexts – even in a liberal democracy – the *fulfillment* of a legal obligation would be unequivocally unreasonable. All the same, many legal obligations do impose moral obligations of obedience (albeit

---

[18] Here and elsewhere in this paragraph, "equally" should be construed as "equally or incommensurably." Note that, although a violation of a moral duty is not unreasonable if the duty has been overtopped or equally balanced by a countervailing moral duty, the violation is still wrong in that the person committing it will have incurred a moral obligation to remedy it in some way. On this point, see Kramer 2004a, 249–94; 2005.

moral obligations that are susceptible to being overtopped by counter-vailing moral duties that are even more pressing). In a liberal democracy, most legal duties produce such an effect, and indeed most of the moral obligations-of-obedience engendered by those legal duties are not over-topped or equally balanced by any countervailing moral obligations or by any hugely weighty prudential considerations. Accordingly, many viola-tions of legal duties in a liberal democracy will be unreasonable. Even in most illiberal countries, quite a few such violations will be unreasonable.

Thus, although objectivity qua rational compellingness is not an aspect of the objectivity of legal systems and their mandates, there is a connection between legal requirements and reason. Anyone can con-travene legal mandates without being irrational – that is, without having become entangled in logical incoherence – but in many cases the unlaw-ful behavior is unreasonable. Although such behavior does not bespeak anything as strong as a self-contradiction in a person's thinking, it does in many circumstances bespeak faulty moral reasoning. It bespeaks a defi-cient grasp of the balance of reasons that should sway a person's actions. Having recognized this frequent connection between unlawfulness and unreasonableness, we can more readily accept that there is generally no connection between unlawfulness and self-contradictoriness.

1.2.7.2. Objectivity qua Invariance

In the eyes of some philosophers, the linchpin of objectivity is invariance (Nozick 2001). Invariance itself is a multifaceted property, of course. Some of its aspects have been probed in some of my previous subsections on dimensions of objectivity. For example, one sense in which a regime of law can partake of invariance is that its norms are uniformly appli-cable to everyone. So construed, the property of invariance obviously falls under my earlier discussion of objectivity qua uniform applicability. Another respect in which a legal system partakes of invariance is that the contents and implications of most of its norms are widely agreed upon (by people generally or specifically by people who have expert knowledge of the law). When people do converge with one another in their percep-tions of the existence and contents of legal norms, the variations among their individual outlooks are subordinated – in their perspectives on the law – to the commonality of those perceptions. Insofar as the property of invariance is explicated along these lines as the broad homogeneity of the ways in which people understand the contents and implications of laws, it obviously falls under my earlier discussion of objectivity qua transindividual discernibility. Still another respect in which a legal system partakes of invariance is that the observational mind-independence of its norms is strong. Because the contents and implications of laws at any given juncture do not necessarily tally with what people individually or collectively believe them to be, they do not vary at that juncture in accordance with any misunderstandings harbored by people individually or collectively. Invariance in this sense obviously falls under my earlier discussion of objectivity qua mind-independence.

Two other aspects of invariance are not subsumable under any of the previous subsections of this chapter. However, those two types of invariance – unchangingness and ubiquity – are not generally characteristic of the substance of legal norms. If laws were invariant in the sense of being unchanging, their existence and contents and implications would remain always the same. Perhaps such a state of affairs obtains in some extremely primitive regimes of law, but it manifestly does not obtain in any legal system that exists in the modern world. Every such legal system includes mechanisms for altering the norms which it currently comprises. Alterations occur most conspicuously through the legislative and quasi-legislative actions of public officials, but they also occur through many actions of private individuals (in forming contracts, for example). Risibly far-fetched is the idea of a modern legal system without some such means for transforming its existent norms. Hence, invariance qua unchangingness is remote indeed from the substance of the mandates and other norms produced by legal-governmental institutions. In that respect, the substance of law differs notably from the substance of morality. Numerous moral precepts, such as prohibitions on the torture of babies and on the deliberate slaughter of unarmed civilians and on the commission of unprovoked assaults and on the defrauding of people for fun and profit, always have been binding and always will be binding. They are timeless. Although the extent of people's compliance with such prohibitions will of course vary markedly from historical era to historical era – and although some of those prohibitions may in fact go virtually unglimpsed in certain eras – the dispositive sway of those prohibitions and of other fundamental moral precepts is temporally invariant. Whenever human beings (or other rational beings) exist, they are bound by those precepts. Objectivity qua changelessness encompasses much of the substance of morality, then, whereas it does not have any similar grip on the substance of legal norms.

Despite what has been said in the last paragraph, there is a grain of truth – albeit only a grain – in the notion that temporal invariance is a property of the substance of laws. As will be discussed in Chapter 2, the very existence of any legal system as such is dependent on limits to the scale and frequency of changes within the system's laws. No ostensible legal system can guide people's conduct with minimal efficacy if its norms undergo transformations so often and so sweepingly as to leave people bewildered. The extreme disorientation induced by persistent and whole-sale changes in the prevailing norms will undermine the central function of law in directing and channeling people's behavior. If a system of law is to perform that function and is therefore to exist at all as a system of law, the rate of metamorphosis of its directives cannot be dizzyingly high. Legal change will occur and should occur, but it has to take place within moderately confining limits if it is to count as *legal* change rather than as chaos. Insofar as a thesis about the temporal invariance of the substance of legal norms is intended simply to highlight the requisite limits on the pace of juridical evolution, its message is quite correct; but any reference to temporal invariance in the thesis is extraordinarily misleading, since an insistence on the aforementioned limits is hardly tantamount to an insis-tence on the absence of change altogether. We are best advised to eschew such a thesis and to acknowledge straightforwardly that objectivity qua temporal invariance is not to be predicated of the substance of law.

Much the same can be said about invariance qua ubiquity. The legal norms of each jurisdiction are specific to that jurisdiction. Though some of the norms of international law in the modern world may be operative in all or most national jurisdictions, the domestic law of each country is peculiar to that country. Within many national jurisdictions, moreover, there are other jurisdictions with their own arrays of legal norms (such as those of the fifty states in the United States). Hence, given the multiplicity and diversity of the legal systems in the world, the quality of omnipres-ence is not generally attributable to the substance of any legal norms. Of course, some such norms may be shared across a number of different juris-dictions, especially when active efforts to bring about such uniformity have occurred (as they have – in certain areas of law – among the states of the United States and among many of the countries in Europe). Even so, countless legal norms do not transcend jurisdictional boundaries in that fashion, and the norms that do cut across those boundaries are far from ubiquitous. Their presence in many jurisdictions is accompanied by their absence from other jurisdictions. Laws of nature and laws of logic are the same throughout the universe, but the laws devised by governmental officials for the regulation of human behavior are not.

A renowned argument by the great legal philosopher H. L. A. Hart may seem to tell against my claim that invariance qua unchangingness and invariance qua pervasiveness are not characteristic of the substance of any legal norms. Hart maintained that, if we are attentive to certain elementary features of human beings and of the world in which they live, we shall conclude that the mandates of every sustainable legal system must include prohibitions on serious misconduct such as murder and unprovoked assaults and arson (Hart 1961, 187–98). A society, especially a sizable society, would not last for more than the briefest span of time if it were without such legal prohibitions. It would lack even minimal cohesion. Hart was surely correct to emphasize this point. Yet, if mandates outlawing the sundry types of serious misconduct are to be found in every viable system of law, my disinclination to ascribe ubiquity and immutability to the substance of legal norms may seem dubious.

I have written at length elsewhere on the argument by Hart that has been laconically summarized above (Kramer 1999a, 262–307). For the purposes of the present discussion, we can simply note something of which Hart himself was well aware. Although legal prohibitions on serious misconduct must indeed exist in any society that is to stand a chance of enduring, the specific forms which the prohibitions take can vary significantly from society to society and from one historical period to another within a single society. For example, the prohibitions can be more inclusive or less inclusive in the extent to which they embrace people within their protective ambit. In any liberal democracy, everyone alike is safeguarded by the laws that proscribe serious wrongdoing. In societies with systematically subordinated groups of people, by contrast, some or all of the laws that forbid serious misdeeds may omit those people from the compass of their protection. As Hart wrote: "These painful facts of human history are enough to show that, though a society to be viable must offer *some* of its members a system of [safeguards against serious misdeeds], it need not, unfortunately, offer them to all" (Hart 1961, 196, emphasis in original).

For another of the many respects in which basic legal interdictions can vary dramatically, a comparison between the Biblical conception of rape and the modern Western conception is illuminating. According to the Torah, a man who rapes an unbetrothed virgin is required to marry the victim and to make a payment to her father (Deuteronomy 22:28–29; Exodus 22:16). Thus, although there was a clear recognition in ancient Israel that rape could not be condoned and left unregulated, the Biblical angle on the problem and on the apposite remedies for dealing with it was profoundly different from modern Western perspectives. In the eyes of the ancient Israelites, the person primarily wronged by an act of rape against an unbetrothed maiden was the father of the hapless victim. For the rectification of such an act, therefore, the suitable remedies lay in a payment to the father and in a marriage ensuring that the victim of the rape would not be doomed to spinsterhood (a condition in which she would remain financially dependent on her father). Attitudes toward the crime of rape in Western countries in the twenty-first century are strikingly different, of course. As a consequence, the remedies for particular instances of that crime – consisting chiefly in lengthy terms of imprisonment and certainly not in marriages – are strikingly different. Instead of being aimed at upholding the pride and financial well-being of the fathers of victims, the legal remedies for rape in any present-day liberal democracy are aimed at vindicating the dignity and humanity of the victims themselves (and at repairing rents in the fabric of a community that have been brought about by the rapists' violent flouting of societal values). Hence, although we find prohibitions on rape both in ancient Israel and in twenty-first-century Western countries, the divergences between the prohibitions are more arresting than the similarities between them. Quite untenable is any suggestion that the proscription of rape is temporally invariant.

Legal mandates outlawing major misconduct can vary in a number of other ways as well. The range of the actions forbidden can be more expansive or less expansive, for example, as can the range of the people on whom penalties are levied when such actions are performed. (In most contemporary societies, the penalties are inflicted solely on the individuals who have engaged in forbidden conduct themselves. In some other societies or in other eras, the penalties have been extended to members of the families of such individuals.) In short, Hart's admirably sound argument about the indispensability of legal curbs on disruptive wrongdoing does not lend any support to the notion that some legal norms or some arrays of legal norms are unchanging and omnipresent. To subscribe to such a misguided notion, as Hart himself never did, is to overlook the multifariousness of the aforementioned legal curbs over time and throughout the world. Certain formal features are present whenever and wherever law exists – as will be recounted in the next chapter – but the substance of law is always malleable.

1.2.7.3. Objectivity qua Corrigibility

Some legal philosophers, such as Nicos Stavropoulos, have submitted that the central dimension of objectivity for jurisprudential purposes is that of corrigibility. According to this conception of objectivity, a domain of enquiry is objective only if there is genuinely room for mistakes within it (Raz 2001, 198–99; Rosati 2004, 278–79). As Stavropoulos writes, "we shall try to test for objectivity by investigating whether the relevant domain is such that there is space for *error.*" He elaborates: "We should expect that for a domain to be objective there should be some logical space between how we understand or judge or perceive or believe things to be and what discriminations we make among different objects or properties in the domain, on the one hand, and what the case is, on the other" (Stavropoulos 2005, 316, emphasis in original).

As should be evident, this conception of objectivity as corrigibility is subsumable under one or more of the conceptions already expounded. Most obviously, it is subsumable under this chapter's subsection on objectivity qua mind-independence. That subsection explains how the domain of law is characterized by exactly the sort of "logical space" to which Stavropoulos refers: the space between how things are thought to be and how they actually are. Although the existential mind-independence of general legal norms is only weak, the observational mind-independence of every legal norm is strong. Thus, within any legal regime, the officials collectively as well as the officials individually can be in error about the contents and implications of legal norms.

Another subsection of this chapter under which Stavropoulos's conception of objectivity can be partly subsumed is that on determinate correctness. As was observed there, a question to which there are no incorrect answers is a question to which there is no determinately correct answer. Consequently, insofar as there are determinately correct answers to legal questions, the domain of law contains the space for error which Stavropoulos perceives as the hallmark of objectivity. Now, given that there are determinately correct answers to the large majority of the legal questions that arise in any functional system of law, there will persistently be ample room for errors within any such system. Law patently satisfies Stavropoulos's criterion for objectivity.

One other portion of this chapter into which the conception of objectivity as corrigibility can to some extent be absorbed is the subsection on impartiality. As was remarked in that subsection, arbitrariness is introduced whenever legal decision-making proceeds on the basis of factors (such as prejudices and surmises and selfish interests) that are generally unconducive to the attainment of correct outcomes. Plainly, the singling out of certain factors as unconducive to the attainment of correct outcomes is premised on the notion that some outcomes are incorrect. Hence, much of my discussion of impartiality presupposes that the workings of a legal system are objective in Stavropoulos's sense.

In sum, the conception of objectivity as corrigibility has already been well covered by this chapter. While the possibility of mistakes within some discourse is indeed crucial for the objectivity of the discourse, there is no need to treat that possibility as a dimension of objectivity that is distinct from all the dimensions explored heretofore. Even if it is not precisely equatable with any single aspect of objectivity that has been investigated in one of the earlier subsections of this chapter, its nature and implications have been captured cumulatively by those earlier subsections.

1.2.7.4. Objectivity qua Nonillusiveness

In ordinary exchanges and in philosophical disputation, objectivity is very frequently taken to consist in nonillusiveness. An entirely illusive thing is a figment of the mind of anybody who seems to be perceiving it. It does not exist at all outside the putative experience of it by some person(s); it does not exist in the external world in any way, but exists only within some of the conscious states of the aforementioned person(s). If something that appears to exist externally is objective in the sense of not being entirely illusive, then it is not a sheer figment of somebody's imagination. It exists in the external world in some fashion, albeit perhaps only as something that is disposed to elicit certain experiences. (Of course, perfectly genuine mental phenomena such as headaches and fear and anguish and elation are devoid of any existence in the external world. Unlike those phenomena, an illusion *appears* to partake of such existence.)

Illusions need not be thoroughgoing. Sometimes what is illusory is not the very existence of something, but its being endowed with some property. Suppose for example that a line appears to somebody to be of the same length as another line, when in fact their lengths are different. What is illusive in such circumstances is not the existence of either of the lines, but each one's ostensible property of being equivalent in length to the other. Still, the opposition between objectivity and illusiveness is essentially the same in regard to partial illusions as in regard to full illusions. An objective property is some feature that is actually present in something that is itself real, whereas an illusory property is a feature which appears to someone to be present in something but which in actuality is not present therein.

Unquestionably, nonillusiveness is a central facet of objectivity. Equally clearly, however, it is a facet that has been covered at a general level by my subsection on objectivity qua mind-independence. Still, the present context is a good juncture at which to refine the account of mind-independence by drawing a distinction that has been pertinently underscored in the work of philosophers such as John McDowell: the distinction between response-centered properties and illusory properties (McDowell 1985, 113–14). Though the properties in each of those two categories are mind-dependent, the nature of the mind-dependence is importantly divergent between the categories.

An illusory property is profoundly mind-dependent in the manner specified above. That is, it exists only in the mind of the person who undergoes the experience of perceiving it. It is not present at all in the world outside that person's psyche. Any appearance to the contrary – however strong it may be – is deceptive rather than veridical. When somebody succumbs to that appearance and consequently believes that the illusory property is real, he or she is straightforwardly mistaken.

Response-centered properties, such as redness and sourness, are quite different. They are genuinely present in the things of which they appear to be features, though they exist as the capacities or dispositions of those things to evoke certain types of experiences in human beings (and some nonhuman animals) who are endowed with normal perceptual faculties. A belief in the reality of a response-centered property is correct rather than mistaken (Fine 2001, 26). For example, when someone with normal eyesight looks at an apple under good visual conditions and ascertains that it is green, he or she is entirely correct in concluding that the skin of the apple really is green. The greenness of the apple is not a figment of the person's imagination with no existence outside his or her mind. On the contrary, it is a fully genuine property of the apple's skin; the microstructural composition of that skin reflects light in a manner that will educe sensations or experiences of greenness in any human being who is possessed of normal visual faculties. In McDowell's useful phrasing, the greenness of the apple's skin is "there to be experienced" (McDowell 1985, 114).

Insofar as a distinction between the objective and the subjective is drawn to correlate with a distinction between real properties and illusory properties or between veridical experiences and deceptive experiences, response-centered properties such as redness and saltiness should clearly be classified as objective. Such properties are real, and one's experiences of them are not deceptive. However, the demarcation between the objective and the subjective can of course also be drawn in other ways. One way of elaborating that demarcation is to differentiate between (i) any property whose nature can be fully specified without reference to certain actual or potential experiences in human beings and (ii) any property whose nature can only be fully specified by reference to certain actual or potential experiences in human beings. Insofar as the objective/subjective dichotomy is understood along these lines, response-centered properties are to be classified as subjective. Although they are perfectly real rather than illusive, and although they are mind-independent in some respects, they are not mind-independent in the respect that is central to this latest formulation of the objective/subjective distinction.

In what ways are response-centered properties mind-independent? At first blush, they may seem both existentially and observationally mind-dependent. A somewhat fanciful thought-experiment, however, can indicate otherwise. Suppose that, as a result of very widespread genetic mutations over a generation or two, all or nearly all human beings in eighty years will lack the ability to perceive redness. In such circumstances, that color will not have ceased to be instantiated. That is, we should not think that roses and tomatoes and rubies will no longer be red. Instead, the continuing redness of those things will no longer be perceptible by normal human beings. As has been noted, the property of redness exists because the microstructural constituents of various objects' surfaces reflect light in ways that will evoke sensations of the color red in people who are equipped with visual faculties that are currently normal. If pervasive genetic mutations will significantly alter the visual abilities that are normal for human beings, it will still be true that the microstructural constituents of various objects' surfaces reflect light in ways that can educe sensations of the color red in any people who are endowed with visual abilities that are normal *at present*. Perhaps there will not be any such people in the aftermath of the mutations; nevertheless, if there were any such people, the objects' surfaces under ordinary conditions would elicit sensations of the color red in them. Because the surfaces retain the capacity to elicit those sensations, they continue to be red. Though their redness will have become imperceptible to all or most human beings, it will still exist as such.

Numerous complications could be introduced into the foregoing thought-experiment. For example, instead of resulting in an outright loss of the ability to perceive redness, the genetic mutations might transpose certain perceptual abilities. In eighty years, all people or nearly all people might experience the color red when looking at things that would currently lead any normal person to experience the color blue, and they might experience the color blue when looking at things that would currently lead any normal person to experience the color red. Were this book an exploration of epistemology or metaphysics or the philosophy of mind, we would be well advised to ponder such complications. For the purposes of the present volume, however, the discussion in the preceding paragraph is enough. What that paragraph suffices to indicate is that, although response-centered properties are mind-dependent in one important respect, they are mind-independent in some other important respects. A response-centered property is mind-dependent in the sense that its nature cannot be fully specified without reference to human beings' actual or potential experiences, but it is mind-independent in the respect highlighted by my scenario of the genetic mutations. That is, it can continue to exist as such even if no human being is any longer capable of perceiving it or its effects.

This discussion should close with a disclaimer. Some philosophers have argued that moral properties – such as rightness and wrongness and legitimacy and obligatoriness – can be illuminatingly analogized to response-centered properties (McDowell 1985; Pettit 2001; Wiggins 1998, 106–08). No such view is favored here. On the contrary, any assimilation of moral and other normative properties to response-centered properties is fraught with insuperable difficulties.[19] Readers should certainly not infer that my terse remarks on response-centered properties have aimed to suggest an affinity between such properties and the main features of law. Rather, those remarks have been a short digression for the purpose of drawing attention to some involutions in the conception of objectivity as mind-independence. Although the distinctions delineated in my main subsection on objectivity qua mind-independence are more important for an understanding of law than is the distinction between illusory properties and response-centered properties, a grasp of the latter distinction is essential for a full understanding of the phenomenon of objectivity. Not only does that phenomenon comprise multiple dimensions, but in addition each dimension is internally complex.

1.2.7.5. Objectivity qua Susceptibility to Reasons

Some major philosophers have contended that the defining characteristic of objectivity is that of susceptibility to reasons. If the claims asserted and positions taken within some domain are susceptible to reasons – that is, if they are open to alteration through rational persuasion rather than only through subrational manipulation – then the domain in question partakes of objectivity. A view along these lines has been articulated by David Wiggins, among others. He writes that the objectivity of a field of enquiry consists in "the existence of publicly accepted and rationally

---

[19] On some of the difficulties, see Blackburn 1993, 159–62; Sosa 2001. In the third chapter of my book-in-progress *Against Meta-Ethics: Moral Realism as a Moral Doctrine*, I have written at length on this matter.

criticizable standards of argument, or of ratiocination towards truth" (Wiggins 1998, 101). Gerald Postema has given voice to a similar outlook on the matter: "Objectivity makes possible, or presupposes, that expressions not only can coordinate or conflict, but also can be in agreement or disagreement, and that this agreement or disagreement can be pursued, articulated, discussed, deliberated about in virtue of genuine joinder of issue on the matter in question." Postema adds: "Where objectivity resides it is reasonable to hope that reasoning can move subjects to agreement. By the same token, it is an important mark of objectivity that consideration of reasons for judgments in an objective domain can move subjects from agreement to disagreement" (Postema 2001, 108).

The epistemic dimension of objectivity championed in these quotations (and in similar pronouncements from a number of other philosophers) is obviously central to a wide range of human activities and institutions. It is especially prominent in legal contexts in Western liberal democracies, for the legal systems of those countries almost always involve high levels of reflective argumentation. Such argumentation proceeds through the deliberations and exchanges – the public practical reasoning – which many philosophers have in mind when they write about objectivity as susceptibility to reasons. Along with universities, legal-governmental institutions are the paramount arena within which that aspect of objectivity is pursued and realized.

Despite the manifest importance of this conception of objectivity for an understanding of law, this chapter does not need to include a separate exposition of it. Though the idea of susceptibility to reasons is not fully captured by any single conception of objectivity that has been explicated hitherto, it has been covered cumulatively in my two main subsections on epistemic dimensions of objectivity: the subsections on transindividual discernibility and impartiality. As was remarked in my discussion of epistemic objectivity as transindividual discernibility, such objectivity exists not only when there is already a consensus on some matter(s) but also when there is agreement on the methods or pathways by which a not-yet-existent consensus can eventually be forged. Those methods or pathways can be highly specialized techniques of investigation in advanced sciences or in other domains of enquiry, but they can likewise be more general channels and touchstones for public deliberations. Public practical reasoning of the sort envisaged by Postema will be a nonstarter unless people converge in implicitly or explicitly accepting various standards for their proceedings – standards that differentiate between relevant and irrelevant considerations or between sufficient evidence and inconclusive evidence or between cogent lines of argument and unpersuasive lines of argument, for example. Of course, such standards are themselves open to modification and amplification as people deliberate. Moreover, except in specialized fields of enquiry (including specialized areas of legal interpretation), there will very seldom be unanimity or near-unanimity on procedural standards. Public practical reasoning is in part an array of debates about its own nature. Still, even in free-wheeling disputation concerning broad matters of public policy and legal principles, the upshot will be chaotic frustration if there is not a sufficient degree of convergence among people on procedural benchmarks and substantive tenets. Rational exchanges cannot unfold in even a minimally rewarding fashion as rational exchanges if they are excessively unfocused. In short, objectivity qua susceptibility to reasons is crucially dependent on objectivity qua transindividual discernibility.

However, as Postema observes, susceptibility to reasons is not only about convergence. In circumstances (such as those of the ancient Egyptian wise men) where transindividual discernibility stems from the sharing of illusions or prejudices, reasoned persuasion should be a vehicle for overturning consensuses rather than for promoting or consolidating them. Even in circumstances in which the unanimity of enquirers is based partly on correct insights but also partly on errors or bias or ignorance, the role of rational deliberation should be at least as disruptive of received opinions as confirmatory of them. Thus, although objectivity qua susceptibility to reasons is dependent on objectivity qua transindividual discernibility, the former goes beyond the latter. Any thorough realization of the ideal of susceptibility-to-reasons must involve not only transindividual discernibility but also impartiality (in the expansive sense expounded by this chapter). Under any such thorough realization, that is, the considerations that influence people's judgments are not to be ersatz reasons grounded in prejudices or ignorance or panic or venality. All such factors foster arbitrariness in decision-making, as they lead people away from reliable processes of enquiry that conduce to the discovery of the truth about this or that matter. Even when the outcomes of arbitrary decisional procedures are fortuitously correct, they will not have been reached for the right reasons. Thus, in any domain in which susceptibility to reasons is both an actuality and a desideratum to be pursued, impartiality is an ideal for which people should strive. The attainment of that ideal can potently contribute to the formation of consensuses, by helping to eliminate disaccord that has arisen from the sway of non-truth-conducive factors such as prejudices and ignorance; but it can also disrupt the existing consentaneity on any particular issue by helping to reveal that people have concurred with one another because of shared illusions or biases rather than because of shared insights.

In sum, given the breadth of the ideal of impartiality as recounted by this chapter, objectivity-qua-transindividual-discernibility and objectivity-qua-impartiality together constitute objectivity-qua-susceptibility-to-reasons. Although a vital element of the objectivity of any discourse is the extent to which the participants therein can undertake reasoned exchanges that affect the formation of their views, that element is not in need of separate treatment within this chapter. On the one hand, rational deliberations and remonstrations are of huge importance in legal contexts. Public practical reasoning is the lifeblood of the law, in liberal democracies and to some degree in any country with a functional legal system. On the other hand, the ingredients of public practical reasoning can best be understood within the theoretical framework which this chapter has already developed. An additional subsection or category would be superfluous.

Much the same can be said about a very closely related conception of epistemic objectivity. Brian Leiter, among other philosophers, has suggested that the epistemic objectivity of a field of enquiry consists in the cognitive reliability of the procedures and mechanisms by which the participants in the field form their beliefs about the objects of their investigations (Leiter 2001, 1). Central to such reliability is the absence or minimization of distortive influences such as narrow self-interest and bigotry and uninformed whims (Raz 2001, 195–96; Svavarsdóttir 2001, 153–54). While Leiter is clearly correct in attaching great importance to this conception of objectivity, my account of impartiality encompasses it and indeed is largely equatable with it. Hence, there is no need here for a separate exposition of objectivity qua cognitive reliability.

1.3. A Pithy Conclusion

As should be evident, the six chief dimensions of objectivity that have been probed in this chapter are characteristic of legal norms or legal systems, though in differing ways. At least one aspect of objectivity, the strong observational mind-independence of legal norms, is not a scalar property. That is, it applies in an all-or-nothing fashion rather than in varying degrees. No legal norm's observational mind-independence is stronger than that of any other such norm; the observational mind-independence of every legal norm is strong *tout court*. Moreover, the strong observational mind-independence obtains willy-nilly rather than as a feature that has to be sought. Other facets of objectivity, such as impartiality and transindividual discernibility, are scalar properties. Nonetheless, although those other facets of objectivity are characteristic of the workings of legal systems only to varying extents, each of them is characteristic of those workings in every legal system to quite a substantial degree. As we shall see in my next two chapters, no legal system can exist as such if it does not partake of every dimension of objectivity (apart from those dimensions that have been set aside in this chapter as plainly inapplicable to the substance of law).

To say that each of the scalar aspects of objectivity will be present in every legal system is hardly to say that those aspects arise automatically or magically. They, like the existence and functionality of a legal regime itself, can be achieved only through deliberate human efforts aimed at their realization. Moreover, insofar as each scalar dimension of objectivity is an ideal, it is something that ought to be pursued. In a benign legal system, each of those scalar dimensions is to be pursued because each is valuable in its own right and likewise because each of them contributes indispensably to the attainment of the desiderata that can be secured through the existence and flourishing of a regime of law. Although objectivity in one of its facets is a property that obtains whether or not anyone consciously tries to bring it about, it is also – in its other facets – a good for which legal-governmental officials should strive.

2

Elements of the Rule of Law

Chapter 1, in its subsection on objectivity qua invariance, has contended that we cannot correctly ascribe either unchangingness or ubiquity to the substance of law. As was remarked at the end of that subsection, however, the formal features of law are quite different from the substance. Certain formal features are present whenever and wherever law exists. No legal system can operate without those essential attributes, regardless of the time or the place.

Even in connection with the formal side of law, nevertheless, any ascription of unchangingness and ubiquity would be more misleading than illuminating. One of the salient themes of this chapter is that, although the fundamental characteristics of the rule of law are always present when a functional legal system exists, their substantive significance can vary considerably. On the one hand, those fundamental characteristics are content-independent in that they structure every legal regime regardless of the benignity or malignity of its norms. A legal system as a legal system partakes of those characteristics, whether the contents of its laws and the purposes pursued by its officials are commendable or deplorable. On the other hand, the substantive import of the essential properties of law is hugely affected by the substance of each legal system in which they are instantiated. Although those properties do not have any inherent moral bearings, they acquire moral bearings from the character of any regime in which they exist. Accordingly, the rule of law – which is constituted by those essential properties – is itself a divided phenomenon. As the set of conditions that obtain whenever any legal system exists and operates, the rule of law is per se a morally neutral state of affairs. Especially in any sizable society, the rule of law is indispensable for the preservation of public order and the coordination of people's activities and the securing of individuals' liberties; but it is likewise indispensable for a government's effective perpetration of large-scale projects of evil over lengthy periods (Kramer 1999a). It therefore lacks any intrinsic moral standing. All the same, when the rule of law is operative within a benign regime, its moral value goes beyond lending itself to worthy uses. It does indeed promote the attainment of worthy ends by enabling governmental officials and private citizens to pursue and realize such ends, but, within a benign regime, it also does more. Instead of merely being instrumentally valuable, it furthermore becomes expressive of the very ideals which it helps to foster. Its basic features take on the moral estimableness of those ideals, for the sustainment of the rule of law in such circumstances is a deliberate manifestation of a society's adherence to liberal-democratic values.

We shall, then, be encountering the rule of law in two principal incarnations (Craig 1997; Summers 1993; Tamanaha 2004, 91–113). Firstly, as a general juristic phenomenon, it amounts to nothing more and nothing less than the fundamental conditions that have to be satisfied for the existence of any legal system. Secondly, whenever that juristic phenomenon obtains specifically in liberal-democratic societies – which exhibit rich diversity among themselves in their detailed institutions and practices – it is a morally cherishable expression of commitments to the dignity and equality of individuals. Yet, because the rule of law is a morally precious desideratum in some settings and not in others, any attribution of invariance to its key features is prone to mislead. Those features are indeed invariant in that every legal system is characterized by them, but the roles which they play can diverge in major respects from one legal regime to another. We need to keep this point clearly in mind as we endeavor to grasp the complicated relationships between objectivity and the rule of law. When seeking to fathom that set of relationships, we shall have to remain alert not only to the multiplicity of the dimensions of objectivity but also to the pregnant division within the idea of the rule of law. Because the essential attributes of the rule of law are protean in their substantive moral-political bearings, the connections between those attributes and the sundry facets of objectivity are likewise importantly variable.

2.1. Of the Essence of Law

This section's discussion of the rule of law as a general juristic phenomenon – in abstraction from the moral-political hues of particular regimes – will draw quite heavily on Lon Fuller's famous exposition of the central elements in the rule of law. Fuller, an American legal theorist, delineated what he styled as the "eight principles of legality" (Fuller 1969, 33–94). With those eight principles, some of which overlap considerably, he distilled the cardinal features that are present whenever a legal system exists. If at least one of his principles is largely or wholly unfulfilled within some society, then the society in question is devoid of any legal system.

While this section will follow the general contours of Fuller's theoretical framework, it will depart from his more textured analyses at a number of junctures. His elaboration of the eight principles of legality is a permanently valuable contribution to legal philosophy, but some of his arguments in support or explication of his principles are confused or otherwise inadequate. His most far-reaching error lay in his belief that his singling out of the fundamental characteristics of law was somehow at odds with legal positivism's insistence on the separability of law and morality. Fuller contended that his eight principles constitute the "inner morality of law" and that they therefore establish an integral connection between the legal domain and the moral domain. I have elsewhere contested at length his efforts to substantiate his antipositivist conclusions (Kramer 1999a, 37–77). We need not concern ourselves here with the debates over the soundness of legal positivism. We can instead benefit from Fuller's reflections in two ways, which correspond to the two versions of the rule of law. First, although some of his lines of argument are

muddled or lacking in rigor, his overall distillation of the essential properties of law is an admirable achievement. With an array of modifications
in matters of detail, his account of the principles of legality will provide the structure for my own exposition of the rule of law as a general
phenomenon. Second, notwithstanding that Fuller's insistence on the
inherently moral character of law's essential features was misconceived,
his exploration of the ties between law and morality will often inform
my account of the rule of law as a liberal-democratic ideal. As I have
suggested elsewhere (Kramer 1999a, 62), his ruminations on the inner
morality of law are frequently astute and illuminating if they are taken
to be focused specifically on the import of law within liberal-democratic
societies. This chapter will construe those ruminations in precisely that
restrictive fashion. It will thus render Fuller's theory a valuable source of
insights not only for an investigation of the rule of law as a general mode of
governance, but also for an investigation of the rule of law as a moral ideal.

Let us proceed, then, to ponder Fuller's eight precepts of legality.
Under those precepts, a system of governance qualifies as a legal regime
only if

1. it operates through general norms;

2. its norms are promulgated to the people whose conduct is to be
   authoritatively assessed by reference to them;

3. its norms are prospective rather than retrospective;

4. the authoritative formulations of its norms are understandable
   (at least by people with juristic expertise) rather than opaquely
   unintelligible;

5. its norms are logically consistent with one another, and the obligations
   imposed by those norms can be jointly fulfilled;

6. its norms do not require things that are starkly beyond the capabilities
   of the people who are subject to the norms;

7. the contents of its norms, instead of being transformed sweepingly
   and very frequently, remain mostly unchanged for periods of time
   long enough to induce familiarity; and

8. its norms are generally effectuated in accordance with what they prescribe, so that the formulations of the norms (the laws on the books)
   are congruent with the ways in which they are implemented (the laws
   in practice).

Before we probe each of these principles of legality in greater depth, a caveat should be entered. Each principle articulates a condition that must be substantially satisfied within a legal system, rather than a condition that must be invariably or comprehensively satisfied. In no legal system is each of the eight principles ever perfectly fulfilled. Perfect compliance with each of them is a will-o'-the-wisp and is in any event unnecessary for the existence of a legal regime. Although conformity with the precepts of legality is essential for the existence of any such regime, the conformity only needs to meet or exceed a threshold level; that threshold level for each of the precepts is quite high, but it falls some way short of perfection. (Such a threshold level, incidentally, cannot be specified precisely. Any attempt to offer a precise specification, for legal systems generally or for some particular legal system, would run afoul of the problem of vagueness that was broached at a couple of junctures in Chapter 1.)

In short, the existence of a legal system presupposes that the satisfaction of each Fullerian principle of legality is not below some threshold level, but it only contingently involves the satisfaction of any of the Fullerian principles above that level. Every vibrant legal system will conform to those principles well above the threshold point for each of them, but the heightened degree of conformity is a matter of the system's vibrancy rather than of its very existence as a regime of law. Such a degree of conformity will render especially clear the status of a system of governance as a legal system, but that status can obtain (albeit less clearly) even when a regime's conformity is at or only slightly above the threshold level.

Some commentators such as Nigel Simmonds, disregarding Fuller's own remarks to the contrary, have suggested that the Fullerian precepts of legality collectively form an archetype to which any actual legal system approximates more or less closely. Simmonds maintains that each such legal system will approach that archetype of perfection to a greater or a lesser extent, just as a disk or a drawing of a round curve will approximate to the conditions specified by the mathematical definition of a circle (Simmonds 2004, 118–19). In his view, legal systems are legal systems to varying degrees, just as disks or drawings of round curves are circles to varying degrees.

One should eschew Simmonds's view of the matter, for it stems from a simplistic understanding of mathematical definitions and a distortive understanding of the Fullerian principles of legality. When a circle is defined mathematically as a curve delimited by the complete set of points equidistant from a common point, nothing in the material world is a circle at all. Mathematical points are each infinitesimal, and any line or curve which they constitute is thus infinitesimal in its width and depth. A circle defined mathematically is a purely abstract entity rather than something that can genuinely be instantiated in the material world. Hence, if Fuller's principles of legality were relevantly analogous to mathematical definitions, we would have to conclude that no legal systems exist or ever can exist in the material world.

Obviously, when the term "circle" is used in ordinary discourse, it is typically employed more loosely. Instead of denoting a purely abstract entity that can never exist in a material form, it typically denotes a material thing with features that are the material counterparts of the features of the abstract entity. Any such thing partakes of roundness to a greater or a lesser degree. However, this evident observation does not tell in favor of Simmonds's position at all. In the first place, Simmonds goes astray in presuming that the material things correctly labeled as "circles" are circles in the strict mathematical sense to a greater or a lesser extent. Material entities are not purely abstract entities to any degree. Simmonds is making essentially the same error that is made by someone who thinks of infinity as a very large quantity or of infinitesimalness as a tiny quantity. There is a difference of kind, rather than merely a difference of degree, between a circle in the strict mathematical sense and a circle in the everyday sense. Hence, if Fuller's principles were an archetype as Simmonds suggests, they would be specifying conditions that are different in kind from those that obtain when any actual legal system exists. Fuller himself would have been thoroughly bemused by such a notion.

Moreover, inquiries about the archetypal status of the principles of legality are separable from the other question to which Simmonds assigns such importance: the question whether the property of being a legal regime is scalar or nonscalar. Let us here glance first at the property of being a circle. When that property is understood in the everyday sense rather than in the strict mathematical sense, we might ask whether it is to be classified as scalar. Perhaps every object or drawing that meets some vaguely specifiable threshold of roundness is a circle in the everyday sense, and perhaps objects or drawings which far exceed that threshold are more clearly circles (instead of being circles to greater extents) than are objects or drawings which only narrowly exceed the threshold. If so, then the property of being a circle in the quotidian sense is a nonscalar property; like the property of being a circle in the strict mathematical sense, and unlike the property of clarity, it obtains in an all-or-nothing fashion. Contrariwise, perhaps round objects and drawings are circles to greater or lesser extents in proportion to the smoothness of their round shapes. If so, then the property of being a circle in the quotidian sense is a scalar property. Similar questions about the scalar/nonscalar divide can be raised about the property of being a legal system, of course. Perhaps every system of governance that satisfies the Fullerian principles of legality at or beyond some threshold level is a legal regime, and any systems that greatly exceed the threshold level – up to some unspecifiably high point – are more clearly legal regimes (instead of being legal regimes to greater degrees) than are any systems which only narrowly meet that level. In that event, as both H. L. A. Hart and Ronald Dworkin have contended, the property of being a legal regime is nonscalar (Hart 1983, 354–55; Dworkin 1965, 676–78). Alternatively, perhaps a system of governance is a legal system to a greater or a lesser extent in proportion to the measure of its conformity with the Fullerian principles. In that case, as Fuller himself believed, the property of being a legal regime is a scalar property (Fuller 1969, 122–23).

Nothing in the preceding paragraph is meant to imply that the questions therein about the scalar/nonscalar division are unanswerable. On the contrary, there is a uniquely correct answer to each of those questions. Although the property of circularity in the everyday sense is doubtless a scalar property – like roundness – the property of being a circle in the everyday sense is nonscalar. Notwithstanding that there are some borderline cases of objects or drawings that are neither determinately circles nor determinately not circles, nearly every object or drawing either is a circle or is not a circle. What obtains as a matter of degree is the *clarity* of the status of something as a circle in the everyday sense, rather than that status itself. In a similar vein, the property of being a legal system is nonscalar. Above an unspecifiable threshold of conformity with Fuller's principles of legality, any system of governance amounts to a legal system. To be sure, there can exist borderline cases of territories in which the rule of law is neither determinately present nor determinately absent, and there can also exist territories in which the rule of law is present in some respects and absent in other respects. There arises a situation of the latter sort (which may well also be a borderline situation of the former sort), for example, when a system of governance partakes of norm-guided regularity in some of its operations while partaking of chaotic irregularity in some of its other operations. These manifest possibilities are fully consistent with the fact that the property of being a legal system is nonscalar. Whenever that property is determinately present or absent, it is determinately present or absent in an all-or-nothing fashion; we should insist as much while readily allowing that the property of being a legal system is sometimes neither determinately present nor determinately absent. In short, what is scalar is not the status of a system of governance as a legal regime, but the clarity or straightforwardness of that status.

Of course, the preceding paragraph has offered mainly assertions rather than arguments. If it were important within the confines of this book to substantiate the conclusions advocated in that paragraph, then arguments would plainly be needed. However, my purpose here has not been to provide any full-blown justification for those conclusions. Rather, one of the chief purposes has been to indicate that those conclusions are consistent with the proposition that the Fullerian principles of legality are an archetype on a par with the mathematical definition of a circle. Also consistent with that proposition about archetypes, naturally, are contrary conclusions about the scalar/nonscalar dichotomy in application to the property of being a circle (in an everyday sense) and in application to the property of being a legal system. One of the key points here is that disagreements over the scalar or nonscalar character of the property of being a legal regime are orthogonal to disagreements over the nature of Fuller's principles as an archetype. Hence, even if Simmonds were correct in characterizing those principles as archetypal, he would not yet have gone any way toward establishing that the property of being a legal system is a scalar property.

In fact, however, what is most objectionable about Simmonds's discussion is his contention that the principles of legality are collectively an archetype. With that contention, Simmonds misrepresents those principles and fails to heed Fuller's own warnings (Fuller 1969, 41, 45) – warnings which Simmonds himself partly quotes (Simmonds 2004, 118 n27). A modicum of reflection should reveal that the eight principles cannot jointly be perfectly fulfilled, even in an ideal world. Consider, for example, the first and fourth principles: the requirement of generality and the requirement of clarity. The very notion of perfect clarity is somewhat obscure. Yet, insofar as we can make sense of that notion, we can discern that it is in evident tension with the notion of perfect generality. If legal norms are perfectly general, they will be so dauntingly abstract as to be quite unclear in their implications for any particular circumstances. Substantial departures from perfect generality will be inevitable if the principle of clarity is to be fulfilled perfectly or even adequately. Patently untenable, then, is any suggestion that Fuller's principles collectively constitute an archetype of perfect legality. Unlike the conditions specified in the mathematical definition of a circle, the conditions specified in the principles of legality do not all coherently fit together when they are understood as ideals that collectively form an archetype of perfection.

Thus, as we proceed to examine Fuller's principles of legality, we should reject both the view that those principles are archetypal and the view that the property of being a legal system is scalar. In lieu of those misconceptions, the best way of understanding the Fullerian principles has already been indicated. Each principle lays down a necessary condition for the existence of any legal system. That is, the condition encapsulated in each of Fuller's principles is satisfied at least up to some threshold level whenever the rule of law prevails in a society. Above that level, up to some considerably higher point, any further compliance with each principle will enhance the clarity and robustness of the status of a legal system as such but will not be indispensable for the very applicability of that status.

2.1.1. Governance by General Norms

Perhaps the most obvious of the eight principles of legality is the first. No system of governance can count as a regime of law unless it operates through general norms, for those norms are its principal laws and are also the sources of its other laws. There can hardly be law without laws.

Two contrasts are germane here. General norms are to be differentiated from situation-specific directives and also from mandates addressed to particular individuals. That is, the generality of a legal norm pertains both to the circumstances on which the norm bears and to the people whose conduct it regulates (Hart 1961, 20–22). The general norms of a legal system – as opposed to the situation-specific directives which any

such system also comprises – each apply to an array of cognate circumstances rather than only to one particular event or state of affairs. For
example, a law prohibiting murder applies to that general type of conduct rather than solely to one particular instance of the type. It applies
to each of the particular instances, of course, but to each of them as
an instance rather than as a free-standing occurrence that has not been
subsumed under any overarching standard. Most of the legal norms that
are general in this first sense (namely, in the sense of not being purely
situation-specific) are also general in the second way; that is, most such
norms are each addressed to a general class of persons rather than only to
some particular individual. Many legal norms are each addressed to the
community as a whole. A law prohibiting murder, for example, typically
regulates the conduct of everyone alike. In sum, each of the general norms
of a legal system applies to a type of conduct rather than solely to some
particular instance of conduct, and most such norms are addressed to
general categories of people rather than to designated individuals.

Of course, to say that every possible legal system must operate through
general norms is scarcely to say that any such system can operate only with
such norms. Directives that are both situation-specific and addressed to
particular persons will be indispensable in any legal regime, not least
for bringing the regime's general norms to bear on particular problems.
Officials charged with effectuating those general norms will be unable to
carry out their responsibilities unless they are authorized to issue orders
to particular persons relating to particular instances of conduct. All the
same, the essential role of individualized directives in the workings of
any legal system is perfectly compatible with the essential role of general
norms.

In what ways, then, is the role of general norms essential? Let us
ponder first their generality of application and then their generality of
address. The presence of norms that are general in their application –
that is, the fact that situation-specific directives are not the exclusive or
principal means of regulating people's conduct – is crucial not only for
the rule of law but also for the sheer functionality of any system of governance, at least in any society more sizable than a handful of families.
If the officials in any regime were to endeavor to govern a society by
dealing with every situation in isolation from every other situation, then
both the society and the regime would be chaotically uncoordinated. The

ostensible system of governance would in fact be a lack of governance. Only through the operativeness of general norms that relate cognate situations to one another, can a regime suitably coordinate its own activities and the activities of ordinary citizens. Only through such norms, moreover, can the rule of law prevail in a society. As has been stated, those general norms are the principal laws of the regime that establishes them, and are the sources of the regime's other laws. Obviously, the rule of law can never be realized without laws. Basic features of law, such as its regularity and uniform applicability, would be altogether missing if a regime relied solely on situation-specific directives for the regulation of conduct. Given that the rule of law is integrally bound up with the idea that we are to be governed by laws and not by men (Tamanaha 2004, 122–26), it would be fatally undermined in any setting in which no general norms are operative. In such a setting, after all, a regime's officials would have to reach case-by-case determinations in a sweepingly discretionary fashion. They would be neither restricted nor guided by any norms that transcend the respective contexts of their case-by-case proceedings. Such a higgledy-piggledy arrangement would be antithetical to the rule of law and would indeed be inconsistent with any minimally effective system of governance.

Squarely unmistakable is the dependence of the rule of law on the existence of norms that are general in their application. Maybe not quite as obvious is the dependence of the rule of law on the existence of norms that are general in their address. Fuller himself, at any rate, did not include the generality of address within his first principle of legality (Fuller 1969, 47). Nevertheless, *pace* Fuller, the requirement of generality expounded here does indeed encompass the generality of address. To be sure, not every legally binding directive is addressed to a general class of persons. As has already been remarked, many of the mandates issued within any functional legal system are orders addressed to particular individuals rather than to any general classes of persons. Still, having perceived the indispensability of directives that relate only to particularly designated persons, we should hardly infer that norms addressed to general classes of persons are not likewise indispensable. In fact, the presence of such norms – like the presence of norms that are general in their application to types of conduct – is essential not only for the rule of law but also for any tenable scheme of governance. If a regime sought to address a different set of norms to every individual or even to every family, its operations would be hopelessly unworkable (save perhaps in a minute and extremely primitive society consisting of no more than a handful of families). In a society with millions of people, the very task of formulating the multitudinous different sets of norms would be wildly beyond the capacity of any credible scheme of governance. Even more ludicrously unmanageable would be the task of administering the myriad packages of norms. To gauge the permissibility or impermissibility of each person's conduct, the officials responsible for policing would have to know the identity of everyone and the contents of the individualized set of norms to which each person is subject. In other words, even if we put aside the fact that any wholesale eschewal of the generality of address in the framing of a regime's norms would be bizarrely pointless and perverse, such an approach to law-creation and law-administration would be utterly infeasible. Norms general in their address as well as in their application will be operative whenever any institutions of governance are operative.

Even more plainly, such norms are unforgoable elements in the rule of law. Any blanket eschewal of the generality of address in the formulating of a regime's norms would scotch many central characteristics of the rule of law. Indeed, the same fundamental properties of law that would be thwarted if a regime were to do without any norms that are general in their application – properties such as regularity and uniformity – would likewise be thwarted if a regime were to do without any norms that are general in their address. If the sets of norms addressed to different individuals are genuinely divergent, then the normative consequences of similar actions performed by different people will vary markedly. Just as the officials in charge of administering a regime's norms will be unable to carry out their responsibilities in a minimally informed and coordinated and efficacious fashion, so too the members of the public in any sizable society will be cripplingly unable to form any confident expectations on the basis of which they can interact with one another. Outside narrow circles of families and close friends, no one will have an informed sense of what anyone else is required or permitted or empowered to do. This preposterous situation would be antithetical to the rule of law, which – in its malign embodiments as well as its benign embodiments – enables each person to gain a reliable sense of what other people are required and permitted and authorized to do.

In sum, although Fuller was certainly correct in thinking that the generality of address for legal norms is often required by considerations of fairness, he stumbled in thinking that such generality is not also a feature inherent in the rule of law. Admittedly, as has been readily acknowledged herein, many legal directives in any system of law do not partake of such generality; no legal system can operate without orders addressed to particular persons. At the same time, countless other legal mandates in any system of law will indeed be addressed to general classes of persons. No legal regime would be functional in the absence of such mandates and other legal norms that are general in their address.

2.1.2. Public Ascertainability

No legal system can guide and direct human behavior if the contents of its norms remain wholly undisclosed to the people within the jurisdiction of the system. As an operative mechanism for regulating human conduct, rather than as a collection of abstract formulations with no effects in the world, a regime of law has to render its mandates and other norms ascertainable by the people to whose conduct they apply. By some means – often by a variety of means – a legal system must comply with Fuller's second principle, the principle of promulgation. In the complete absence of such compliance, an ostensible legal system would be thoroughly inefficacious in channeling people's behavior. The existence of the system would make no difference to anyone's reasoning about appropriate courses of conduct. Indeed, so long as we construe the principle of promulgation expansively, we should recognize that it specifies a necessary condition not only for the rule of law but also for any viable mode of governance.

Within the requirement articulated by the principle of promulgation, there is ample room for diversity in the techniques by which the norms of legal systems are made ascertainable. At an extreme, which I have discussed elsewhere (Kramer 1999a, 45–48), the promulgation of a regime's norms might occur solely through the concrete decisions whereby the norms are brought to bear on people's conduct. In any regime of law, the officials will have to resolve disputes and penalize wrongdoing and gauge people's legal positions in other respects. Given that their regime is a regime of law, the officials will typically be carrying out those functions by reference to general norms that pertain to people's conduct. In an

ordinary setting, all or most of those norms will be directly ascertainable
by the members of the public to whom they apply; although the members of the public might not be capable of taking advantage of their direct
access to the contents of the prevailing norms without assistance from
legal experts, and although some members of the public might seldom
or never seek to avail themselves of that access, they will retain it and can
resort to it if they so wish. In an extreme setting, however, there would
be no such direct access. Instead, the only manifestations of the contents
of the prevailing laws would be the decisions reached by adjudicative and
administrative officials as they give effect to those laws. If the decisions
were to be sufficiently numerous and regularized, the patterns of those
decisions would serve as the indicators through which ordinary citizens
could become indirectly apprised of the general norms under which the
legal consequences of their conduct are assessed. Officials' determinations
in such circumstances would not be random events devoid of meanings.
On the contrary, they would be the intelligibly patterned expressions of
the legal mandates and other legal norms to which the people in a jurisdiction are subject. Moreover, insofar as the officials' judgments and their
rationales would have precedential force, those judgments and rationales
themselves would constitute directly ascertainable legal norms.

Obviously, the outcome-centered mode of promulgation just discussed is at an extreme of austerity. It will not be tenable as a method of
promulgation unless the decisions explicitly reached by officials are sufficiently plentiful and regularized to create clearly intelligible patterns. If
the decisions are few and far between, or if a number of them are aber-
rant, they will not be adequately reliable and informative as conduits that
provide indirect access to the norms that lie behind them. Nor will an
austerely outcome-focused method of promulgation be sustainable if the
underlying norms quite frequently change. When the general norms of
a legal system are directly ascertainable by the people who are subject
to them, a reasonably substantial degree of changeableness is compatible
with the chief function of law in guiding and channeling people's conduct;
by contrast, when those general norms are only indirectly ascertainable
through concrete applications of them, any significant degree of changeableness will frustrate the efforts of people to infer the contents of the
norms from the applications. Because gaining knowledge of the contents
of those norms is a far more difficult task when one's access to them is

indirect rather than direct, the epistemically disruptive effects of any transformations of the norms will be greatly accentuated. Note, furthermore, that the indirect access is opened up only if the officials' law-applying decisions are themselves publicly ascertainable. If those decisions were somehow to remain undisclosed, then citizens would have no way of becoming acquainted with the contents of the laws to which they are subject – in which case those putative laws would not figure in anyone's reasoning about appropriate courses of conduct.

Because of the considerations adumbrated in the preceding paragraph, an austerely outcome-focused method of promulgation is far from optimal in any but the most primitive legal system. It is precarious at best as a technique for conveying to citizens the terms of the legal norms that regulate their behavior; in a moderately dynamic regime of law, it will very likely prove to be almost entirely otiose. Still, the austere mode of promulgation should not be dismissed altogether as a hopelessly problematic approach that would never be adopted to any degree in a functional legal system. After all, in some respects, it is distinctively the approach of the common law – though, of course, major common-law decisions and their patterns are themselves very often treated as general norms rather than as mere indicators of such norms.

In common-law jurisdictions as in other jurisdictions, the austerely outcome-focused method of promulgation is by no means the lone way of conveying to citizens the contents of the legal norms that govern their interaction. Statutes and administrative regulations and constitutional provisions and indeed judicial doctrines are all directly ascertainable by members of the public. Though specific interpretations of such laws must await the concrete applications of them by judges and various administrative officials, their general terms (which are sometimes very detailed) are accessible in advance of those applications. In what does their direct ascertainability consist? Clearly not required is that each citizen is actually familiar with the terms of those laws. Most people at any given time are ignorant of the vast majority of the legal norms that bear on their behavior, and even legal experts are individually ignorant of many such norms. If the actual acquaintance of citizens with the substance of each of the prevailing legal norms were a necessary condition for the existence of a legal system, then no such system would ever exist. In fact, of course, the principle of promulgation does not envisage such actual acquaintance on any significant scale. What that principle requires is simply that such acquaintance *can* be gained by any member of the public who desires it. Laws must be ascertainable, even though most people very seldom devote much time or energy to ascertaining them.

Devices for making the contents of laws accessible to citizens vary from one legal system to another, and also vary within any single legal system over time. Of greatest importance, in any legal system beyond the tiniest and most primitive, is the presentation of laws in authoritative written formulations. Those formulations, which can be available not only in traditional publications (and on stone tablets) but also more recently in electronic repositories, are the principal objects of attention for most people who endeavor to apprise themselves of the legal consequences that attach to various courses of conduct. Whether such people study the authoritative formulations directly or learn of their contents through intermediate expositions, the existence of those written formulations is what enables each person to acquire knowledge of the law's general demands and permissions and authorizations. It is therefore what enables the law to affect everyone's practical reasoning. It is also what enables legal officials themselves to become and remain apprised of the manifold laws which they are responsible for administering. In any society beyond the tiniest and most primitive, the existence of authoritative written formulations is indispensable for the functionality of a legal system. (Of course, what has just been said does not imply that every law in an advanced legal system will be associated with an authoritative written formulation. As jurisprudential philosophers have long recognized, some laws in virtually any legal system are not encapsulated in canonical written renderings. Examples in the English-speaking part of the world include some customary norms with the status of laws and some common-law rules. The immanence of customary norms in people's activities is itself a suitable means of promulgation that offsets the absence of canonical written expressions, and the variations among judges' formulations of some common-law rules are unconfusingly minor in application to most circumstances. Moreover, those customary norms and common-law rules exist alongside many other laws for which there are authoritative written formulations. Hence, when one recognizes the existence of some laws that are not covered by such formulations, one is scarcely thereby retreating from the view that canonical written statements of legal norms are generally crucial for a regime's compliance with the principle of promulgation.)

My terse reference in the preceding paragraph to intermediate expositions of the contents of laws should alert us to another crucial element in any effective fulfillment of the principle of promulgation: the presence of legal experts in a society. As sources of advice and assistance, specialists in sundry areas of a society's law help to ensure that the authoritative formulations of legal norms are meaningfully accessible. Were citizens left to their own devices in discerning the contents of the laws that are applicable to their doings, the practical significance of the ascertainability of those laws would be virtually nil for many people. Especially in an advanced legal system, but even in quite a crude legal system, the availability of advice and assistance from lawyers (and other legal experts) is something without which the system's norms would remain largely opaque. Chapter 1's discussion of impartiality touched upon the vital role of lawyers in drawing the attention of adjudicators and administrators to the sundry relevant details of any matter on which some authoritative decision is to be rendered. Here we see that lawyers are central to the operations of a legal system at earlier stages as well. They are the vehicles through which the complicated norms of such a system can become familiar to citizens and can thus become live factors in the citizens' practical reasoning.

Any number of more detailed measures for the promulgation of legal norms may be essential in some societies and not in others. At a time before the authoritative written formulations of such norms became readily available in electronic repositories, the widespread distribution of texts containing those formulations was indispensable for the public ascertainability of the norms. In the present era, when virtually all legal experts and many ordinary citizens in Western liberal democracies enjoy electronic access to a huge variety of legal materials, the distribution of printed texts containing those materials is plainly of less importance. Nevertheless, even in the Western liberal democracies, there are still some people who are unable to afford the costs of electronic access to legal materials. In connection with those people, the availability of printed texts is still crucial for the satisfaction of the principle of promulgation.

In much of the world beyond the Western liberal democracies, many people have little or no electronic access to authoritative formulations of the laws of their societies. In some non-Western countries, indeed, illiteracy is rampant. (Even in the Western liberal democracies, illiteracy is quite a pressing problem.) For people who cannot read, neither electronic repositories of legal materials nor printed texts will be of direct value. These difficulties would seldom be greatly alleviated through the production of recordings in which the authoritative formulations of legal norms would be read aloud. Even if such recordings were to be provided free of charge to destitute people who have never attained literacy, very slim indeed (in most cases) is the likelihood that those people could absorb and retain much of what is being recited. Such people will have to rely almost entirely on the advice and assistance of more knowledgeable parties, including legal officials. Given that they will almost certainly not be able to purchase the advice and assistance out of their own meager funds, some charitable or governmental arrangements for the delivery of legal services will typically be necessary.

At any rate, as has been emphasized, what is essential for the existence of a legal system is not the perfect fulfillment of the principle of promulgation (or of any other Fullerian principle); what is essential, rather, is the *adequate* fulfillment of that principle. Even when we take account of the fact that the principle of promulgation requires only ascertainability rather than actual ascertainment, we should recognize that limited departures from perfection will be far from fatal. A legal system can straightforwardly exist even if not all of its laws are ascertainable by everyone. A small number of its laws might be inaccessible to most people, and virtually all of its laws might be inaccessible to people who are too impoverished and ignorant and socially isolated to gain any knowledge of them. Deviations of these sorts from the principle of promulgation are fully compatible with the robust existence of a legal system as such, and indeed they occur in every actual legal system. A regime of law can perform its central guiding role with ample efficacy even though some of its demands and authorizations may be unknowable (and not merely unknown) by some people within its jurisdiction.

2.1.3. Prospectivity

The idea of a legal system without any prospective norms is as bewilderingly absurd as the idea of a legal system without any general norms or without any means of promulgating its laws. Compliance with Fuller's third principle of legality is essential not just for the efficient functioning of a legal regime but also for the very existence of such a regime. If all the ostensible laws in some society were retroactive, then at any given juncture there would not yet be any laws that determine the legal consequences of conduct undertaken at that juncture. Such laws would not materialize until later, if at all. Those putative laws, whenever they might eventually appear, would be wholly inefficacious in guiding the conduct of people at the time to which the putative laws pertain. An ersatz legal system operating entirely through such pseudo-laws would not be a legal system at all. Indeed, such a system would be completely nonfunctional, since the absence of any prospective norms would entail the absence of any norms that authorize and obligate the apparent legal officials to carry out their supposed responsibilities. Not only would citizens at any given juncture be unable to find any legal guidance on the basis of which they might act, but, in addition, the ostensible officials at any given juncture would have no basis for their status as officials at that juncture. None of the norms of the system could be given effect, then. At any time t when those norms might be implemented, no one (*ex hypothesi*) would yet be officially authorized to implement them at t. In short, the notion of a functional legal regime with only retroactive norms is forbiddingly incoherent. In any functional regime, all or most of the laws must be prospective rather than purely retrospective. Plainly, all or most of the laws that authorize certain people to act as legal officials will have to be prospective if the authoritative functions of a legal regime are to be performed. Similarly, all or most of the other laws in a society will have to be prospective if the society's legal system is to impinge in any significant fashion on the choices and behavior of the people who are subject to its sway.

Perfect compliance is no more to be expected with the principle of prospectivity than with any of Fuller's other principles. Indeed, as Fuller himself incisively observed (Fuller 1969, 53–54, 56–57), departures from this third principle of legality can be salutary in quite a few credible circumstances. For example, such departures can sometimes be advisable as devices for rectifying any untoward consequences that have ensued from previous muddles in the creation or administration of laws; in some contexts, the best way of coming to grips with those untoward consequences might be to eliminate them retroactively. Moreover, the introduction of retroactively effective laws is both unavoidable and (on balance) desirable in the relatively small number of private-law cases that hinge on questions to which there are no determinately correct answers. In any such case, in the absence of a settlement between the parties, either the defendant or the plaintiff will ultimately prevail. Any judge hearing such a case is obligated to reach a decision, whatever the decision may prove to be. Yet, up to the point when the case has been heard and resolved, there is no determinately correct answer to the question whether the defendant should win or the plaintiff should win. Accordingly, if the defendant loses and is therefore ordered to pay compensation to the plaintiff, the new legal norm introduced by the precedential force of that decision will have been applied retroactively against the defendant. Conduct that was not determinately unlawful at the time of its occurrence has retroactively been deemed unlawful. Contrariwise, if the plaintiff loses and is thus denied any compensation, the new legal norm introduced by the precedential force of *that* decision will have been applied retrospectively against him in favor of the defendant. A type of conduct that was not determinately lawful at the time of its occurrence has retroactively been deemed lawful.

This feature of unavoidable retroactivity is not similarly present in the small number of criminal-law cases that hinge on questions to which there are no determinately correct answers. In any benignly liberal-democratic system of law, a background norm – a rule of closure – prescribes that no one is to incur criminal penalties for conduct that was not determinately unlawful at the time of its occurrence. Hence, when a court decides that a thitherto indeterminate question about the culpability or permissibility of a certain kind of conduct should be resolved through the classification of such conduct as criminally culpable, the norm articulated by that decision will be applied only prospectively. Within a liberal-democratic scheme of things, the defendant in the case immediately before the court will be acquitted.

In any private-law litigation that revolves around indeterminate legal questions, by contrast, the prospect of retroactive detriments cannot be dodged. If a private-law defendant's conduct is retrospectively deemed to be determinately lawful, then the plaintiff will have suffered a detriment through that retrospective determination of the conduct's status. Conversely, if a private-law defendant's conduct is retrospectively deemed to be determinately unlawful, then the defendant will have suffered a detriment. Were a court to remove that hardship from the defendant by decreeing that the norm articulated in the decision will apply only prospectively and not to the case at hand, the plaintiff in the case would suffer a detriment. As far as that particular plaintiff is concerned, the court would in effect be retroactively classifying the particular defendant's conduct as determinately lawful. After all, at least in Anglo-American law, no general background rule prescribes that a defendant will never incur any compensatory obligations for conduct that was not determinately unlawful at the time of its occurrence. In the absence of such a background rule, a decision against the retroactive burdening of the defendant would amount to the retroactive disadvantaging of the plaintiff. (Note that the absence of the specified background rule in Anglo-American law is hardly an inexplicable anomaly. If the courts were regularly disposed to decline to issue compensatory orders against defendants in cases of the sort just envisaged, they would markedly impair the incentives for potential plaintiffs to pursue lawsuits in such cases. Indeterminacies in the law would less frequently give rise to litigation and would thus tend to remain unresolved. Indeed, since the courts would probably quite often fail to heed the distinction between indeterminacy and uncertainty – a distinction highlighted in my opening chapter's discussion of objectivity qua determinate correctness – they would probably be inclined not to issue compensatory orders in some cases that hinge on questions to which there are determinately correct answers. The incentive-impairing effects of their stance would thus be especially problematic. For these reasons, Anglo-American judges are justified in being disposed to apply newly determined legal norms to the detriment of defendants in the private-law cases immediately before them.)

My discussion of private-law litigation in the last few paragraphs has concentrated on some legal norms that are not purely retrospective. Indeed, those norms are principally prospective. Retroactive applications of such norms are not as glaringly at odds with Fuller's third principle as are laws that are introduced purely for the purpose of altering people's legal positions retroactively. All the same, the main claims advanced in the opening paragraph of this subsection on prospectivity are still pertinent. Just as there cannot exist a functional legal regime with nothing other than purely retroactive laws, so too there cannot exist such a regime with nothing other than retroactive applications of seemingly prospective laws.

If a regime operated solely through successions of such applications, then its purportedly prospective laws would not really be prospective at all. Those laws would be continuously undone and superseded by retroactive applications of other purportedly prospective laws, which would in turn be continuously undone and superseded. The general role of law in guiding and directing human conduct would thus be negated. Even in a system where most rather than all of the applications of the prevailing norms are retroactive, the general role just mentioned would be undermined. In any functional legal system, then, most of the applications of legal norms – as well as most of the legal norms themselves, of course – have to be nonretrospective. We should recognize as much while also recognizing that some departures from the principle of prospectivity are salutary.

As has been argued, indeed – and as Fuller himself observed – departures from the principle of prospectivity are sometimes not only salutary but also unavoidable, at least in any legal system with procedures for private-law adjudication that yield proper incentives for litigation. Given as much, we can perceive the stark untenability of the thesis that Fuller's eight precepts form an archetype of perfection. Such a thesis obscures the actual character of those precepts. Instead of laying down a standard of perfection, the principle of prospectivity is like the other Fullerian precepts in proceeding along the two tracks mentioned earlier. That is, it delineates a necessary threshold condition for the existence of any legal system, and it fixes upon a property whose greater and greater presence (up to some high level well above the threshold) will increase the straightforwardness of the status of a legal system as such. A bit of reflection on the principle of prospectivity helps to sharpen one's understanding of Fuller's whole theoretical framework. Any characterization of that framework as an archetype is misconceived.

2.1.4. Perspicuity

Unless the mandates and other norms of a legal system are formulated in reasonably lucid language, the system will largely or completely fail to perform the basic function of law as a means of channeling people's behavior along certain paths and away from other paths. One of the hallmarks of the rule of law is that it conveys to people a clear sense of what is demanded of them (and what is permitted and what is authorized).

That cardinal aspect of the rule of law will be stymied if statutes and administrative regulations and judicial opinions and other expressions of legal norms are not drafted perspicuously. People do not receive adequate guidance from the workings of a legal system if its directives are darkly incomprehensible or nonsensical or muddled.

Of course, the clarity of legal language is not to be gauged principally by reference to an ordinary person's understanding and knowledge. Legal language, the parlance of a specialized profession, abounds with terms and phrases that are unfamiliar to people who lack juridical expertise. Some of those terms and phrases get incorporated into the law's public pronouncements (statutes, regulations, and the like). Hence, if we were to take the ordinary person's comprehension as the touchstone for the lucidity of legal directives, we would significantly overestimate the unclarity of the law in virtually every society. Instead, the chief touchstone for the understandability of the formulations of legal norms is the competent legal expert's comprehension. If such an expert would regard the wording of some statute or regulation as clear and precise, then the statute or regulation is squarely in compliance with Fuller's fourth principle of legality – even if most people without legal training would find the wording pretty formidable.

One of the paramount reasons for my intermittent emphasis on the centrality of lawyers and other legal experts in the operations of any legal system is precisely that those operations are often quite technical. As such, they tend to involve a technical argot. The widespread availability of assistance from experts is thus vital for the proper functioning of a legal regime. Without the availability of such assistance, many of the law's directives would not be meaningful sources of guidance for ordinary citizens – even if the citizens knew where to locate the formulations of those directives and endeavored to locate them. However, given that the advice and help of legal experts are indeed generally available, the intelligibility of the language in the formulations of legal norms should not be gauged as if citizens had to fend entirely for themselves. Since formulations opaque to the layman may well be transparently clear to the specialist, and since most laymen typically have ample opportunities to consult specialists, the perspective of the latter rather than the perspective of the former should be our benchmark when we judge whether the wording in various legal materials is in conformity with the Fullerian principle of perspicuity.

Even when the formulations of legal norms are assessed from the perspective of a competent expert, of course, any actual legal system will almost certainly contain some formulations that are insufficiently clear to furnish any informative guidance. Instances of murkiness and imprecision are virtually inevitable. As has already been suggested, one important reason for the presence of some unclarity in every legal regime is the tension between the fourth and the first of Fuller's principles: the principle of perspicuity versus the principle of generality. In a number of circumstances, the aims of the officials who run a legal-governmental system can most effectively be realized (with suitable flexibility) through the adoption of broadly abstract standards rather than through the devising of more detailed and precise rules. Now, keeping in mind my opening chapter's distinction between indeterminacy and uncertainty – and the related distinction between indeterminacy and indemonstrability – we should not hastily assume that the abstract standards will give rise to large-scale indeterminacy in the law. However, such standards may well give rise quite often to uncertainty and disagreement over their concrete implications. Their abstractness can make them unclear, even in the eyes of legal experts. Fuller himself was well aware of this tension between the requirement of generality and the requirement of clarity (Fuller 1969, 64–65).

Unclarity is to some degree unavoidable in any legal system, then. Within appropriate bounds, it need not detract from the efficiency of a legal system's workings, and it can even enhance those workings. To say as much is not to say anything at odds with the principle of perspicuity; that principle is not a counsel of perfection, and was certainly not propounded as an element of an archetype. Nevertheless, when unclarity occurs in inapposite contexts, or when its intensity goes beyond certain limits (which, of course, cannot be specified precisely), it does detract from the efficient operations of a legal regime. Indeed, if the unclarity is both severe and wide-ranging, it can undermine the very existence – rather than merely the efficiency – of a functional legal system. Not all departures from the requirement of perspicuity are undesirable, and *a fortiori* not all such departures are fatal to a legal system's existence, but a minimum level of compliance with that requirement is indispensable. The minimum level, like the minimum level for each of the other Fullerian precepts, is quite high.

2.1.5. *Against Conflicts and Contradictions*

The fifth principle of legality is more complicated than Fuller grasped. He characterized it as a principle of noncontradictoriness, but in most of his discussion he concentrated instead on conflicts. Nonetheless, despite his inapt terminology, his fifth principle should undoubtedly be construed as an admonition both against conflicts and against contradictions in the law. So construed, the fifth principle is structurally similar to the other Fullerian precepts. That is, it articulates a necessary condition for the existence of any viable legal system, and it indicates a property – the property of logical tidiness – whose greater or lesser realization (above some threshold level, and up to some much higher level) will render a legal system a more straightforward or less straightforward specimen of the rule of law.

Let us begin with the distinction between contradictions and conflicts (Kramer 1998, 17–19; 1999a, 52–53; 2001, 73–74). A conflict exists in the law whenever someone is legally obligated to do X and legally obligated to abstain from doing X.[1] Conflicts between legal duties can and sometimes do occur, but the conflicting duties can never be jointly fulfilled. One and only one of any pair of conflicting duties will ever be fulfilled, at any given juncture. All the same, the coexistence of conflicting duties is perfectly possible. No logical improprieties are involved in their coexistence, though of course some moral improprieties may well be (since a person who is under conflicting legal duties will face the prospect of penalties irrespective of how he or she behaves).

Contradictions are different. What is in contradiction with a duty to do X is not a *duty* to abstain from doing X, but a *liberty* to abstain from doing X. Unlike conflicting duties, a duty and a liberty that contradict each other can never genuinely coexist. It can never be the case that someone is both genuinely under a duty to do X and genuinely at liberty to abstain from doing X; at any given time, one and only one of those states of affairs is actual. In other words, someone is under a legal duty-to-do-X if and only if he is not legally at liberty to abstain from doing X.

---

[1] Throughout this discussion, for stylistic reasons, I use the phrase "to abstain from doing X" as if it were interchangeable with "not to do X." As understood here, that is, an abstention from doing X does not necessarily involve a refusal to take advantage of an opportunity to do X; it can equally well ensue from one's unawareness of an opportunity or from the absence of any such opportunity altogether.

The truth of the proposition "I am currently under a duty to do X" entails the falsity of the proposition "I am currently at liberty to abstain from doing X," and vice versa.

Now, although there cannot be veritable contradictions within the workings of a legal system, there can be apparent or ostensible contradictions (Kramer 2001, 73–78). That is, a legal system can contain formulations of legal norms – such as some unrepealed statutes or some provisions within a single statute – which together affirm *both* that each person is legally obligated to do X *and* that each person is legally at liberty to abstain from doing X. Naturally, it can never be the case that both of the norms expressed in these inconsistent formulations are actually given effect in relation to any particular person P at any given time. At any juncture, in application to anybody who has abstained from doing X, one and only one of those norms will be given effect. When P abstains from doing X, then either he will be subjected to penalties or he will not be. If he is subjected to penalties, then the norm endowing him with a legal liberty-to-abstain-from-doing-X is inoperative in application to him at that juncture. Operative instead is the contemporaneous legal norm under which he bears a legal duty-to-do-X. Contrariwise, if P is not subjected to penalties in the aftermath of his abstention from doing X, then the legal norm placing him under a legal duty-to-do-X is inoperative in application to him at that juncture (either because the duty is unenforceable or because it is waived). Operative instead is the contemporaneous legal norm that bestows upon him a legal liberty-to-abstain-from-doing-X. In sum, although the norm imposing a legal duty-to-do-X and the norm conferring a legal liberty-to-abstain-from-doing-X can never both be operative at the same juncture in relation to the same person, the formulations expressing those norms (such as two unrepealed statutes) can simultaneously belong to a legal system as some of its authoritative materials.[2] Contradictions in the law's formulations are quite possible, then, even though genuine contradictions in the law's operations are not.

---

[2] Here and elsewhere, the phrase "authoritative materials" refers to the various formulations that are treated by juridical-governmental officials as legally binding. They include statutes, administrative regulations, constitutional provisions, executive orders, public and private contracts, adjudicative orders, judicial doctrines, rules of civil or criminal procedure, wills, deeds of title, and treaties.

As has been stated, Fuller devoted most of his remarks on the principle of noncontradictoriness to conflicts rather than to contradictions. (One of his examples, concerning two provisions in an American food-regulation statute – in Fuller 1969, 67–68 – does not in fact involve either a conflict or a contradiction.) Nevertheless, as has likewise been maintained, his fifth principle should be understood as an insistence on non-conflictingness *and* noncontradictoriness. If either conflicts or contradictions abound within the authoritative materials of some system of governance, then its very existence as a legal system is at stake. Hence, a principle which requires that conflicts and contradictions be kept below some level (a level that cannot be precisely specified) is enunciating a necessary condition for the status of a legal regime as such.

Should conflicts pervade the norms of some system of governance, the paramount function of law in guiding people's conduct might well be frustrated within the particular jurisdiction. In such a pass, the system's status as a legal system will have come undone. Crucial in this context are the penalties attached to the various duties that are in conflicting pairs. If the penalty that will be incurred for a breach of a person's duty-to-do-X is markedly heavier or lighter than the penalty that will be incurred for a breach of her duty-to-abstain-from-doing-X, then there will be strong incentives for the person to comply with one duty as opposed to the other. If there is a similarly gaping disparity between the penalties attached respectively to the two duties in virtually every other conflicting pair, then the rampant numerousness of the conflicting pairs is not incompatible with the fulfillment of law's guiding role. In that event, the system of governance comprising the myriad conflicting duties can still be a legal system, albeit an unappealing and peculiar legal system. If instead the penalties attached respectively to the two duties in virtually every conflicting pair are equivalent or approximately equivalent, then there will be no legally created incentives (or virtually no legally created incentives) for anyone to favor either of the two elements in each conflicting pair over the other. If the pairs of conflicting duties cumulatively cover large swaths of human behavior, then the putative system of governance that includes those multitudinous pairs will be failing to direct people's conduct. It is probably not a system of governance at all, much less a legal system.

One's conclusions about contradictions should be similar in most though not all respects. Let us assume that the authoritative formulations of the norms in some system of governance teem with contradictions. Pairs of contradictory formulations in the system's authoritative materials cumulatively cover vast areas of human conduct. Within each pair of contradictory legal positions, as has been indicated, one and only one of those positions will be operative at any given time in application to any particular person. A genuine contradiction can never obtain as a state of affairs in the world. Now, if the operativeness and inoperativeness of sundry contradictory legal positions occur in regularized patterns that are amply predictable, the system with norms that establish those positions might conceivably be able to operate as a system of governance. It will hardly be a model of efficient functioning, but it might attain sufficient regularity to keep its society from anarchic unrule. Notwithstanding, for reasons that should be evident from Chapter 1's discussion of the distinction between determinacy and predictability (or between indeterminacy and unpredictability), any system of governance along the lines hypothesized here does not qualify as a legal system. The possible predictability of its workings is not accompanied by the determinate correctness of any answer to any of the principal questions on which its contradictory legal norms decisively bear. If one authoritative norm of the system provides that each person is required to do X, and if another authoritative norm of the system provides that each person is at liberty to abstain from doing X, then there is no determinately correct answer to the question whether any particular person is required to do X. Since we are assuming that contradictory norms of this sort are rife within the system, we have to conclude that its authoritative materials do not yield any determinately correct answers to manifold questions concerning most areas of human behavior. Thus, even though the envisaged system of governance might conceivably display a moderate degree of regularity in its workings – and even though it might therefore furnish sufficient guidance to citizens to coordinate and direct their activities – the regularity is not that of a legal system. Rampant indeterminacy is incompatible with the existence of a legal regime. Even in circumstances (far-fetched circumstances) in which the indeterminacy does not subvert the functionality of an apparatus of governance, it negates the status of that apparatus as a system of law.

In short, whenever the authoritative norms of a regime teem with contradictions, its status as a legal regime is undermined. Exactly how abundant the contradictions must be in order to produce such an effect is of course not something that can be pinned down precisely. There is no talismanic point of transition, immediately past which a legal system ceases to be a legal system. All the same, although no such point can be specified precisely, there is a qualitative difference between a system of governance whose norms are replete with contradictions and a system of governance whose norms contain few or no contradictions. Only the latter is a legal system (if it satisfies the other Fullerian principles of legality).

Fuller's fifth principle, then, is certainly in part a principle of non-contradictoriness. No legal system can comprise norms that are in contradiction with one another on a large scale. In addition, however, the fifth principle is a principle of nonconflictingness. As has been argued, the pervasiveness of conflicting duties can be inimical to the existence of a legal system (and indeed, most likely, to the existence of any system of governance). If the penalties attached respectively to the two duties in virtually every conflicting pair are quite evenly balanced, then the presence of myriad conflicts in a regime's normative matrix will thwart the ability of the regime to guide conduct with minimal efficacy. Unlike the problem engendered by profuse contradictions, the problem engendered by profuse conflicts is not one of indeterminacy. Anybody who bears a duty to do X and a duty to abstain from doing X is determinately required to do X and determinately required to abstain from doing X. Rather, the problem is one of muddled guidance. In a situation marked by throngs of conflicting duties with quite evenly balanced penalties along the lines just mentioned, a regime will not adequately be steering people's conduct away from any particular paths and toward other paths. It will not adequately be affecting their practical reasoning. When somebody faces the prospect of being penalized for doing X and the prospect of being similarly penalized for not doing X, his choice between doing and not doing X is unaffected by the existence of the regime that stands ready to impose the penalties. *Pro tanto*, then, the regime is not performing the guiding and directing function of law. If the normative structure of the regime pullulates with a host of such conflicts, then its general performance of the directing and coordinating function of law is too meager to warrant our classifying it as a legal regime. In sum, when Fuller's fifth precept is construed as a principle of nonconflictingness (with a focus on evenly counterpoised penalties), as much as when it is construed as a

principle of noncontradictoriness, it lays down a necessary condition for
the existence of any system of law. Some conflicts within such a system
are tolerable, but their overabundance is fatal to its continued existence
as a minimally effective mode of governance.

2.1.6. Compliability

As Fuller readily acknowledged (Fuller 1969, 70 n29), several of his precepts of legality call for the possibility of citizens' compliance with legal
norms. People cannot fulfill both of two conflicting duties, for example,
and they likewise cannot conform to a legal mandate that is unintelligibly
obscure. Nor can they comply, except fortuitously, with a legal mandate
that is unpromulgated or purely retrospective. Still, although his sixth
principle of legality does clearly overlap with some of the other principles, it also plays a distinctive role. Even when a legal directive is clear and
prospective and publicly ascertainable and unentangled in any logical
conflicts, its demands might be such as to lie flatly beyond the capabilities of all or most citizens. What Fuller's sixth principle maintains is that
such unfulfillable mandates cannot be pervasive in any functional legal
system.

   As Fuller emphasized, and as should be plain from my first chapter's
discussion of the uniform applicability of legal norms, some departures
from the principle of compliability are virtually inevitable and are in any
event salutary. Within Anglo-American tort law, for example, the standard of reasonable care is incumbent on all adult human beings – apart
from insane people and people with severe physical disabilities – even
though some adult human beings are not capable of living up to that
standard. For the reasons recounted in Chapter 1, the uniform applicability of the law in this respect is generally desirable. Whereas some
considerations militate in favor of tailoring the law's requirements to
individuals' unameliorable weaknesses, a number of more weighty considerations militate against such an approach. A move toward a more
accommodating approach in order to satisfy Fuller's sixth principle would
be misguided.

   Nonetheless, although some deviations from the principle of compliability are advisable – especially when, like the uniform applicability
of the standard of reasonable care, they adversely affect only a small

proportion of a society's population – the deviations in any functional legal system cannot be too numerous and sweeping. To be sure, if the only role of a legal regime were the resolution of disputes among people, the extensive use of unfollowable mandates could be serviceable (Kramer 1999a, 46–47). So long as those mandates would differentiate among people in ways that would enable legal decision-makers to classify disputants as winners and losers, they would be consistent with the fulfillment of the posited role. Consider, for instance, a legal norm which provides that any human adult shorter than six feet in height must grow taller in order to reach that stature (without any surgical or prosthetic enhancement) or else lose certain legal entitlements *vis-à-vis* anyone whose height is at least six feet. Such a norm would be ridiculous if it were adopted as a means of channeling people's behavior into certain courses of action and away from other courses of action. No fully grown adult who is shorter than six feet in height would be able to do anything to comply with the norm's requirement. Only in a highly indirect fashion could that requirement meaningfully affect people's behavior. Over time, that is, it might impel parents to have their children exercise vigorously and eat more heartily in order to increase the likelihood that the children will grow taller than six feet. Even if the silly legal mandate were eventually to produce such an upshot, it would be ludicrously less efficient and fair and straightforward than a legal mandate directly enjoining parents to induce their children to exercise more vigorously and eat more heartily. Still, although the silly mandate would be ridiculous as a source of guidance for people's conduct, it could facilitate the dispute-resolving role of a legal system. After all, it would differentiate among people along clear-cut lines, and its effect of removing various legal entitlements from shorter people *vis-à-vis* taller people could bear decisively on the outcomes of quite a few legal disputes. Hence, if the only function of a legal regime were to pronounce on people's respective entitlements in concrete controversies, the law requiring short people to grow taller would not be nearly as outlandish as it initially appears. Were it not flagrantly invidious, it could indeed be quite sensible. Along with a host of other unfollowable directives, it could greatly promote the fulfillment of the aforementioned function.

In fact, however, a legal regime's primary function is to direct the conduct of people by presenting them with mandates and other laws to which they are capable of adjusting their behavior. Its dispute-resolving function is activated only when its primary function has broken down in some respect and when the regime has consequently not succeeded in coordinating people's behavior (Hart 1961, 38–41). Given as much, a plethora of utterly unfollowable directives in the normative matrix of some system of governance will be incompatible with the performance of law's cardinal role. Such a system of governance would not be a legal system – and would probably not be a system of governance at all, since so many of its mandates in their stark uncompliability would not affect anyone's practical reasoning and decisions. If a legal regime is to operate as a legal regime, its normative structure has to consist mainly of laws that can be followed. If its normative structure is such that all or most of its norms cannot possibly be heeded, then those norms are ersatz laws, and the regime overall is a travesty of the rule of law rather than a genuine embodiment thereof.

Like most of Fuller's other principles of legality, then, the principle of compliability is integrally connected to law's paramount function. It articulates a necessary condition for the existence of any legal system because it captures something that is indispensable for the minimally effective guidance of human conduct. Any arrangement that fails to provide such guidance is not an instantiation of the rule of law. No single departure from the principle of compliability is fatal to the existence of a legal system, of course, but wide-ranging and protracted departures are.

2.1.7. Steadiness over Time

If any further rebuttal of Simmonds's view of the Fullerian principles as an archetype were needed, the seventh principle – requiring the steadiness or constancy of legal norms through time – could supply it. Fuller did not preposterously suggest that a perfect legal system would be one in which nothing ever changes. Rather, he simply sought to indicate that limits on the pace and scale of the transformations of the sundry norms in a legal system are essential for the system's functionality. If changes in the law are bewilderingly sweeping and rapid for an extended period, then the capacity of the law to direct the behavior of people within its sway will founder. Fuller aptly pointed out that the problems engendered by excessively frequent and massive dislocations in the law are akin to those engendered by an overabundance of retrospective enactments (Fuller 1969, 80). In each case, the difficulty lies in the inability of people to orient themselves by reference to what the law requires and permits and authorizes. When the law's requirements and permissions and authorizations are altered with dizzying celerity on a large scale for more than a very short period of time, people do not have opportunities to absorb the law into their practical reasoning. Their conduct is thus largely or wholly unguided by authoritative legal norms. In such circumstances, then, the basic function of law is unrealized.

To an even greater extent than most of the other principles of legality, this seventh principle is meant to be flexible rather than absolute. Manifestly, not every change in the law threatens the existence of the legal system in which it occurs. Most changes in the law do not impair the operativeness of a legal system at all, and many of them improve and strengthen it. Fuller's principle of constancy, understood as a general jurisprudential thesis, is but an admonition against too much of a (potentially) good thing. It warns against transformations of legal norms that are disconcertingly frequent and far-reaching; it certainly does not warn against the more modest changes that occur from time to time in any legal regime.

Indeed, the stagnancy resulting from any wholesale eschewal of those modest changes would bring Fuller's seventh principle quite seriously into tension with his eighth principle, which requires congruity between the formulating and the implementing of legal norms. If a legal system's matrix of norms were somehow to go unaltered for decades or centuries, then – in any society that is not itself ossified in virtually all respects – many of the system's mandates and authorizations would become obsolete as a consequence of changes in technology and social interaction. Gaps between the law on the books and the law in practice would yawn widely, maybe to the point of reducing the legal system to a grotesquely empty shell that has in fact been superseded by an alternative regime of law. That alternative regime, dynamically evidenced in the decisions that constitute the law-in-practice, would itself be gravely hampered by the simulacrum of a legal system that exists alongside it and overlaps with it. (For example, given that the alternative regime's norms have *ex hypothesi* not displaced the rigidly unchanging norms as the law on the books, its arrangements for the promulgation of its demands and prescriptions and allowances are plainly inadequate.)

Thus, although Fuller's seventh principle lays down a necessary condition for the existence of any functional legal system, we need to be especially attentive to the confinedness of that principle's injunction. On the one hand, significant curbs on the rate and extent of changes in the law are vital. We cannot pin down exactly how much change is too much, but we can be sure that transformations of laws become ruinously inordinate at some level. On the other hand, an openness to innovations within the requisite curbs is likewise vital. If a legal system is to endure as such, it has to avoid the overwhelming disorientation that ensues from excessive flux; however, the fierce resistance of a legal system to every transforming influence would produce its own sort of disorientation, bred by a gaping disconnection between the appearance and the actuality of legal regulation.

2.1.8. Congruence between Formulation and Implementation

Fuller's eighth principle of legality is in many respects a summation of the other seven principles, but it is also a distinctive precept that covers and raises an array of attendant problems. Any satisfactory fulfillment of it will involve objectivity qua impartiality on the part of legal officials, in the expansive sense delineated by Chapter 1. Furthermore, any such fulfillment will involve proficiency in legal interpretation. Unless legal officials can competently ascertain what statutes and other expressions of legal norms mean, they will hardly be in a position to give effect to those norms persistently in accordance with the terms thereof.

As has been recounted in my opening chapter, the various factors that lead away from impartiality – such as self-interestedness, prejudices, ignorance, and impulsiveness – are strongly unconducive to accurate perceptions and correct decisions. Somebody swayed by one or more of those factors might still arrive at a correct decision and an accurate understanding of some particular matter, of course, but that happy outcome would occur despite the absence of impartiality rather than because of that absence. In general, an outlook wanting in impartiality is cognitively unreliable. It tends to lead away from justified perceptual and practical responses. Specifically in connection with the effectuation of legal norms, officials who lack impartiality will be inclined toward misunderstandings of the legal norms themselves and of the situations to which those norms apply. Often because of such misunderstandings, the officials will likewise be inclined toward inappropriate judgments in their handling of disputes and other matters. Moreover, even when they have not strictly misunderstood the relevant laws and situations, the officials who lack impartiality will be inclined toward inappropriate judgments in order to indulge their ignoble promptings (such as self-interestedness or bigotry). A dearth of impartiality, then, fosters decision-making that frequently deviates from any tight correspondence between the law as it is formulated and the law as it is administered. Because quite a firm correspondence of that kind is indispensable for the existence of a functional legal system, impartiality on the part of legal officials – not perforce as something that they invariably maintain, but at least as something that they typically maintain – is itself indispensable for the rule of law. An ample degree of impartiality in the authoritative activities of legal officials is a necessary condition for the status of a regime of law as such.

Similarly a necessary condition is the officials' possession of an ample degree of proficiency in legal interpretation. Their being endowed with such proficiency, like their being endowed with impartiality, is essential for the sustainment of any lasting congruence between the law on the books and the law in practice. Indeed, given the capaciousness of my conception of impartiality, interpretive competence is best regarded as one key element of an impartial stance. Officials devoid of such competence are on a par, at least for present purposes, with officials whose ignorance leaves them prone to go astray in their judgments. Their perceptions of the actualities of the law in their jurisdiction are skewed by their maladroitness in grasping what the formulations of legal norms mean. Any congruence between their law-administering decisions and the contents of the prevailing legal norms is fortuitous – and therefore almost certainly meager – rather than a properly informed achievement that comes about reliably.

Before we mull over the matter of interpretive proficiency in somewhat greater depth, we should ponder the broader question raised by Fuller's eighth principle. Why is congruence between the articulation and the implementation of legal norms a crucial condition for the rule of law? The answer to this question, which will shed light on the nature of interpretive competence in juridical endeavors, has been adumbrated in the preceding subsection's discussion of legal constancy. If the law in practice diverges markedly from the law on the books, then a weirdly bifurcated system of governance has supplanted any genuine legal system that may have existed. Such a situation will be marked by an array of formulated and promulgated norms that are seldom given effect, and by an array of largely unpromulgated norms that are regularly effectuated. The former array will not constitute a functional legal regime or even a part of a functional legal regime. When putative laws that form an overall scheme of governance are systematically unimplemented – either because they are sweepingly ignored or because they are sweepingly misconstrued – they are not veritable laws, and the scheme of governance which they form is a mere carcass.

Such a state of affairs is very different from that which obtains when scattered laws such as jaywalking ordinances are seldom or never applied in accordance with their terms. As has been noted near the outset of Chapter 1, the jaywalking ordinances retain their status as laws notwithstanding the extreme rarity of the occasions (if any) on which they are enforced. They retain that status exactly because they are elements of a wide-ranging matrix of norms that are mostly given effect quite regularly. Though in some jurisdictions the prolonged desuetude of a legal norm can deprive it of its status as a legal norm, such an effect is purely contingent. It is hardly preordained by the sheer nature of law. In any jurisdiction where desuetude over a long period is not a ground for the invalidation of a law as such, a limited number of disused laws can continue to be laws because they exist in a network with many other laws that are not disused. By contrast, they would not remain legally valid if all or most of the accompanying laws in the network had also fallen into disuse over a substantial span of time. Legal validity is something conferred on a norm by an operative legal system; it is a property of which the norm partakes by dint of being classifiable as a law under the efficacious system's criteria for legal validity.[3] If the system as a whole has been pushed into obsolescence by some alternative array of norms at the level

---

[3] Within any jurisdiction J, a norm is legally valid – that is, it has the status of a law – if and only if it satisfies the criteria by reference to which the officials in J's legal system fix upon the norms that belong to the system as its binding bases for their substantive and procedural decisions.

of judicial and administrative decision-making, then the norms in the obsolete network have ceased in effect to be legally valid (except insofar as any of those norms are also elements in the new array). Whether or not this upshot is overtly acknowledged in the formulations of the law on the books, it obtains as the reality of the law in practice. Since a functional legal regime comprises not only the law on the books but also the broadly congruent law in practice – as is evident in my discussion of prosecutorial and administrative discretion in Chapter 1 – the state of affairs envisaged here does not amount to such a regime. Of major importance, as has been suggested, is the difference between the unimplementedness of a small proportion of the norms in an overall matrix and the unimplementedness of all or most of those norms. In the former case, the overall matrix can sustain the legal validity of the uneffectuated norms; in the latter case, there is no comparable base of support for the legal validity of the uneffectuated norms or for the operativeness of the matrix itself.

When we view the matter from the other direction and concentrate on the law in practice that has displaced the law on the books, we find similarly daunting impediments to the existence of a functional legal system. In the scenario under consideration, most of the norms given effect by the concrete decisions of officials are not the norms that constitute the law on the books. They are only the law in practice. One of the major problems with such a situation, then, has been mentioned near the end of the preceding subsection. That is, the law-in-practice in such circumstances is largely or wholly unpromulgated – in which case its status as the *law*-in-practice is undone. It cannot adequately perform the guiding and coordinating role that is characteristic of any veritable legal regime. Let us now suppose that the decisions of the officials are sufficiently copious and patterned to enable experts (and perhaps ordinary citizens as well) to descry the norms which the officials are implementing. In that event, the situation involves a variant of the austerely outcome-focused method of promulgation that was discussed in Section 2.1.2. For all the reasons adduced there, any such method of promulgation will be precarious even in the most favorable of settings. In the much less propitious setting of a large and fairly dynamic society, such a method of promulgation – unsupplemented by any other methods – would be preposterous. There would be a logical possibility of its succeeding, but there would be no credible possibility.

Moreover, the difficulties explored in that earlier discussion of an outcome-centered mode of promulgation are greatly exacerbated here. In the present context, we are not ruminating on a situation where there is only the law in practice and no law on the books (apart from the law-in-practice itself in the form of discretely ascertainable decisions). In the present context, rather, we are ruminating on one array of norms that collectively constitute the law in practice and another array of norms that collectively constitute the law on the books. The serious shortcomings in the promulgation of the former array of norms will be hugely intensified by the simultaneous existence of the latter array. Either the prevailing regime's adjudicative and administrative officials are permitted and authorized to effectuate the norms in the latter array (the law on the books), or they are not. If they are not, then any outcome-centered promulgation of the operative norms of the regime will be accompanied by the full promulgation of norms that are truly dead letters. Even worse problems loom if the aforementioned officials are indeed permitted and authorized to give effect to the norms that make up the law on the books. In such a situation, the severe confusion bred by the outcome-centered promulgation of one set of norms and the straightforward promulgation of another set of norms will consort with arrant indeterminacy. If the officials are authorized to have recourse to one set of norms and are also authorized to have recourse to a markedly divergent set of norms, there will be no determinately correct answers to a wide range of legal questions. In response to each of those manifold questions, the officials are entitled to render an affirmative verdict but are equally entitled to render instead a negative verdict. Each verdict would be correct, and therefore neither is determinately correct. Hence, in addition to muddling the processes of promulgation, the existence of the unimplemented law on the books will have given rise to massive indeterminacy within the normative structure of the prevailing regime. Even if there were no other grounds for the proposition that such a regime is not a legal regime, the massive indeterminacy itself would be a sufficient ground for the truth of that proposition.

In sum, far-reaching incongruities between the law as it is articulated and the law as it is administered will be fatal to the existence of a legal system. Though there may be a logical possibility of a legal system's operating with such extensive incongruities, there is not any credible possibility. Those incongruities will accentuate the crippling drawbacks of an outcome-focused method of promulgation, and will generate indeterminacy on a large scale whenever a regime's officials are permitted and authorized to draw upon each side of the yawning division between the law on the books and the law in practice. For all these reasons, then, Fuller's eighth principle of legality distills a necessary condition for the functionality of a system of law. Quite a number of deviations from the terms of the law on the books are tolerable, and some of those deviations are clearly promotive of the ends of the legal system within which they occur; but at a certain point (an unspecifiable point) the divergences between the law on the books and the law in practice become so gaping as to scotch the very existence of such a system.

Let us now return to the matter that was deferred above. What is the nature of interpretive proficiency in the operations of a legal regime? That is, what are the interpretive approaches with which the officials of such a regime can best seek to ensure that the implemented law tallies with the formulated law? On the one hand, not very much can usefully be said about this matter at the high level of abstraction on which this book is proceeding. Appropriate interpretive techniques vary from legal system to legal system, and likewise vary over time within each such system. On the other hand, a few general points follow from the foregoing reflections on the rationale for Fuller's eighth principle. Although the specifics of the interpretive methods that commend themselves to officials will depend on the particular contexts of the officials' endeavors, the fundamental objective is to square the directing and coordinating function of the law-on-the-books with the directing and coordinating function of the law-in-practice. Only when the guidance furnished by the law's formulations is largely at one with the guidance furnished by the law's applications, do officials avoid the pitfalls recounted in the last several paragraphs. A comprehensive match between the formulations and the applications is hardly required, of course, but a considerable degree of correspondence is. Given as much, two constraints are met by any genuine legal system. First, a key aim of the officials is to interpret and apply the formulations of the norms of their legal system in accordance with what would be expected by a dispassionate observer who knows those formulations and who also knows the interpretive canons that prevail within the system. Second, naturally, those canons themselves – which consist of technical conventions for dealing with specialized legal terminology and concepts, but which also draw upon all or most of the ordinary conventions of the language in which the formulations of the legal norms are written – are such as to satisfy rather than dash the expectations of a dispassionate observer who is familiar only with the formulations and with the language (such as English) in which they are written. This second constraint is a crucial supplement to the first, since it rules out interpretive canons that would license and indeed require significant aberrations from the terms of the law on the books. The second constraint leaves ample room for variations among legal systems in the technical conventions under which the officials of those systems construe specialized juridical parlance and categories. Such technical conventions can and do differ in line with other differences among legal regimes. Their diversity is not at all precluded by the second constraint. What that constraint closes off, instead, are interpretive approaches that in effect displace the law on the books with alternative arrays of norms. That second constraint is met in any genuine legal system, since no such system will involve any large-scale displacement of the sort just mentioned.

Also implicitly if not explicitly informing the interpretive judgments of legal officials are the common-sense assumptions that were fleetingly touched upon in Chapter 1's discussion of determinate correctness. That is, legal officials will be drawing on a medley of background beliefs concerning the typical desires and inclinations and projects of human beings generally and more specifically of human beings in their society. Those assumptions will enable the officials to ascribe more concrete purposes to the legal norms which they are called upon to apply, and will further enable them to grasp the nature of the conduct on which those norms are being brought to bear. The attunedness of adjudicators and administrators to the purposive character of the behavior undertaken by lawmakers and by ordinary citizens will not always be overtly expressed, but it will always figure in the interpretive endeavors of these law-applying officials. Any satisfactory attempts to sustain a state of congruence between the law on the books and the law in practice will inevitably rest partly on such attunedness. Fuller recognized as much when he devoted most of his exposition of his eighth principle to a discussion of juridical interpreters' efforts to unearth the purposes and intentions of lawmakers.

An emphasis on purposes in legal interpretation is consistent with many different elucidative techniques that vary from one legal system to another. In some jurisdictions, for example, the interpretation of statutes is often informed by certain pronouncements of the legislators who were chiefly responsible for the enactment of those statutes – or by other legislative pronouncements that have occurred outside the confines of the statutes themselves. In other jurisdictions, adjudicators and administrators are not allowed to make reference to such pronouncements. They are required to focus on the wording of the statutes and to infer legislative purposes exclusively therefrom (with the aid of the common-sense assumptions mentioned above, of course). Variations along these lines and along many other lines are perfectly consistent with the two constraints broached in the penultimate paragraph above. Whatever may be the details of the prevailing techniques for the ascertainment of legislative intentions and the elucidation of the statutes that are the products of those intentions, the adjudicative and administrative officials in a legal system can warrantedly attribute a general awareness of those techniques to the system's legislators. Consequently, the adjudicative and administrative officials are on solid ground in presuming that statutes are meant to be interpreted in accordance with the aforementioned techniques. Legislators intend that statutes should be understood as the legislators expect them to be understood. Much the same can be said in connection with other types of laws such as judicial doctrines and administrative regulations – and even in connection with the countless private contracts that are drafted by experts in full awareness of the regnant interpretive approaches to such documents. When legal officials resort to the established exegetical devices of their profession within their jurisdiction, then, they are construing laws in conformity with the general intentions of the makers of those laws (Raz 1996, 266–67). Such a result ensues from the officials' compliance with the two constraints broached above. Their compliance secures congruity between the law on the books and the law in practice, by treating the law on the books as something purposive.

This discussion should close with a caveat. Much of what has been said here might lead some readers to infer that the fulfillment of Fuller's eighth principle typically involves arduous feats of interpretation that unlock obscure meanings. Such feats are indeed sometimes needed, but very often the tasks of officials in applying the law are much more straightforward. We should not join the Critical Legal Scholars and the Legal Realists in thinking that the knotty cruxes addressed by judges in difficult appellate cases are representative of the questions that arise from day to day in a legal system. Quite the contrary. A large majority of the decisions that have to be taken by administrative and adjudicative officials are routine to the point of being humdrum, and do not confront those officials with any perplexing interpretive puzzles. Of course, while recognizing as much, one should accept that most of the factors which influence officials' deliberations in cases centering on tricky interpretive problems are also at work in unexcitingly quotidian cases. The constraints applicable in difficult cases are likewise applicable in the innumerable routine circumstances that are handled by legal officials daily. However, because the satisfaction of those constraints is so easily accomplished in the presence of the routine circumstances, it there goes ahead with virtually no conscious reflection and deliberation on the part of the relevant officials. In such contexts, the officials can preserve congruence between the law on the books and the law in practice quite perfunctorily, without any carefully focused processes of exegetical contemplation. They draw on the same assumptions that underlie their responses to more problematic circumstances – assumptions such as the common-sense beliefs that have been noted above – but they do so in a predominantly unreflective manner. What should be underscored here is that most of the situations faced by the officials in any functional legal system are of this boringly straightforward kind. When coming to grips with the implications of legal norms for various sets of facts, legal officials do not usually have to engage in agonized interpretive deliberations. They can usually carry out their interpretive responsibilities, which form a key part of their broader responsibility to abide by the Fullerian principle of congruence, with barely any thought and with no hesitation. Thus, although the effecting of correspondences between the law on the books and the law in practice does sometimes require a considerable degree of interpretive perspicacity on the part of legal officials (especially appellate judges), it much more often requires simply the routine performance of each official's role.

2.2. The Rule of Law as a Moral Ideal

Heretofore, this chapter has explored the rule of law as the state of affairs that obtains when every one of Fuller's principles of legality is satisfied above some threshold level. Whenever such a state of affairs does obtain, a functional legal regime is in existence. In other words, we so far have pondered the rule of law in complete abstraction from the benignity or malignity of particular legal norms and legal systems. My conception of the rule of law, as it has been expounded hitherto, belongs to the domain of legal philosophy rather than to the domain of political philosophy. It is a jurisprudential conception. It sets forth the individually necessary and jointly sufficient conditions for the existence of a regime of law. In so doing, it is neutral on all moral and political questions – questions, for example, concerning the uses to which law should be put, the appropriate limits on legal regulation of individuals' lives, the legitimacy or illegitimacy of various patterns of differentiation among people under the terms of legal norms, the conditions under which a regime of law is a just regime, and so forth. The rule of law, as the realization of the necessary and sufficient conditions for the existence of a legal system, is itself morally neutral. It is indispensably serviceable for the pursuit of benevolent ends on a large scale over a sustained period, but it is also indispensably serviceable for the pursuit of wicked ends on such a scale over such a period (Kramer 1999a; 2004a, 143–222; 2004b).

In the second half of this chapter, we shall be shifting our scrutiny to the rule of law as a moral-political ideal. To mark the distinction between the jurisprudential conception of the rule of law and the moral-political conception, I shall henceforth use upper-case letters to designate the phenomenon encapsulated by the latter conception: "the Rule of Law." Although the rule of law is of course fully consistent with the Rule of Law and is indeed a vital prerequisite of it, the latter goes beyond the former. To apprehend the nature of the Rule of Law, we have to discern how matters of form can become matters of substance.

My discussion will proceed afresh by reference to Fuller's eight principles of legality. Here, however, those principles will be considered not as specifications of individually necessary and jointly sufficient conditions for the existence of a legal regime, but as precepts of political morality. Not every legal system complies with all of those principles when they are reelaborated as precepts of political morality; not every legal system instantiates the Rule of Law.

Reconceived as doctrines of political morality, the Fullerian principles express the values of the liberal-democratic tradition. This book is scarcely the place for an exhaustive survey – or even a laconically selective survey – of the many different strands of that tradition. Let us simply note that the liberal-democratic tradition comprehends thinkers such as John Locke, John Stuart Mill, Immanuel Kant, Friedrich Hayek, John Rawls, and Robert Nozick. Those thinkers and the numerous other distinguished proponents of liberal democracy during the past four centuries have disagreed with one another over many issues, but there are some points on which most of them concur. Central to the liberal-democratic tradition has been an emphasis on the liberty and autonomy and dignity of the individual, on the fundamental legal and political equality of persons, on equality of opportunity, on the responsibility of governments to protect the lives and basic well-being of their citizens, on the importance of reasoned deliberation and justification in the domain of public power, on opportunities for adults to participate in elections and in other forms of political activity, and on the separation of powers of government. These values come to fruition in the Rule of Law. They are the values whose formal dimensions are enshrined in Fuller's principles, insofar as those principles are presented as a compendium of the Rule of Law. As we shall see, the shift of our focus from the rule of law to the Rule of Law brings with it a shift – an enrichment – in the significance of each of the aforementioned principles.

2.2.1. Governance by General Norms

When the first principle of legality is advanced as a strictly jurisprudential thesis, it lays stress on the key role of general norms in enabling and constituting the existence of any legal system. Without denying the need for countless individualized directives in every such system, the principle of generality – qua jurisprudential thesis – maintains that no legal regime could function as such in the absence of general norms. Those norms are the principal laws of any such regime, and most of the individualized directives therein are applications of them. Without generality in its normative structure, a system of law would not be a system of law at all.

The jurisprudential significance of generality, which has been examined at much greater length in Section 2.1.1, is certainly not denied or discounted when Fuller's first principle is reunderstood as a tenet of the Rule of Law. However, that significance is supplemented by the moral-political import of the property of generality in legal institutions. Before we investigate that import, we should briefly take account of a distinction highlighted in other contexts by the moral philosopher Richard Hare: the distinction between the generality/specificity dichotomy and the universality/particularity dichotomy (Hare 1963, 38–40; 1981, 41; 1989). This distinction has heretofore been left aside in my remarks on generality, and it went entirely unnoticed by Fuller. For my purposes, moreover, the contrast drawn by Hare can and should be somewhat softened. Nevertheless, a terse summary of that contrast will help to sharpen the focus of the present discussion.

Generality, which is always a matter of degree, consists in abstraction from the more concrete or detailed features of things. If two features can be ranked in their generality, and if the possession of one of them entails the possession of the other, the entailment always runs from the more specific feature to the more general feature rather than vice versa. Thus, for example, the property of being a lion entails the property of being an animal but not vice versa. General laws prescind from many concrete qualities of the instances of conduct to which they apply. A law proscribing murder, for example, will have abstracted from the specific features that earmark various types of murders (strangulations versus shootings versus stabbings, and so forth).

Universality differs from generality. A formulated norm is universal if and only if it contains no named references to particular entities such as individuals or times or places. A named reference to Abraham Lincoln or to the year 1922 or to France, for instance, would deprive a formulation of its universality. Still, although any named reference to a particular person or thing is inconsistent with universality, specificity is not; a universal norm can be highly specific. A law prohibiting anyone with red hair and brown eyes from watering rhododendrons on Thursdays, for example, is expressive of a universal norm in spite of its detail. Such a law contains no named references to particulars, even though its references to types (types of hair, eyes, flowers, and days) are quite concrete.

As has been readily avouched, my expositions of generality have until now ignored the contrast between the generality/specificity dichotomy and the universality/particularity dichotomy. There has not really been any need to take account of that contrast, since – for my purposes – particularity can be regarded as an extreme form of specificity. In the present context, however, the distinction between specificity and particularity is worthy of attention for the very reason why it has hitherto been pretermitted. That is, we should take note of that distinction in order to be attentive to the affinities between specificity and particularity. If most named references to particular persons in laws are pernicious or invidious, then so too are most highly specific but unnamed references to particular persons. From a moral-political perspective, the effects of a reference of the latter sort will typically be as objectionable as the effects of a reference of the former sort.

Of especially grave concern here are so-called definite descriptions: descriptions that each employ a suitable formulation (usually with the definite article "the") to single out a particular person or entity without naming him or her or it. Thus, "the tallest man who has ever watered rhododendrons on a Thursday" is a description that picks out some particular individual without naming him or any other particular entity. Though such a description is universal, its bearings as an object of moral assessment are pretty much the same as the bearings of a description that does include a named reference to an individual. (Notwithstanding that definite descriptions single out particulars, many of them are not useful guides for identifying those particulars. The example of a definite description just above is hardly a very useful guide for identifying the man to whom it uniquely refers. Even more obviously of little value for identification would be the definite description "the largest galaxy that has not yet been discovered by anyone." A definite description along those lines will become inapplicable to its unique referent as soon as that referent has been identified as a galaxy.)

Similarities among definite descriptions, named references to particulars, and highly specific descriptions are of course important for the rule of law as well as for the Rule of Law. As was argued earlier, the basic functioning of law will be fatally impaired by sustained and sweeping departures from the Fullerian principle of generality. That result will ensue irrespective of whether the departures have occurred through definite descriptions or through named references to particulars or through highly specific descriptions or through some combination of these generality-forsaking devices. If an overabundance of the norms in a legal regime are divested of generality by being formulated with any of those devices, the regime will have lost its functionality as a system of law. Similarities among the effects produced by such devices are thus of great jurisprudential significance. However, those similarities are especially important in the present subsection, where we are focusing on the Rule of Law and where we have thus moved from solely jurisprudential concerns to concerns of political morality. Although the potential deplorableness of each one of the generality-forsaking devices in the law is distinct in some respects from that of each of the others, the potential deplorableness resides mainly in what is common among those devices. We should be aware that the evils of named references to particular persons in the formulations of legal norms are not eliminated or even alleviated when the aims of such references are accomplished instead through the other generality-forsaking means. Indeed, those evils are to some degree compounded when the other generality-forsaking means have been employed.

Before we consider the special vices of the means just mentioned, we should mull over the broader moral-political drawbacks of deviations from generality in the law. At the outset, let it be emphasized that not all such deviations are regrettable. Many of those deviations in the form of individualized directives are necessary for the functioning of a legal system, as has already been observed. Quite a few other departures from generality are likewise salutary, in that they reflect morally significant differences among people in apposite ways. Anyone should happily acknowledge as much. However, we are interested here in the countless other derogations from generality that are not salutary – the derogations from generality that detract from the Rule of Law.

Of course, one key respect in which the undesirable deviations from generality are objectionable is directly related to their jurisprudential significance. They impair the rule of law; that is, they impair the functionality of any legal system in which they occur. Cumulatively, they can be fatal to that functionality. Consequently, they endanger the realization of the desiderata for which a legal system is indispensable – desiderata such as public order, the coordination of people's activities and of a society's institutions, and the preservation of individual freedom. That detrimental effect is certainly one of the ills against which the Fullerian principle of generality (as a principle of the Rule of Law) is an admonition. Even if that pernicious effect is left aside, however, there are solid moral-political grounds for wariness of legal norms that are individualized or highly specific in their compass. Some such norms are benign, of course, but many are not.

Individualized directives and highly specific formulations, precisely because of their peculiar limitedness, lend themselves to nefarious purposes. Save where they are the vehicles for implementing general norms – that is, save where they are judicial orders or administrative decrees that apply general laws to particular cases and individuals – they cut against the aspiration of the Rule of Law toward fundamental legal equality and fairness. They are serviceable for nepotism and other varieties of favoritism (such as tax loopholes for people who fit very narrowly specified descriptions), and they are equally serviceable for invidious modes of discrimination against members of despised groups. They can amount to stratagems for circumventing adjudicative processes or other procedures that might stand in the way of the accomplishment of legal-governmental officials' objectives; such stratagems, which are exactly what the American Constitution's prohibition on bills of attainder was designed to avert, are antithetical to the basic liberal-democratic value of due process. When legislators or other officials decline to subject themselves to the discipline of coming up with a law that is addressed broadly (to all people within the jurisdiction or to some sizable subset of those people), and when they opt instead for a law that is addressed very restrictively, they lessen their own incentives for ensuring that the legal norm in question is recognizable as fair from many different perspectives.

Named references to particular individuals in laws can seem especially odious because they run so strongly against the ideal that people who are similarly situated should be treated alike (in the sense of being subject to the same requirements and endowed with the same entitlements concerning the respects in which they are similarly situated). However, definite descriptions and highly specific descriptions can be disingenuous means of subverting that same ideal, even though their terms are universal rather than particularistic. Indeed, it is the deviousness of such devices – when they are put to illegitimate purposes – that intensifies their disreputability. The straightforwardness of named references to particular individuals in the formulations of legal norms is more conducive to public scrutiny than is the circuitousness of the other generality-forsaking devices. Insofar as the named references are morally dubious, their dubiousness is undisguisedly open for debate. Definite descriptions and highly specific descriptions are often not comparably transparent. As has already been mentioned, definite descriptions are not always handy guides for the identifying of their referents; much the same can be said, of course, about highly specific descriptions. Although the opacity of laws containing such descriptions will probably be quite easily penetrable in most circumstances, it adds an extra degree of unsavoriness to the other grounds for a distrust of such laws.

In at least one respect, to be sure, named references to particular persons in the formulations of legal norms can be singularly deplorable. When incorporated into laws that prescribe forms of harsh treatment for the designated persons, such references can serve (and be intended to serve) the purpose of public humiliation. In that role, the named reference itself is a form of punishment and is thus an especially nasty way of circumventing the normal adjudicative and administrative procedures that determine when and how punishments are to be levied. Still, even though the other generality-forsaking devices are not quite as blatant and effective as named references in drawing down public opprobrium upon certain individuals, they too can powerfully perform that function. Except in contexts where their relative obliqueness thwarts any ready identification of their referents, the other generality-forsaking devices – in laws that impose disadvantages – will provocatively call attention to the individuals whom they are singling out. The very disingenuousness of any such device, which is objectionable in itself, can also convey a slyly taunting message.

At any rate, although the different generality-forsaking tactics diverge in some respects, their principal effects are the same when they are used improperly in the formulations of legal norms. They are in tension if not outright conflict with some of the central values of liberal democracy, such as equality and fairness and due process. Accordingly, the standing laws of a system of governance – as opposed to the orders and decrees through which those laws are applied to particular individuals or groups – should rarely be formulated with the generality-forsaking devices. Fuller's first principle, understood not only as a jurisprudential tenet but also as a precept of political morality, warns against those devices. They are not always to be eschewed, of course, but they are to be used very sparingly and cautiously. If they are used frequently in the standing laws of a society, then they will imperil the sheer existence of the society's legal system and will likewise imperil some key liberal-democratic values that may be instantiated by that system. Even when they are used only

infrequently – and therefore even when they do not endanger the existence of a legal regime – they can dismayingly encroach upon those
liberal-democratic values. In short, the moral-political reasons for dis-
trusting the generality-forsaking devices are even more far-reaching than
the jurisprudential reasons.

2.2.2. Public Ascertainability

As we have seen, a regime's compliance with the Fullerian principle of
promulgation is essential for the performance of law's guiding and coordinating function. If people (including any expert assistants) are kept in
the dark about what they are legally required and permitted and authorized to do, then the norms of their ostensible legal regime will not be
directing their behavior. That regime will not be operating as a genuine
regime of law.

In a nutshell, the foregoing paragraph recounts the main grounds
for the strictly jurisprudential version of Fuller's second principle. Those
grounds will be supplemented here by considerations of political morality, as we turn to the version of the second Fullerian principle that articulates a requirement of the Rule of Law. Considerations of political morality do not, of course, call for apprising every citizen of the content of
every legal norm. Such a ridiculously burdensome aspiration does not
follow from liberal-democratic values any more than from jurisprudential concerns. What is required instead is precisely what is needed for the
existence of a functional legal system: the public ascertainability of the
system's norms. Most citizens at any given juncture will be unfamiliar
with the terms of most laws, but they persistently have opportunities
to become familiar with the terms of any of those laws (probably with
the assistance of experts). Reasonable ascertainability, rather than actual
ascertainment, is the desideratum to be sought.

Moral-political considerations weighing in favor of the promulgation of laws are several. In the first place, of course, the goods that are
made possible by the existence of a legal system – public order, social
coordination, secure individual freedom, and so forth – will be atten-
uated by significant departures from the principle of promulgation. If
the departures are sweeping and sustained, and if the very existence of a
functional legal system is consequently undermined, those goods may be

lost altogether. Beyond such concerns relating directly to the necessary conditions for the functionality of a legal regime, however, some central liberal-democratic values are at stake.

If duty-imposing laws are not promulgated, then citizens will not have been given any fair opportunities to conform their behavior to the terms of those laws. Unless the citizens are lucky enough to comply unknowingly with the undisclosed legal mandates, they will unwittingly have rendered themselves liable to be penalized for acting athwart the duties established by those mandates. Without any adequate warnings, the coercive might of legal-governmental institutions will have become directed against them. From the perspective of the citizen, the wielding of that coercive might by legal-governmental officials in any such situation is arbitrary. It is undertaken in effectuation of some legal requirement, but the requirement could not have been known to the citizen at the time of his transgressive conduct. His status as a moral agent – his moral autonomy – has not been properly respected. Because he is such an agent, his society's legal-governmental institutions should present him not just with reasonable options but also with reasonable opportunities to learn what the options are. When a regime does not promulgate a legal mandate, it withholds those crucial opportunities. Hence, even if the unascertainable mandate itself is fair, the regime has shown disrespect for the people whom it governs.

Another virtue of the promulgation of laws was touched upon by Fuller (Fuller 1969, 51). When the contents of legal norms are accessible to members of the public in a society that allows ample latitude for the expression of political sentiments, those norms are open to debate and challenge. The ability of people to inform themselves of the terms of various laws is invaluable not only because they can then adjust their behavior, but also because they are then in a position to impugn those laws on the basis of solid knowledge rather than on the basis of ignorance and uninformed speculation. Public scrutiny of the products of legal officials' doings is dependent on the regularized disclosure of those products and doings. Such scrutiny is typically salutary both *ex post* and *ex ante*. It naturally helps to improve laws that are already on the books, but it also tends to work its ameliorative effects beforehand. When legislators and other legal officials in a liberal democracy know that the laws which they devise are going to be subjected to the gaze of the public at large,

they will have strong incentives to come up with laws that are not manifestly unfair or dubious. Such officials will have incentives to anticipate
plausible objections to their formulations of legal norms, and to defuse
or satisfy those objections by addressing the concerns from which they
would stem. The proneness of governing officials to develop an arrogant
sense of their own wisdom and rectitude will therefore be somewhat
checked.

Admittedly, the openness of legal norms to public scrutiny might
be more detrimental than salutary in some contexts that are not wholly
outlandish. In a society where racist sentiments are widespread among
the citizenry, for example, the public ascertainability of laws may well
inhibit legislators and other officials from adopting legal norms that run
against those repugnant sentiments. Still, even if a practice of concealing
certain laws or certain portions of laws might embolden the officials to go
further in tackling the hardships of racial minorities than they otherwise
would – an upshot that is hardly inevitable – such a subterfuge would
also involve considerable disrespect for the moral agency of the members
of the public. Instead of engaging with citizens through exhortation and
rational persuasion, the officials would be stealthily dodging the citizens'
rational faculties. A tack of that sort might be justifiable if the good
achieved is substantial and if the likelihood of its being achieved in a more
candid fashion is nil. Nonetheless, the chicanery of such an approach is a
regrettable aspect of it. Moreover, the potential justifiability of a practice
of concealment in relation to some legal norms would scarcely warrant the
extension of that practice to other legal norms. (Note that nothing in this
paragraph presupposes that honesty is invariably a virtue. If somebody
passes vital state secrets to a loathsomely aggressive and tyrannical enemy,
his communication is not made morally better by being sincere and
accurate.[4] What has been presupposed here is simply that frankness is
normally a virtue in the interaction between legal-governmental officials
and citizens. When circumstances are such that the officials have to eschew
frankness in order to accomplish some morally compelling objective, the
need for dissimulation is a matter for regret though not for remorse.)

---

[4] For a much longer argument against the view that honesty is inherently or invariably a virtue,
see Kramer 2004a, 208–10.

Yet another moral-political factor militating in favor of the promulgation of laws is that members of the public will then be in a position to ascertain whether the laws are being implemented in accordance with their terms. In other words, promulgation facilitates public scrutiny not only of the laws themselves but also of their applications. This point is of particular importance in connection with legal mandates that are never enforced, and in connection with laws which establish public powers that are never exercised or private powers that are never effectuated. If citizens are unable to learn of the existence of those mandates and those power-conferring laws, they will not be able to know that the officials are being remiss. Laxity in giving effect to certain laws is by no means always undesirable, but its desirability or undesirability is usually a proper topic for public debate. If the laws themselves are withheld from the ken of citizens, then only the officials will be able to gauge whether their own diligence or slackness in giving effect to those laws is appropriate. Except in rare circumstances, judgments on a matter of that sort are not best reserved solely for an elite coterie of officials. Administrators' and adjudicators' views on such a matter should often carry special weight, of course, but ordinary citizens should be able to have a say as well.

To be sure, these sundry moral-political considerations in favor of the principle of promulgation do not support the notion that every law should be publicly ascertainable. Fuller's second principle, construed as a precept of political morality, is no more an uncompromising dogma than are any of his other principles. We have already considered one context (of widespread and inveterate racism) in which some degree of dissimulation might be morally optimal. Some other credible contexts – involving concerns of national security, for example – might similarly be handled best through furtive approaches. The point of this discussion has not been to suggest that the factors in favor of promulgation always overtop any countervailing considerations; indeed, my purpose has not even been to suggest that those factors invariably weigh to some extent in favor of promulgation. Such blanket claims are neither necessary nor tenable. Instead, the aim here has simply been to highlight some moral-political values that will typically call for the public accessibility of laws. Fuller's principle of promulgation, in its moral-political version, encapsulates those values.

2.2.3. Prospectivity

Like the principle of promulgation, the principle of prospectivity does not articulate an unremittingly across-the-board requirement. As was argued earlier, some retroactivity in law-making is unavoidable and desirable. All the same, the potential injustices of retroactive laws are evident, and consequently the moral-political considerations that frequently militate against retroactivity are evident as well.

Some retroactive modifications of the law might conceivably be so predictable that everyone affected by them will have had a fair opportunity to take account of them at the time to which they pertain (rather than only at the time when they occur). Such a situation is not inconceivable, but it is extremely unlikely in any actual legal system. Far more likely is that any retroactive modification of the law will have caught unawares some or all of the people who are affected by it. Given as much, those people will have had no fair opportunity to bring their behavior into conformity with the law's new prescriptions. Nobody can go back through time to adjust his or her behavior retroactively. Fuller commented on this problem exclusively in connection with duty-imposing laws – he dwelt on "the brutal absurdity of commanding a man today to do something yesterday" (Fuller 1969, 59) – but the problem also arises in connection with other laws. For example, if a significant change in the contract law of a jurisdiction is made retroactive, and if the change was not fully predictable at the time to which it reaches back, it will almost certainly disadvantage some people who followed the then-prevailing procedures for contractual formation to the letter. Their fate is as unfair (in most circumstances) as the fate of people to whom a retroactive duty-imposing law applies detrimentally. In each case, the addressees of the law are in effect told today to do something yesterday. Such an upshot devalues the capacity of each addressee to deliberate and choose as a moral agent. Legal consequences supposedly determined by individuals' choices are actually determined after the fact by the countermanding decrees of officials. People's expectations, which might be admirably reasonable at the time when they are formed, will have been dashed.

Any frequent disruptions of legitimate expectations are not only unfair to the individuals directly involved but are also inimical to the efficient workings of an economy. If the legal framework of an economy is unreliable because of retroactive reversals, producers will typically be less inclined to engage in venturesome undertakings, and consumers will typically be less inclined to engage in major transactions. This point is applicable regardless of whether an economy is predominantly capitalistic or predominantly socialistic. Hence, the integrity of the status of every sane adult as a moral agent is not the only important moral-political factor that weighs against many retroactive changes in the law. Also at stake is the prosperity of a society as a whole. Though retroactive legal norms in appropriate contexts can promote a society's flourishing, their presence in inappropriate contexts will produce an opposite effect.

More widely, of course, an overabundance of retroactive legal norms will tend to subvert the continued functionality of a regime of law. In that event, the deleteriousness of such an overabundance will be felt not only in a society's economy but also in virtually all other aspects of the lives of the people therein. If a legal system ceases to exist and operate as such, then its ordering and coordinating and stabilizing effects will have fallen by the wayside. The jurisprudential momentousness of such an eventuality is matched by its moral-political gravity.

Quite sharp restrictions on the use of retroactive laws, then, are dictated by several considerations of political morality: the salutariness of fair notice for those who receive it and for those who are required to undergo the discipline of providing it; the dignity of the moral agency of each individual; the importance of upholding people's legitimate expectations; the pursuit of efficiency in a society's economic activities; and the general desiderata to which the existence of a legal system is prerequisite. None of these factors comes close to warranting the wholesale disallowance of retroactive laws, of course. It is sometimes necessary or desirable (or both necessary and desirable) for the law to reach backward in time. All the same, the moral-political factors that militate against the use of retroactive laws are germane and weighty in many contexts. We do not need to look at extreme examples of iniquities – such as the Nazis' retroactive legalization of the carnage committed by Adolf Hitler and his followers on the Night of the Long Knives (Fuller 1969, 54–55) – in order to grasp the potential harmfulness of legal retroactivity. Even in much more humdrum settings in far more commendable legal systems, after-the-fact alterations of legal requirements or of legal authorizations are very often at odds with a proper respect for the moral agency of the law's addressees.

2.2.4. Perspicuity

Moral-political considerations broadly similar to those just invoked are linchpins of Fuller's fourth precept – the principle of perspicuity – when that precept is understood as recounting a key element of the Rule of Law. If the terms of laws are hopelessly obscure or uninformative (even when perused by legal experts), then citizens will not be able to ascertain what they are being authorized or required or permitted to do. If the unclarity afflicts large swaths of the law in some jurisdiction over sustained periods of time, then it will be of jurisprudential significance; it will fatally undo the functionality of the jurisdiction's legal system. Well before any unclarity proliferates on that scale, however, the moral-political grounds in favor of the principle of perspicuity will have been triggered.

On the one hand, laws sometimes have to be framed in uninformatively abstract terms in order to preserve flexibility. In certain areas of legal regulation (for example, in areas relating to advanced technology), some statutes and judicial doctrines might be inadvisably confining if they were to be enunciated in narrowly focused language. Insofar as narrowness and concreteness would indeed undesirably cramp the achievement of the purposes of those laws, the adoption of wispily open-ended formulations may well be justified. Such departures from the principle of perspicuity are to be regarded with circumspection, but there is no reason for thinking that they will never be warranted. Legislators sometimes act most wisely in leaving administrators and adjudicators with very little informative guidance, so as to allow them to develop more detailed standards in the course of dealing with concrete situations and problems.

On the other hand, although a very high level of abstraction in legislation and some other sources of law is doubtless desirable in certain areas, it almost always carries drawbacks as well as advantages. Chief among those drawbacks, manifestly, is that the abstractly formulated laws present a dearth of clear-cut guidance to citizens. Such a state of affairs detracts from a legal system's fulfillment of its role in directing and coordinating human behavior, and thereby detracts from the provision of citizens with fair notice of what they are legally obligated or permitted or empowered to do. When citizens have to await the devising of perspicuous standards by administrators at some later juncture, they will have to rely heavily on conjectures in the meantime. In fields such as medical experimentation and high-technology communications, people (including lawyers) for quite long periods may be largely at a loss in gauging the legal consequences of their own actions and other people's actions. Note that the problem here does not arise from indeterminacy in the law. Abstract standards can be just as determinate in their implications as are much more concrete standards. Rather, the problem consists in uncertainty. Once again, that is, the distinction between indeterminacy and uncertainty has an important bearing on the matters discussed by this book. Although laws formulated at a rarefied level of abstraction can yield determinate implications for a wide array of concrete cases, the task of identifying those implications will very likely be fraught with uncertainty and controversy. Even if the unclarity in the law and the consequent uncertainty are not nearly so severe and extensive as to threaten the existence of a legal system, they obviously compromise the ideal of giving people fair notice of the legal consequences that attach to various modes of conduct. In that respect, any reliance by legislators and other lawmakers on uninformatively abstract formulations is in tension with a due regard for the moral agency of the law's addressees.

Moreover, while a very high degree of abstraction in the law is sometimes amply justified in order to accommodate the dynamic character of certain fields of human endeavor, there is no comparable justification for outright obscurity in the terms of legal norms. To be sure, legal officials often have to draw upon a technical jural vocabulary in their formulations of legal norms – both for the sake of precision and for the sake of succinctness. However, although that technical parlance is probably opaque to most ordinary citizens, it is readily intelligible by lawyers and other legal experts. As was indicated in my earlier discussion of Fuller's fourth principle, the point of reference for gauging the perspicuity of laws is the legal expert's understanding rather than the ordinary citizen's understanding (provided that the assistance of legal experts is affordably available to all or most citizens). Hence, the need for some specialized juridical jargon in the phrasing of laws is not indicative of any need for obscurity therein. Nor is there any other basis for an acceptance of genuine obscurity. If laws are drafted in terms that nonplus legal experts as well as ordinary people, their murkiness is a shortcoming without any concomitant advantages. Such murkiness impairs the efficiency of a legal system's operations – and thus impairs the realization of the goods that are attainable through those operations – and it clashes with the ideal of fair notice recounted in my last paragraph. It stymies the capacity of each citizen to become aware of the legal obligations or authorizations or permissions that are formulated in the impenetrable language. *Pro tanto*, it accordingly stymies the capacity of each citizen to make informed choices about the legal implications of his or her actions.

In short, the principle of perspicuity – put forth not only as a jurisprudential thesis but also as a precept of political morality – does not categorically disallow the use of wispy abstractions in the formulations of legal norms, but does categorically disallow the use of murkily unintelligible phraseology. There is never any adequate justification for the latter. Whereas the tension between generality and clarity is sometimes to be resolved in favor of uninformative abstractness, there is no comparable reason for ever resolving the conflict between opacity and clarity in favor of incomprehensible obscurity. Such obscurity, whether on a small scale or on a jurisprudentially significant scale, is always at odds with the Rule of Law.

2.2.5. Against Conflicts and Contradictions

More than some of the other Fullerian principles of legality, the principle of nonconflictingness and noncontradictoriness differs importantly in its moral-political guise from its jurisprudential counterpart. As was argued earlier, the rule of law is consistent with a state of affairs in which every person is under myriad pairs of conflicting legal obligations, so long as the penalties within each pair are lop-sided. However, although such a state of affairs is consistent with the rule of law, it is incompatible with the Rule of Law. No one should frequently find himself in situations in which he will be liable to undergo penalties for his conduct regardless of what the conduct may be. If somebody is legally obligated to do X and legally obligated to abstain from doing X, his dignity as a moral agent is compromised even if he faces a meaningful choice because of the disparity between the threatened penalties. If a predicament of that sort confronts him in many an aspect of his life, then his dignity as a moral agent is being flouted unacceptably. To show due esteem for that dignity, a legal system must not only enable meaningful choices but must also permit them. When somebody is under conflicting legal duties, any possible course of conduct on his part is legally impermissible. That state of inescapable impermissibility obtains whether or not one of the two options open to him (doing X or not doing X) is preferable to the other because the penalties attached to it are less severe. No legal system that instantiates the Rule of Law can allow situations of inescapable impermissibility to occur with frequency. Intrinsic to the Rule of Law is that every person will normally be able to act in such a way that he can avoid any violations of the law. If instead legal impermissibility is regularly inescapable, the prevailing legal regime is exerting a repressively far-reaching hold over the lives of the people who are subject to its control. It too seldom leaves them any respite from the sway of its requirements. No regime with such an unremitting grip over its citizens can be liberal-democratic.

We should not quite conclude, however, that conflicting duties will be absent altogether whenever the Rule of Law is realized. On the one hand, various techniques of legal interpretation can indeed eliminate conflicts from the law of a jurisdiction (Fuller 1969, 66–69; Williams 1956, 1140–41). When confronted with legal materials that appear to impose on someone both a duty to do X and a duty to abstain from doing X, adjudicators and administrators will typically be inclined to do their best to construe the materials in such a way as to resolve the conflict. For example, if the conflicting duties are respectively imposed by statutes enacted at different times, the adjudicators or administrators may treat the relevant provisions of the later statute as superseding those of the earlier. Through such methods, legal interpreters can smooth away conflicts in order to ensure that at least one course of action open to anyone will not involve an infraction of the law. Nobody will face the prospect of inescapable impermissibility. On the other hand, such an upshot is hardly preordained, and it will not always be optimal on moral-political grounds. Within any large legal system, there will almost certainly arise some situations in which the finessing of conflicts between legal obligations is undesirable.

For instance, suppose that Jeremy has formed a contract with Susan whereby he undertakes to be present at a certain place on a certain day during a certain stretch of time. Suppose further that he subsequently forms – or has previously formed – a contract with Melanie whereby he undertakes not to be present at the specified place on the specified day during the specified stretch of time. Each of his contractual partners has spent money or made arrangements in reliance on the undertaking

received. Now, in these circumstances, the officials responsible for giving effect to legal requirements could undoubtedly handle the conflict
between Jeremy's contractual duties by holding that in fact only one of
those duties exists. They might, for example, declare that his first contract
takes priority over the second. Nonetheless, although a conflict-resolving
approach (of the sort just mentioned or of some other sort) would manifestly be feasible, it would most likely be unacceptably unfair to one or
the other of the two contractual partners. In the absence of special mitigating factors, Jeremy should not so leniently be absolved of the burden
of dealing with the quandary in which he has placed himself. His moral
agency is not compromised by his being directed to live up to the obligations which he has incurred. Inevitably, of course, he will breach one
of those two obligations. Either he will be present at the specified place
during the specified span of time, or he will not. Accordingly, regardless
of how he acts, he will be liable to incur an additional legal obligation to
remedy his breach (most likely through the payment of compensation).
In the circumstances depicted, however, such an outcome is maximally
fair to all parties concerned. Given the credible possibility of situations
of this kind, we should not construe Fuller's fifth principle as a blanket disallowance of conflicting duties. Any such constraint would be too
rigid for the Rule of Law. In some cases, the Rule of Law – with its
expressed values of human equality, individual dignity, and fairness – is
promoted rather than hindered by the preservation of conflicting duties in
the law.

As the example in the last paragraph suggests, the inadvisability of
eliminating all conflicts between legal duties is particularly evident in
connection with duties that have been voluntarily incurred. Even in connection with obligations that are imposed by statutes or administrative
regulations, however, there can conceivably arise conflicts that should
not be smoothed away by interpretive maneuvers. Still, although such
innocuous conflicts are certainly possible and sometimes actual, they
are exceptional. In general, the existence of conflicting duties is something to be avoided rather than something to be sought or encouraged.
No liberal-democratic system of governance can condone a situation in
which the pairs of conflicting duties incumbent on people are numerously
wide-ranging. As has been remarked, such a situation would spread the
interdictory sway of the system far too broadly. Not all conflicts between

legal duties should be averted or dispelled, but no liberal-democratic scheme of things can countenance the proliferation of such conflicts.

Everything said so far in this subsection is applicable to pairs of conflicting duties even if the penalties attached to the duties in each pair are grossly unbalanced. Whether the penalties associated with two conflicting duties are approximately equivalent or gapingly disparate, somebody in a situation marked by those duties will be subject to penalties irrespective of how he behaves. Only exceptionally can the occurrence of such a plight be squared with liberal-democratic values. *A fortiori*, then, the prevalence of pairs of conflicting duties will be irreconcilable with liberal-democratic values if the penalties within each pair are evenly balanced. Not only would such a state of affairs be redolent of the chief vice that has just been highlighted – the vice of the overextension of a legal regime's duty-imposing grip on its citizens – but in addition it would imperil the very existence of the rule of law (and thus the very existence of the Rule of Law). As was argued in my exposition of the jurisprudential version of Fuller's fifth principle, the basic function of law as a system of authoritative direction for channeling and coordinating human behavior will be undermined if conflicting duties that carry equivalent penalties are pervasive rather than very uncommon. A regime will be failing to guide the conduct of citizens with minimal efficacy, if it supplies them with equally strong reasons for doing X and for not doing X in many areas of their lives. This point is a jurisprudential point, but it is also a pregnant point of political morality. After all, the Rule of Law cannot exist without the rule of law. If the rampancy of conflicting duties subverts the functionality of a legal regime as such, it precludes the attainment of the desiderata for which the functional existence of a regime of law is a necessary condition (at least in any sizable society). It precludes, among other things, the attainment of the values whose realization constitutes the Rule of Law.

Similarly damaging would be the prevalence of contradictions within the authoritative materials of a legal system. We should first note that, unlike some conflicts, contradictions are always detrimental to the Rule of Law even if they are not abundant. Whereas the preservation of some conflicts between legal duties can be promotive of the Rule of Law – because individuals are thereby impelled to assume responsibility for their obligation-incurring actions, or because the legitimate expectations of innocent third parties are thereby protected – the presence of contra-dictions in the authoritative materials of a legal system is never salutary, even defeasibly. Of course, as has been observed, a legal system in its adjudicative and administrative workings can never contain any genuine contradictions. Whenever the formulated norms of such a system appear to establish two contradictory legal positions, one and only one of those positions is actually operative in application to any particular person *P* at any given juncture; the other position at that juncture is strictly inoperative in application to *P*. However, contradictions can obtain at the level of the formulated norms themselves. When contradictions are present at that level (the only level at which they can be present), they are never worthy of being preserved. They give rise to out-and-out indeter-minacy in the law, and they tend to muddle the guidance afforded by the normative matrix of the system in which they appear. That is, they invari-ably engender indeterminacy, and they usually engender uncertainty. Their existence in abundance within a legal system's normative matrix will imperil the very sustainment of the rule of law, but they weaken the Rule of Law even when they are present only on a much smaller scale.

In a system of governance that conforms to the Rule of Law, the authoritative formulations of the system's standards will indicate straight-forwardly what people in the jurisdiction are required or permitted or authorized to do. No less is necessary as a means of showing proper regard for the moral agency of the law's addressees. Yet any such requisite indication of legal consequences is missing when two of the authoritative formulations of a system's standards are in contradiction. Together, the two contradictory laws affirm and deny the existence of some legal norm. If the contradiction between those laws is isolatedly anomalous, then it will detract from the rule of law only to a trivial extent. By contrast, it detracts from the Rule of Law more significantly by evincing disrespect for the capacity of each citizen to make reasoned choices. Perhaps the manifestation of such disrespect derives from carelessness or perhaps it derives from arrogance, but, whatever its origin, any knowing retention of it would bespeak a cavalier attitude – rather than a properly solici-tous attitude – on the part of the officials involved. Officials complying with the Rule of Law will not be so insouciant about retaining in the law something that generates bemusement and needless indeterminacy.

Whereas officials are sometimes justified in giving effect to both of two conflicting duties, they can never give effect to two contradictory laws simultaneously in application to any particular person *P*. As has been stated, one and only one of those laws will be operative in application to *P* at any given time. As a consequence, contradictory formulations of legal norms may engender reasonable expectations that cannot all be satisfied. Should Jack reasonably rely on a law which provides that he is at liberty to do *X* at some time *t*, and should Jill reasonably rely on a law which provides that she has a legal right against anyone else's doing of *X* at *t*, then the two sets of reasonable expectations cannot be jointly satisfied within the confines of private-law institutions if Jack in fact does *X* at *t*. Either Jack's expectations or Jill's expectations will be frustrated. If adjudicative officials hold that Jill has a right against Jack's doing of *X*, and if they then lighten the compensatory award of damages against Jack in order to take account of the reasonableness of his reliance on the liberty-conferring law, they will not only have foiled his expectations but will also have partly foiled her expectations. The only way to avoid the dashing of either party's reasonable expectations is to provide compensation to Jill from some public fund rather than from Jack or his insurer. However, such a "solution" will have foisted onto taxpayers the costs of coming to grips with legal contradictions.

So long as any contradiction is retained in the authoritative materials of a legal system, the potential for Jack-and-Jill situations – situations in which the nonsatisfaction of some reasonable expectations is inevitable within private-law institutions – will abide. Contradictions differ from conflicts in this respect, and are thus especially sharply at variance with the Rule of Law. Whereas the reasonable expectations possibly aroused by laws that impose conflicting duties are always susceptible in principle to being jointly met within private-law arrangements (in part through compensation), the reasonable expectations possibly aroused by legal formulations that contradict each other are not always susceptible to being jointly met within such arrangements.

Hence, even when contradictions are present in a legal system's authoritative materials on far too small a scale to impede the realiza-tion of the rule of law, they mar the Rule of Law. Of course, if they were to multiply hugely, their effects would be far more serious. They would then threaten or scotch the sustainment of the rule of law, and they would completely undo the Rule of Law (not least because the Rule of Law depends on the rule of law). However, Fuller's fifth precept of legality, presented as a tenet of political morality, is not aimed solely at overabundant contradictions. It counsels against any contradictions at all in the formulated norms of a legal regime. There are no reasons in favor of the inclusion of contradictions, and there are strong moral-political reasons for excluding them.

In most respects, then, the principle of nonconflictingness and non-contradictoriness is less flexible than the other Fullerian precepts when it is construed as a tenet of political morality. Unlike its jurisprudential counterpart, it is no more accommodating toward pairs of conflicting duties with lop-sided penalties than toward pairs of conflicting duties with evenly balanced penalties. Moreover, while it allows that some conflicts between legal duties are better preserved than eliminated, it counsels strictly against the presence of contradictions in the authoritative materials of a legal system. On the whole, then, this principle comes closer to laying down a categorical prohibition than do any of the other principles of legality.

2.2.6. Compliability

As we have seen, the Fullerian principle of compliability in its jurisprudential version is concerned primarily if not exclusively with the guiding and coordinating function of law. As was remarked in my earlier discussion of the matter, a wide-ranging bevy of unfollowable mandates could be consistent with the rule of law if the only function of a legal regime were that of resolving disputes. However, because the cardinal function of any legal regime is actually that of directing and channeling human behavior, no such throng of unfulfillable directives would ever be reconcilable with the rule of law. That cardinal function would be stymied if most of the requirements laid down by a regime could not ever be obeyed. No minimally effective legal system would exist in such circumstances.

When we understand the principle of compliability as a tenet of the Rule of Law rather than only of the rule of law, we can discern further reasons for distancing ourselves from the prospect of a legal system in which most of the duty-imposing norms establish obligations that lie wholly beyond the capacities of all or most citizens. On the one hand, as has been contended in this chapter and the preceding chapter, the officials in a legal system should not seek to ensure that every mandate of the system is followable by everyone to whom its requirements apply. Such a goal would be debilitatingly unrealistic, and the attainment of it would be undesirable even if it were not a will-o'-the-wisp. Some mandates should be applied uniformly even though not everyone is capable of abiding by them. On the other hand, laws that cannot ever be obeyed by anyone are without any proper place in a liberal-democratic legal system. Plainly, such laws should not be pervasive within a legal system; what is more, they should not exist at all. Quite apart from their deleterious effects on the directing and coordinating function of law, the demands which they set forth are unfairly overweening.

Suppose for example that a law requires each person daily to jump straight into the air at least forty feet above the ground without mechanical assistance or any other assistance. As a vehicle for guiding and channeling people's behavior, such a law will be pointless. No one will adjust his or her conduct in order to try to comply with a directive that is patently unfollowable. In addition to being pointless and indeed ridiculous, however, the law on jumping is grossly unfair and is inimical to the value of liberty. It will render everyone liable to be subjected to penalties for having failed to comply with the obligation which it imposes. If the penalties are levied against everyone, then everyone will unjustly suffer some hardship for not having carried out a requirement that is well beyond everybody's capacities. To be sure, as has been remarked in Chapter 1, the notion that "ought" implies "can" – the notion that nobody is ever morally obligated to achieve anything which he is genuinely incapable of achieving – is unsustainably strong. If "ought" truly implied "can," then the uniform applicability of the negligence standard in tort law could not be morally justified. All the same, although "can" is not always a necessary condition for "ought," it often is so. When all or most people in a jurisdiction are made legally responsible for living up to a standard (such as the law requiring forty-foot jumps) that cannot ever be fulfilled by any human being, the effect is to render them liable to undergo penalties for partaking of human limitations.

The situation is markedly different from that in which an oafish person has to pay compensation for injuries inflicted as a result of his slipshod conduct. In that latter situation, admittedly, the oaf is held accountable by reference to a standard of reasonable care with which he is incapable of conforming; nonetheless, he has hardly been rendered liable to undergo penalties simply for partaking of the limitations shared by all human beings. Rather, he has been rendered liable to incur compensatory duties for acting in accordance with his oafishness. Of course, his maladroitness is most likely a component of his physical and mental constitution that he cannot transcend. Nevertheless, it is not something that assimilates him to his fellows. On the contrary, it marks him out as someone who is unusually prone to injure them and himself through his actions. It is thus an aspect of his physical and mental constitution that should not be indulged by legal officials, on occasions when it eventuates in harm to other people. Penalizing him legally for not performing superhuman feats would be morally preposterous, but perfectly sensible is the burdening of him legally for not sustaining a level of care and proficiency that is within the reach of ordinary human beings. Because of his failure to sustain that level, his conduct is properly regarded as slipshod. (No similarly disapproving characterization of his conduct would be apposite if he had simply failed to do more than is humanly possible.) Though his inability to overcome his own clumsiness is probably sufficient to exclude any moral case for criminal-law proceedings against him, it does not negate the moral basis for his incurring of compensatory obligations – a moral basis outlined in my opening chapter.

The preceding two paragraphs have pondered the moral shortcomings of an utterly unsatisfiable law on the assumption that that law will be enforced against everyone who breaches it. Much more likely is that such a law will go unenforced or that only some breaches of it will be penalized. If it goes wholly unenforced, then the officials responsible for applying it are effectively acknowledging its moral dubiousness. If breaches of it are selectively penalized, then the selectiveness introduces an additional element of unfairness toward those people who do incur penalties. In sum, a law requiring people to perform feats physically impossible for every human being is deplorable whatever the pattern of enforcement may be. Even when such a mandate is entirely unenforced, the retention of it as an element of the law on the books will redound to the law's discredit. Such a state of affairs will also of course detract from a regime's conformity with Fuller's eighth principle of legality (which calls for congruence between the law on the books and the law in action).

The foregoing arguments about compliability have focused on a law – a mandate requiring each person to jump forty feet off the ground daily – that is ludicrously unfollowable by any human being. Furthermore, that particular law does not serve any discernible purpose that is worthy of pursuit. My clear-cut conclusions about unfulfillable mandates might have to be slightly qualified if we were to focus instead on a law which is not blatantly unfulfillable and which is potentially promotive of some commendable purpose. Suppose that a legal directive imposes a requirement that is beyond the capacities of everyone or virtually everyone. Suppose further, however, that the unfollowability of the mandate is not obvious and that the mandate's existence as a legal norm might be salutary in some respect. Fuller offered a helpful analogy when he noted that a schoolteacher sometimes demands more from her pupils than they can actually achieve. She does so in order to stretch their capacities, with the aim of inducing them to improve their skills and knowledge (Fuller 1969, 71). In a limited number of contexts, the norms of a legal system could conceivably play a similar role. To that extent, the firm conclusions stated in this subsection might have to be somewhat softened. However, any such qualifications would be minor. As Fuller himself observed straightaway, the analogy between the schoolteacher and the lawmaker can easily lead us astray. Indeed, he introduced the analogy in order to warn against it. He remarked that "the teacher whose pupils fail to achieve what [she] asked of them can, without insincerity or self-contradiction, congratulate them on what they did in fact accomplish," and he contrasted her situation with that of a legal-governmental official who "faces the alternative of doing serious injustice [by imposing penalties on people for not performing superhuman deeds] or of diluting respect for law by himself winking at a departure from its demands" (Fuller 1969, 71). Fuller's reservations are well put. If any qualification to this subsection's broad conclusions is needed, it will be very modest. The existence of a law requiring humanly impossible conduct might in some unusual circumstances be morally justifiable – especially if the impossibility of the obligatory conduct is not evident – but the circumstances will certainly be unusual.

In fact, the conclusions advanced heretofore within this subsection are in a significant respect too narrow. So far, we have concentrated on compliability as a virtue of legal *mandates*. We should now recognize that compliability is likewise generally essential for the moral justifiability of legal norms of other types. Procedures prescribed for the formation of contracts, for example, should be within the capacities of ordinary human beings (with the assistance of legal experts, if necessary). Of course, once again, compliability need not encompass everyone. For instance, the fact that some people are incapable of signing their own names will hardly mean that the rules for forming contracts or bequeathing property should not specify the inclusion of signatures. Indeed, this point about not having to encompass everyone directly is especially clear with reference to such power-conferring rules, since the procedures deriving from them can be carried out by people of sound body and mind on behalf of people who are physically or mentally incapacitated. Hence, although a law would be pointless and morally indefensible if it were to prescribe contract-forming procedures that cannot ever be followed by any human being, a law can quite sensibly prescribe procedures that are unfollowable by certain people on their own behalf. Indeed, some procedures of the latter kind will have to be prescribed if any procedures are, given that even the simplest steps will exceed the capacities of certain people. Both as a jurisprudential thesis and as a precept of political morality, the principle of compliability acknowledges as much. While admonishing against laws that require or prescribe superhuman achievements, it does not itself call for the impossible (and undesirable) feat of devising a law with which absolutely everyone can comply.

Before moving on, we should note one other respect in which the principle of compliability is more accommodatingly realistic than it might at first appear. It does not militate against the imposition of strict liability in Anglo-American tort and contract law. Strict liability is legal responsibility for remedying the harmful effects of one's actions – usually through the payment of compensation – irrespective of whether those actions were faulty (negligent, reckless, knowingly indifferent, or malicious) in any way. Under a regime of strict liability, in other words, the incidence of remedial obligations is fault-independent. In many areas of Anglo-American tort law, remedial obligations are incurred only by people whose conduct has been faulty; but strict liability prevails in much of contract law and in the remaining areas of tort law. In American tort law, for example, people who carry on certain ultrahazardous activities will be legally responsible for repairing any harmful effects of those activities, even if they have been impeccably careful throughout. Under English tort law, similarly, a keeper of an animal that belongs to a dangerous species will be legally responsible for remedying any harm caused by the animal, whether or not the keeper's conduct has been faulty. Although these and other instances of strict liability in Anglo-American law might appear to be at odds with the principle of compliability, there is no genuine conflict between them.

To perceive why strict liability is compatible with the principle of compliability, we need to take account of a distinction between two versions of the "ought"-implies-"can" thesis. Everything hinges on how we construe "can." On the one hand, we might take "can" to mean "be able to achieve as a matter of physical possibility," and we might therefore take "cannot" to mean "be unable to achieve as a matter of physical possibility." Alternatively, we might take "can" to mean "be able to achieve through the scrupulous exercise of care and good will," and we might therefore take "cannot" to mean "be unable to achieve through the scrupulous exercise of care and good will." When the "ought"-implies-"can" thesis is interpreted in the latter way – as a claim that there is no moral basis for anyone to be legally obligated to avert harmful occurrences which he or she is unable to avert through the exercise of scrupulous care and good will – it is far too strong. So construed, it would impugn any moral justification for strict liability in the law. Now, although strict liability in the law is often inapposite, it is by no means always so. If someone engages in a distinctive type of activity that engenders peculiarly high risks of harm to other people, or if someone voluntarily incurs an obligation to bring about a certain state of affairs (rather than merely to endeavor to bring about that state of affairs), there may very well be a moral basis for holding the person legally responsible independently of any fault on his or her part. Nothing in the Fullerian principle of compliability will have ruled out the existence of such a moral basis. Quite the contrary.

Rather, the principle of compliability is associated with the first version of the "ought"-implies-"can" tenet. That is, it generally admonishes against the imposition of legal penalties on people for having failed to do things that are starkly beyond the physical capabilities of every human being. Given that it is physically possible for anyone to forbear from engaging in some special activity (such as dealing with ultrahazardous substances or keeping a dangerous animal), and given that it is likewise physically possible for anyone to forbear from promising to bring about a specified state of affairs, the "ought"-implies-"can" tenet that underlies the principle of compliability is entirely consistent with the presence of strict liability in Anglo-American tort law and contract law. Of course, the principle of compliability does not itself insist that any particular areas of tort law or contract law should involve strict liability. Instead, it leaves the matter open – open for determination by other moral-political considerations. While warning that legal penalties for the nonperformance of superhuman feats are seldom if ever morally justified, it neither disallows nor prescribes the establishment of strict liability anywhere in the law.

2.2.7. Steadiness over Time

As my earlier discussion of Fuller's seventh principle of legality has maintained, what is required under this principle is a balance between constancy and adaptability. On the one hand, the efforts of legal officials to guide and coordinate people's behavior through the operations of a legal system will be devastatingly derailed if most of the system's mandates and other norms are repeatedly transformed with stupefying rapidity. On the other hand, the absence of any changes within the normative matrix of a legal system that presides over a moderately dynamic society – to say nothing of a highly dynamic society – will itself be deeply problematic, as it leads to far-reaching discrepancies between the law on the books and the law in action. Accordingly, the functionality of a legal regime depends on the forging of a *via media* between destructive dislocation and preposterous ossification. Such, in a nutshell, is the jurisprudential elaboration of Fuller's seventh principle.

Moral-political factors in support of that principle are similarly evident. If it is not the case that most of the norms in some system of governance are reasonably constant over time, then the major desiderata attainable through the operations of a legal regime will go unrealized. Not all of those desiderata will be secured by every legal system, but none of them can be secured in any sizable society in the absence of such a system. Among the valuable things that would be lost through the excessive transiency of legal norms is a suitable degree of respect on the part of legal officials for the moral agency of citizens. If the successive arrays of norms laid down by a regime are each so ephemeral as to leave citizens frustrated and bewildered, the officials in the regime are preventing rather than facilitating the exercise of each citizen's capacity to make informed choices. That precious capacity, when given appropriate latitude among reasonable options, is the cornerstone of each citizen's legal and moral responsibility. If citizens cannot make informed choices about their legal obligations and opportunities (because the information available to them and to their lawyers is unreliably transitory), then their actions, qua responses to the law rather than qua patterns of conduct that occur independently of the law, are not susceptible to moral assessment. Hence, overabundant transmutations of legal norms will have terminated the basic moral relationship that obtains between citizens and their government under the Rule of Law. Such a relationship consists partly in each citizen's moral responsibility – based on his or her moral agency and on ample leeway for the exercise of that agency – and partly in legal-governmental officials' esteem for the agency and responsibility of each citizen. Officials evince no such esteem when they woefully befuddle citizens by changing the law sweepingly and persistently. Far from endowing the citizens with ample leeway for the informed exercise of their moral agency in response to legal requirements and authorizations, the officials in these circumstances are thwarting any such exercise.

Many other moral-political desiderata will likewise be imperiled when Fuller's seventh principle is not heeded. For instance, the efficiency of a society's economic arrangements will be in jeopardy if excessively frequent and wide-ranging metamorphoses of legal norms unsettle the security of people's proprietary and contractual entitlements. As was remarked in my earlier discussion of the seventh principle of legality, the problems posed by transgressions of this principle are broadly similar to those posed by retroactive laws. Just as people will be loath to engage in economic ventures or in other arduous undertakings if they fear that their efforts will retroactively be deemed illegitimate, so too they will be loath to engage in any such endeavors if they fear that their legal entitlements will have altered dramatically by the time those endeavors are completed. Such a state of uncertainty will offer no solid basis for any long-term planning or even medium-term planning. As a result, the robustness of a society's economy will suffer grievously.

Of course, the numerous detrimental effects of inordinate changes in a legal system's normative matrix should not impel us to conclude that very few changes therein will ever be justified. As has been emphasized, the Fullerian principle of steadiness over time does not favor petrifaction any more than relentless fluxion. In addition to the jurisprudential considerations that support the striking of a balance between stagnancy and chronic upheavals, there are sound moral-political reasons for pursuing such a tack. If the normative framework of a legal regime were somehow to become static, the dire consequences would be manifold. Since the very existence of the legal regime as such would be threatened (in ways recounted in Section 2.1.7), the sundry goods made possible only through the existence of such a regime would in turn be at stake. At any rate, even if the regime were to continue to operate as a totteringly inefficient legal system, its moral-political drawbacks would be egregious. Gross inefficiency is one such major drawback, of course, but a number of other moral-political vices as well would tarnish the system.

For example, whenever antiquated laws are left on the books, they can become traps for the unwary. Even legal experts might not be able to avoid those traps, for they might not be sufficiently attuned to the implications of laws that were brought into existence hundreds of years ago. Hart adverted to a colorful instance of an unexpected application of a hoary statute (Hart 1961, 60). In 1944, Helen Duncan was prosecuted and convicted in England under the Witchcraft Act of 1735. During the period leading up to the D-Day landing in World War II, the British authorities suspected that she was acquiring and revealing secret military information for the purpose of enhancing her reputation as a clairvoyant. After she was arrested during one of her séances, she was eventually charged with the crime of fraudulently conjuring the dead – an offense under the 1735 Act. Whether or not her charlatanry posed any genuine danger to the planning of the armed forces, the important point here is that the existence of the ancient statute provided the authorities with a disconcertingly convenient route for dealing with her. The element of surprise in their invocation of the statute was greatly to their advantage and to the disadvantage of the citizen against whom they were proceeding. Though Helen Duncan herself was hardly an admirable person, her case illustrates the potential for injustices when laws are kept on the books well past their obsolescence. (Of course, whether anything along the lines of the Witchcraft Act should ever have been on the books is a pertinent question.) Injustices through surprises from the past are rare in a dynamic liberal-democratic legal system like that of England, in which most laws on the books are still germane rather than obsolete. Thus, although those injustices are each repugnant in isolation, they do not cumulatively affect the fundamental character of the legal system in which they occur. In a society with an illiberal regime whose regulatory structure contains a multitude of obsolete norms, by contrast, the presence of those myriad norms is likely to affect the whole character of the regime profoundly for the worse. Those norms will present the regime's officials with a host of opportunities for catching citizens unawares. Even if those opportunities are seldom seized, their very existence – and the common knowledge of their existence, despite their not being separately identifiable beforehand by most citizens – will tilt the relationship between the government and the citizens sharply toward the dominance of the former. Not only will a stagnant, antiquated normative matrix contribute very little to the beneficial direction and coordination of human conduct; in addition, it can easily play a sinister role as a source of leverage for a nefarious government.

Hence, the principle of steadiness over time is an integral component of the Rule of Law because it counsels against any blinkered defiance of human mutability as well as against any unmitigated embrace thereof. Steadiness is not stagnancy. Still, although the seventh principle of legality does not countenance stagnancy, its most salient message is a warning against the evils of immoderate rates of change in a jurisdiction's law. Keeping things stable in order to let people know where they stand is scarcely a sufficient condition for the Rule of Law, but it is undoubtedly a necessary condition.

2.2.8. Congruence between Formulation and Implementation

As the pivotal precept in Fuller's exposition of the rule of law and the Rule of Law, the principle of congruence is a fitting capstone for this chapter's discussions. Moral-political considerations in favor of that principle are legion. Those considerations become evident as soon as we recall how congruence between the formulation and the implementation of legal norms is generally brought about. As was indicated in my account of the jurisprudential version of Fuller's eighth principle, a key ingredient in the fulfillment of this principle is the sustainment of impartiality on the part of adjudicative and administrative officials. My earlier account highlighted the epistemic virtues of impartiality. Impartiality is cognitively reliable, whereas the factors that vitiate impartiality – such as self-interest and bigotry and ignorance and capriciousness – tend to lead officials (and other people) away from correct understandings of the matters with which they are confronted. Though that epistemic point is still of major importance in the present subsection, the principal emphasis here is on the moral-political virtues of impartiality.

On top of being cognitively unreliable, the impartiality-vitiating factors are morally and politically dubious. Officials motivated by selfishness or prejudices or whimsicalness will not only be prone to misunderstand the laws and situations which they encounter, but will also be likely to deviate from what is morally obligatory or appropriate. To be sure, there are notable exceptions to this generalization. In particular, the pertinence of the generalization will depend to some degree on the benignity of the law in any relevant jurisdiction. In a legal regime with many heinous laws, promptings that divert officials from the strict enforcement of those laws – even if they are ignoble promptings – may be morally better than a posture of steadfast dedication to such enforcement (Kramer 2004a, 191 n10). Suppose, for example, that the adjudicative and administrative officials in a wicked regime are charged with the task of effectuating many laws that call for harshly oppressive measures against some despised group of people. Suppose further that some of the officials are willing to accept bribes from members of the downtrodden group in return for declining to inflict the fierce persecution that is prescribed under the terms of the prevailing laws. In a context of this sort, the corruptly self-interested departures from a stance of strict impartiality are morally superior to any disinterested implementation of the noxious laws. Even more plainly superior to the impartial enforcement of those laws would be decisions by officials against enforcement that are based on preferentially favorable attitudes toward the members of the subordinated group. Such attitudes, which of course are biases, might be essential for emboldening the officials to hazard the wrath of their more zealous fellows (who will object to any laxity in the enforcement of the discriminatory laws). In that event, the biases are inclining the maverick officials toward the satisfaction of the demands of morality rather than toward the flouting of those demands.

To quite an extent, then, the moral-political tenor of adjudicative and administrative impartiality will hinge on the substance of the law in each jurisdiction. However, in the second half of this chapter we are concentrating on the Rule of Law rather than on the rule of law. That is, we are here focusing specifically on the state of affairs that obtains when a liberal-democratic regime of law is flourishingly in existence. We are not at this juncture seeking to take account of the characteristics of any legal systems that are markedly illiberal and undemocratic. Thus, for present purposes, this chapter can pretermit scenarios in which the norms of certain legal regimes are so odious as to render morally suspect any stance of impartiality in the application and enforcement of those norms. We are confining our attention here to regimes that comply with liberal-democratic values.

Given as much, adjudicative and administrative officials who strive for impartiality will thereby increase their prospects of arriving at morally correct determinations. Because the laws to be effectuated by the officials are themselves benign, and because the impartiality of the officials' outlooks will enhance their ability to understand and implement those laws correctly, their impartiality is morally valuable instrumentally; that is, it serves as a means to the morally valuable ends that are pursued by the aforementioned laws. It is also instrumentally valuable in another respect, for it helps to fulfill people's legitimate expectations. Since citizens and the legal experts advising them have been able to ascertain the terms of various laws, and since the impartiality of the officials will strengthen the likelihood of their giving effect to those laws in accordance with the terms thereof, the impartiality promotes the morally worthy end of upholding the citizens' reasonable beliefs concerning the legal consequences of their actions. More broadly, of course, the officials' adherence to an impartial stance reinforces the vitality of their legal system. By indispensably furthering a state of congruence between the law on the books and the law in practice, their impartiality averts the difficulties posed by major discrepancies between the two – difficulties threatening the very existence of the rule of law (and thus the existence of the Rule of Law). Official impartiality enables the smooth performance of law's guiding function, and it therefore enables the realization of the precious desiderata for which the functionality of a legal system is essential.

Furthermore, apart from being instrumentally serviceable in these several respects, the officials' impartiality is of intrinsic moral value. It helps to ensure not only that the officials reach morally correct decisions, but also that they arrive at those decisions for the morally correct reasons. As was argued near the end of my discussion of impartiality in Chapter 1, the motivational and cognitive deformations that negate impartiality are at odds with any proper respect for the people who are adversely affected. For example, when adjudicative or administrative officials place their own selfish interests ahead of the interests of citizens who deserve to be treated favorably, they are acting athwart the elementary constraint of human equality. Admittedly, they might not be aware that they are so acting. They might be so blinded by their own self-absorption that they are genuinely not conscious of the ways in which they are unjustly devaluing the concerns and projects of other people. Alternatively, they might be fully aware of their own rapacity and might be disdainfully unperturbed by that awareness. Whatever may be the degree of their alertness to their own self-indulgence, their having succumbed to that discreditable propensity is enough to taint any decisions taken on the basis of it. Even if some of those decisions happen to be correct in their substance, the selfish promptings that underlie them will have sullied the relationship between the governors and the governed. In such circumstances, the officials will have reached the right outcomes for the wrong reasons. Their acting on the basis of those self-centered reasons is what renders their conduct so objectionable (even on occasions when they have arrived at the correct outcomes), for it establishes that the officials attach importance to any citizen's well-being only insofar as his or her well-being is derivative of their own. By reducing each citizen in this manner to a means for their own selfish ends, the officials evince a lack of basic respect for the dignity of each citizen as a moral agent. Thus, whether or not they recognize how warped their perspective is, their devotion to their own interests is violative of the parity between themselves and other human beings.

Much the same can be said about the other impartiality-subverting factors such as prejudices and ignorance and capriciousness. When citizens are treated unfavorably because of biases against them or against some group(s) to which they belong, the denigration of them is palpable. Again, the denigration takes place whether or not the biased officials are aware of the negativeness of their attitudes. For example, some officials might harbor demeaningly prejudiced attitudes toward women – whom they regard as fragile creatures in need of domesticity – while believing that their own outlooks on the matter are especially solicitous and noble.

However well-intentioned their condescension may be, it is condescension all the same and is thus a blot on the relationship between the officials and the citizens.

Indeed, even when prejudices are preferentially favorable rather than disparaging, they blight the aforementioned relationship. Of course, the regrettableness of such prejudices partly resides in the fact that they typically redound to the detriment of people to whom they do not apply. When an adjudicative or administrative official treats Hispanic people in undeservedly generous ways, for example, he is usually thereby according less than is due to non-Hispanic people. Even when that consequence of the preferential treatment is not in prospect, however, any favoritism toward Hispanic people qua Hispanic people by an adjudicative or administrative official would remain objectionable.

On the one hand, to be sure, any such official may encounter a situation in which the morally optimal course of action for him is to be exceptionally generous or lenient when bringing the law to bear on somebody's conduct. On the other hand, the considerations that motivate the extralegal generosity or leniency – on the part of a legal-governmental official acting in his public capacity – should never include a person's ethnicity. When such a factor inflects an official's deliberations concerning the appropriateness of extralegal generosity or leniency, it besmirches those deliberations by focusing them not on a citizen's status as a person but on his or her status as a person of some particular genealogy. Though a private citizen can in some contexts legitimately take into account the ethnicity of other people when deciding how generous to be toward them (with charitable donations, for example), there is no similar leeway for a public official who has to ponder whether to be more complaisant toward some citizen than is prescribed by any applicable laws. Such an official in a liberal-democratic society properly governs in the name of everyone, and is both legally and morally obligated to deal with everyone as juridically on a par. (Note that nothing in this paragraph rules out the potential legitimacy of processes by which the officials in some regime apply general laws that themselves differentiate among people on ethnic grounds. Although the tenets of liberal-democratic governance will seldom be consistent with laws that do call for any preferential treatment of some people on grounds of ethnicity, there is no compelling reason for us to presume that those tenets will disallow all such laws. At least within the confines of my present discussion, the potential legitimacy of some such laws should be left an open question. In the event that a general law does favor certain people by reference to their ethnicity, any impartial implementation of that law by adjudicative or administrative officials will obviously involve their adverting to people's ethnic backgrounds. Nothing that has been said here is meant to suggest otherwise. What this paragraph has been discussing is not the impartial implementation of general laws that differentiate among people on the basis of ethnic affiliations, but instead the impartiality of officials' decisions to go beyond or outside the law.)

Likewise deplorable are official determinations stemming from ignorance or whimsicalness. Of course, some degree of ignorance is inevitable. No credible system of governance will have the resources to enable adjudicators and administrators to acquaint themselves with all relevant facts of every situation with which they are confronted. In certain cases, moreover, some relevant facts might remain unascertainable even if limitless resources were to be expended on efforts to unearth them. Nonetheless, although complete knowledge of the material facts of every situation is a chimera, legal-governmental officials cannot correctly claim to be impartial unless they take all reasonable steps to apprise themselves of those facts. Ignorance resulting from hastiness or remissness or lackadaisical indifference is something that undermines the impartiality of officials, for it leaves their judgments dependent on their surmises and impulses rather than on their open-minded attentiveness to germane facts. Chapter 1, in its discussion of impartiality, has emphasized this point. What should be underscored here afresh are the moral-political costs of ignorance in the decision-making processes of officials.

Given that at this stage we are concentrating on regimes whose laws conform to liberal-democratic values, one principal drawback of ignorance is that it decreases the chances that those benevolent laws will be applied in accordance with their terms. Instead, insofar as officials lack any informed sense of what they are doing, they will be prone to misapply the laws and consequently to frustrate or weaken the realization of the purposes thereof. Furthermore, beyond retarding the realization of those specific purposes, officials who are frequently mired in ignorance will impair or even destroy the overall functionality of their regime as a legal regime. By persistently declining to inform themselves adequately of the complexities of the problems which they are addressing, the officials substantially increase the probability of discrepancies between the law on the books and the law in practice. They thereby impede the performance of law's guiding and coordinating role, perhaps to the point of undoing the status of their regime as a system of law. *Pro tanto*, they place in jeopardy the desiderata for which the existence of such a system is indispensable.

One major vice of remediable ignorance on the part of adjudicative or administrative officials, then, is that their benightedness tends toward bad effects. It is instrumentally of disvalue, particularly when it clouds the officials' deliberations continually rather than only occasionally. As regrettable as the instrumental shortcomings of alleviable ignorance, however, are its intrinsic shortcomings. When officials do not reasonably endeavor to become familiar with relevant facts of the matters on which they have to pass judgment, they are failing to show proper respect for the citizens whose interests are at stake in those matters. In any such cases, the relationship between the officials and the citizens is one of high-handedness. Whether or not the officials are aware of the unreasonableness of their disinclination to acquaint themselves with readily discoverable facts, that disinclination is cavalier. It might not be the product of conscious haughtiness – it might, for example, ensue from lazy remissness – but it bespeaks the inadequacy of the officials' concern to prevent their decisions from being arbitrary. That is, it bespeaks the inadequacy of their concern to ensure that their treatment of each citizen is in accordance with his or her moral standing (which, in a liberal democracy, will be closely though not perfectly correlated with his or her legal standing). Such indifference is overbearing, regardless of its ultimate wellspring. It lessens the moral decency of any system of governance in which it inflects officials' determinations.

We need not consider here separately the impartiality-confounding factor of whimsicalness or capriciousness, since any discussion of it would largely echo what has just been said about avoidable ignorance. Indeed, a dominant theme runs throughout my brief exploration of the various states of mind that are counter to impartiality. Whenever one of those states of mind has significantly influenced an official decision, it has displaced the requirements of law and morality as the effectual basis for a legal-governmental system's authoritative interaction with some citizen(s). It has displaced the rule of law (and therefore the Rule of

Law) with the rule of men, within the scope of the decision in question. Such a displacement contravenes the liberal-democratic axiom of fundamental human equality, for it brushes aside the status of any affected citizen as a moral agent whose conduct is regulated by general norms that are themselves legitimate. It elevates the errant officials to a position of unwarranted dominance, by substituting the arbitrariness of their predilections and peculiarities in lieu of those general norms. It thus perverts the relationship between officials and citizens, which – on the side of the adjudicative and administrative officials – should always be mediated through benevolent general laws and moral principles rather than through idiosyncrasies and fiat.

To close my remarks on the virtue of impartiality in adjudicative and administrative processes, a word of caution is advisable here. These remarks do not entail the proposition that laws should always be effectuated in accordance with their terms. On the contrary, sometimes an impartial assessment of a situation will militate against the conclusion that the applicable laws should be given effect. Although the morally correct course of action for officials in a liberal-democratic regime will usually be to enforce any laws in circumstances to which they are applicable, a different course of action will sometimes be morally requisite. Suppose for example that a municipality's anti-jaywalking ordinance, whose terms are of blanket applicability, is never enforced on quiet streets and almost never enforced on much busier streets. Suppose further that a policeman charged with administering the municipal laws has observed someone transgressing the anti-jaywalking ordinance on an extremely sleepy street. At the time of the infraction, as at virtually every other time of each day, no cars or other vehicles are proceeding along the street. In these circumstances, the policeman is under a moral obligation to refrain from giving effect to the ordinance. Measures of enforcement in such a context would be morally unacceptable for a number of reasons. Those measures would violate rather than uphold the tenet of basic human equality, since they would single out some pedestrian for punitive treatment that has not been similarly meted out to other people who have behaved in the same fashion. Any such measures would dash, rather than vindicate, the legitimate expectations which the pedestrian has formed about the patterns of law-enforcement in the municipality. They would serve no morally worthy purpose whatsoever, since the benefits of an anti-jaywalking ordinance in relation to busy streets are beside the point in relation to a street on which there is virtually no traffic at any time of the day. Nor would the enforcement of the ordinance in the envisaged situation tend to keep the law from falling into disesteem. On the contrary, such an act of enforcement would tend to cast the law into disrepute by bringing its requirements to bear on somebody in an inequitable and ridiculously pointless manner. In sum, the policeman who espies the infraction of the ordinance is both morally permitted and morally obligated to abstain from pursuing any measures of enforcement. (He is also legally permitted, though probably not legally obligated, to forgo such measures.) If the policeman adopts an impartial perspective on the matter, he will recognize that the law should go unenforced.[5]

Impartiality in official decision-making, then, will sometimes eventuate in the condonation of unlawful conduct. Much more often in a liberal democracy, however, an impartial stance will call for the effectuation of legal norms in conformity with their prescriptions. To that end, the officials in a liberal-democratic regime will need to be possessed of interpretive proficiency. Their being endowed with such proficiency is crucial not least for the reasons recounted in Section 2.1.8; without a healthy degree of interpretive skill, the officials will not be able to operate a functional legal system and will therefore not be able to maintain the advantages that follow from the existence of such a system. That earlier account can be supplemented here, for we are now in a position to see why interpretive competence is vital not just at the level of a legal system as a whole, but also in each particular case.

Whenever legal officials interpret laws incompetently, either they arrive at incorrect verdicts or else they arrive at correct verdicts purely coincidentally. Incorrect verdicts will frustrate the legitimate expectations formed by citizens and legal experts. After all, as my earlier discussion of interpretive proficiency has contended, a central feature of such proficiency for any particular case lies in the correspondence between the interpretation that is rendered and the interpretation that could reasonably have been anticipated. Hence, when interpretive processes go awry and yield unwarranted outcomes, the affected citizens are quite right if they feel that they have been misled. Their having been misled is itself

---

[5] For a more extended discussion of the example of jaywalking, see Kramer 1999a, 285–87.

an evil – even though it occurs as a result of blundering rather than as a result of malice – for the defiance of their apposite expectations has turned their own capacities as moral agents against them. Moreover, since a misapplication of a law created by a benignly liberal-democratic regime will usually counteract a worthy substantive purpose underlying that law, the misapplication will usually be substantively as well as procedurally regrettable. That is, quite apart from the misapplication's foiling of legitimate expectations, its substantive bearings considered in themselves are likely to be dismaying. Furthermore, insofar as the misapplication and the misinterpretation whence it derives are endowed with precedential force, they mar the future direction of the law. Thus, even if misapplications arising from botched interpretations are too rare to pose any threat to the functionality of the liberal-democratic system of law in which they occur, they generally tarnish that system.

Fortuitously correct outcomes that stem from incompetent interpretations of legal norms are not as markedly problematic as incorrect outcomes. They will not dash the legitimate expectations of the citizens who are immediately affected by them. Similarly, since they are correct (albeit fortuitously correct) applications of benevolent legal norms, their substantive bearings are likely to be morally sound. However, although verdicts that are correct-by-happenstance do not carry all the disadvantages of verdicts that are incorrect, the interpretive maladroitness of their underpinnings is not without costs. Insofar as any bungled interpretation that generates such a verdict is invested with precedential force, it casts a distortive shadow over the future course of some area of the law. The distortion will not inevitably be for the worse, but it very likely will be so. What is more, even in isolation from any precedent-setting effects, misguided interpretations serve as flawed bases for decisions that may be impeccable in all other respects. As has been remarked, adjudicative and administrative officials should not only be rendering the right determinations but should also be rendering them for the right reasons. An official who reaches an otherwise impeccable decision by way of a confused interpretive approach has in effect substituted his own muddled thoughts for the terms of the relevant law(s) as the grounding for his decision. Notwithstanding that his deliberations culminate in an unexceptionable outcome, they detract from the moral authority of his regime by tending to supplant the rule of law – and the Rule of Law – with the rule of men.

In short, both impartiality and interpretive proficiency on the part of adjudicative and administrative officials are indispensable for the flourishing of the Rule of Law. Any wide-ranging and persistent departures from impartiality or any wide-ranging and persistent failures of interpretive proficiency will imperil the very existence of a legal system as such. More probable are isolated departures or failures. They will not endanger the general functionality of a system of law, but, within their limits, they almost always debase the system's overall moral standing. Even though they may occasionally prove to be salutary in certain respects, they will prove to be detrimental in other respects. They typically prove to be only detrimental. Accordingly, Fuller's eighth principle of legality does indeed lend itself to being construed as a precept of political morality. It sets forth a necessary condition for the overall decency of a regime of law, and a usually necessary condition for the moral propriety of the handling of each particular case by legal officials. Both at the broad level and at the narrowly focused level, it articulates a keynote of the Rule of Law.

2.3. Conclusion

This chapter has explored the jurisprudential phenomenon of the rule of law and the moral-political ideal of the Rule of Law. Fuller's principles of legality have structured each half of the discussion, and have thereby enabled me to highlight many affinities and some dissimilarities between the jurisprudential phenomenon and the moral-political ideal. The affinities are more numerous and conspicuous than the dissimilarities, of course. In part, they stem from the sheer fact that the rule of law is a *sine qua non* of the Rule of Law. Albeit the realization of the former is not a sufficient condition for the realization of the latter, it is a necessary condition. As a result, whatever threatens the former will also threaten the latter. Important though that point is, however, it does not fully capture the extent of the homologies between the rule of law and the Rule of Law.

Central to both the jurisprudential significance and the moral-political significance of each of the Fullerian principles is law's basic role in guiding human conduct by presenting human agents with demands and opportunities. One key reason why all of those principles are fundamental to the rule of law is precisely that they are vital for the performance of law's role. Each of them is vital for sustaining the integral connection between the sway of law and the exercise of human agency (on the part of those who are subject to that sway). Yet such a connection is also of profound moral-political importance. It distinguishes legal governance from any purely manipulative mode of governance that would treat people as unwitting pawns by circumventing their agency. When there occur breakdowns in the connection between legal norms and the agency of the norms' addressees, they impair the legitimacy of the law by indicating that the relevant legal officials do not adequately respect that agency. Even if some of those breakdowns produce beneficial effects, they constitute lapses in the law's treatment of people as responsible moral choosers.

Of course, the fact that a regime addresses itself perspicuously to the agency of each individual is hardly sufficient to establish the legitimacy of its demands. After all, a gunman typically expresses pungently the choice which he is offering to his victim, and a kidnapper typically articulates vividly the choice which he is offering to the family or friends of his captive (Kramer 1999a, 59–60). Still, as has been emphasized, my whole exposition of the moral-political import of the Fullerian principles is premised on the assumption that the prevailing regime of law is liberal-democratic in its substance. Given as much, those principles distill the procedural morality of such a regime. Combined with the benign substance of the law, the proper fulfillment of those principles will have clinched the law's legitimacy and moral authority. It will have done so by ensuring that the benign substance of the law is meaningfully presented to citizens as an array of requirements and opportunities with which they can become familiar and about which they can make effectual choices. In other words, it ensures that the operations of a liberal-democratic system of law are an arena in which the governing officials display due respect for the moral agency of the governed. (Recall, incidentally, that the proper fulfillment of the Fullerian principles does not consist in the perfect fulfillment of each of them. Quite realistic is the role ascribed here to the conditions that are encapsulated in those principles; that role does not belong to some elusively utopian archetype.)

A focus on the rational agency of the law's addressees is, then, a unifying thread that ties together the two main components of this chapter's investigations. That focus has enabled us to discern what is necessary for law's functional existence and also what is necessary for law's legitimacy

and moral authority. Worth noting here is that which the Fullerian theoretical framework omits as well as that which it includes. Fuller has
sometimes been criticized – for instance, in Harris 1997, 150 – on the
ground that his principles do not cover some key characteristics that are
intrinsic to the rule of law or to the juridical dimension of the Rule of Law.
Such criticism, however, is misplaced. On the one hand, certain things
not expressly comprehended in any of his principles are indeed prominent features of many liberal-democratic legal systems. One example is
the strict institutional separateness of courts, and another is the vesting
of people with entitlements to appeal the objectionable rulings of lower
courts to higher courts. On the other hand, no such features are generally indispensable for law's very existence or for its legitimacy and moral
authority. Arrangements for securing the conditions that are articulated
in Fuller's principles (especially in his eighth principle) will vary to some
degree from one liberal-democratic legal system to the next. Features of
the sort just mentioned may be crucial to those arrangements in some
societies, but in other societies the arrangements may be different and
may nevertheless be equally well suited for effecting compliance with the
Fullerian precepts. When certain procedural or institutional safeguards
are present in some society X but not in some society Y, they might obvi-
ate in X certain alternative procedural or institutional safeguards that are
present in Y. Hence, Fuller was wise to refrain from designating some specific set of such safeguards as essential for every instantiation of the rule
of law or the Rule of Law. He recognized that, however deeply entrenched
a certain institution or practice might be in one liberal-democratic system of governance, its salutary role can be played by quite a different
institution or practice in some other liberal-democratic system of governance. For example, although the entitlement to be tried by a jury of
one's peers in any serious criminal case is a longstanding element in the
Anglo-American incarnation of the Rule of Law, it is not an element in
the Rule of Law as embodied in some other liberal-democratic countries.
Unacceptably provincial, then, would be the inclusion of trial by jury
as a fundamental principle of legality. Fuller showed good judgment in
keeping such concrete institutional matters out of his enumeration of
fundamental principles.

Thus, Fuller's theoretical framework compendiously summarizes all
the essential properties of the rule of law. Admittedly, it does not likewise

offer a complete conspectus of the essential elements in the ideal of the Rule of Law, since it does not aim to expound fully the liberal-democratic substance of that ideal (relating to economic justice or civil rights and liberties, for example). Nonetheless, although the basic substantive characteristics of the Rule of Law have been only partly explicated herein, its formal or procedural essence is admirably captured by Fuller's principles of legality. This chapter's reelaboration of his principles – which often goes beyond what Fuller himself wrote – can be set alongside my first chapter's examination of the chief dimensions of objectivity. Connections between the two chapters have already been touched upon at many junctures. Chapter 3 will look more searchingly at some of those connections.

Objectivity and Law's Moral Authority

In this final chapter, we shall ponder in greater depth how some of the principal dimensions of objectivity bear on the rule of law and the Rule of Law. Many of the connections between objectivity and law (law in general or liberal-democratic law specifically) are already apparent from the foregoing two chapters, and are therefore not in need of further exposition here. For example, we have already explored at length the crucial role of objectivity-qua-impartiality in fostering congruity between the law on the books and the law in practice within any particular jurisdiction. Some other aspects of the relationships between objectivity and the rule of law or the Rule of Law, however, stand in need of additional investigation. The analyses presented heretofore in this book will provide the requisite framework for this closing chapter's reflections.

3.1. Preliminary Remarks on the Matter of Observational Mind-Independence

As has been argued in my opening chapter, the observational mind-independence of legal norms is always strong rather than merely weak. That is, the nature of every legal norm in any legal system does not depend on what any observers (such as the system's officials) individually *or collectively* take that nature to be. As has also been contended, strong observational mind-independence is a nonscalar property; it applies in an all-or-nothing fashion rather than to varying degrees. Although strength and weakness are usually scalar properties, the terms "strong" and "weak" in this context are used in the technical senses specified in Section 1.2.1. In those senses, the terms denote nonscalar properties. Objectivity qua observational mind-independence, then, is different from most of the other dimensions of objectivity. For example, the impartiality of legal officials and the transindividual discernibility of legal truths vary in their extents among different systems of law. By contrast, the strong observational mind-independence of legal norms does not vary within any system of law or among any such systems. If a legal regime exists at all, its norms are strongly mind-independent observationally. In that respect, its norms are at one with those of every other legal regime.

Because the impartiality of legal officials and the transindividual discernibility of legal truths are scalar, the operations of legal systems exhibit those properties to differing degrees. In no small part, the efficiency and vibrancy of any legal system – even a heinous legal system – will depend on the levels of those two types of objectivity within it. Indeed, if those levels do not remain quite high, the very existence of a legal system will be in jeopardy; in such a plight, some of Fuller's principles of legality (such as the principle of congruence and the principle of perspicuity) would be going unfulfilled. Consequently, legal officials who wish to secure the robustness and the very continuation of their regime will need to strive for the sustainment of those dimensions of objectivity. Their striving will make a difference to the effectiveness of their regime and to its longevity.

Observational mind-independence is quite another matter. In regard to this dimension of objectivity, admirably efficient legal systems and dismayingly inefficient legal systems are indistinguishable. A greater degree of vibrancy in a legal system is not accompanied by any greater degree (or lesser degree) of observational mind-independence for the system's laws. Nor is there any distinction, in regard to the observational mind-independence of laws, between a legal regime that is laudably benevolent and a legal regime that is deplorably malign. In each case, the observational mind-independence of the regime's laws is strong. When officials strive to ensure that their regime's norms are benign and that its workings are efficient, they are not thereby doing anything that will increase (or decrease) the observational mind-independence of those norms and workings. So long as a legal system endures at all, its laws and operations are strongly mind-independent observationally.

We should obviously not conclude, on the basis of what has just been said, that there is no relationship between objectivity-qua-observational-mind-independence and the rule of law or the Rule of Law. On the contrary, as is evident, both the rule of law and the Rule of Law inevitably partake of such objectivity. Still, precisely because of the unvaryingness of the relationship between observational mind-independence and the rule of law or the Rule of Law, nothing of practical importance will be settled by reference to that mind-independence. Regardless of the character of a legal system – regardless of whether it possesses or lacks moral authority – its norms are endowed with strong observational mind-independence. Even if officials' decisions are wicked or wrong-headed, the strong observational mind-independence will persist. For all the matters of practical importance that confront a legal system, then, the strong observational mind-independence of legal norms is a given rather than something that has to be worried about and sought.

3.2. The Authoritativeness Doctrine

Consequently, quite unilluminating and extremely misleading is the following proposition:

> **Authoritativeness Doctrine**: No legal regime can be morally authoritative unless the norms in such a regime are strongly mind-independent observationally.

A thesis of this sort is unilluminating because it does not really go beyond the uninformative claim that a legal system can never be morally authoritative without existing as a legal system. More precisely, it does not really go beyond the claim that a legal system can never be morally authoritative unless a certain basic and unavoidable feature of every legal system is a feature thereof. We may as well be told that a legal system cannot be morally authoritative unless its operations occur in space and time. Furthermore, the Authoritativeness Doctrine is extremely misleading because it naturally suggests that, although the strong observational mind-independence of laws is necessary for any legal regime's moral authority, such mind-independence is not similarly necessary for a legal regime's wickedness. Yet, given that no legal system can ever be present without that mind-independence, and given that the existence of a legal system is necessary for the existence of a heinous legal system, the strong observational mind-independence of legal norms is necessary for the heinousness of a system of law. Any legal system in the absence of such mind-independence is impossible, and thus any evil legal system in the absence of such mind-independence is impossible.

Now, the fact that the strong observational mind-independence of legal norms is a necessary condition for benign legal systems and iniquitous legal systems alike may not initially seem to render the Authoritativeness Doctrine unilluminating. After all, I have argued elsewhere that compliance with each of Fuller's principles of legality is necessary for any benevolent regime's attainment of morally vital desiderata and also for any evil regime's fulfillment of nefarious purposes on a large scale over a long period (Kramer 1999a, 62–77; 2004a, 172–222; 2004b). My arguments have not been uninformative and trivial, but have instead attempted to counter the prevailing wisdom on the matter by showing at length that the rule of law – unlike the Rule of Law – is not possessed of an inherent moral status. Yet those arguments may seem quite closely parallel to the Authoritativeness Doctrine, and may therefore seem no less vulnerable to objections than that doctrine. Given that the features distilled in Fuller's principles are essential properties of every legal system, my arguments about the rule of law may seem to be making the trivial claim that a legal system has to be a legal system if it is to realize the good or evil purposes that are achievable only through the existence of such a system. If in fact my arguments are not trivially jejune, then the resemblances between them and the Authoritativeness Doctrine may indicate that that doctrine too is much more meaty than I have contended. Such, at least, is what the proponents of the Authoritativeness Doctrine might urge.

Let us leave aside here the fact that quite a few jurisprudential theorists had failed to recognize the indispensability of the rule of law for the realization of many wicked aims (and had therefore failed to recognize that evil rulers bent only on reinforcing their own exploitative sway will have strong reasons for complying with each of Fuller's principles to a substantial degree). Even if we pretermit that important point, there are decisive dissimilarities between the Authoritativeness Doctrine and my arguments about conformity with Fuller's principles. Each of the Fullerian principles encapsulates a scalar property that is to be sought and attained by legal officials to varying degrees. Although each such property must be instantiated at least at some threshold level whenever a legal system is functioning as such, the level of each above the relevant threshold is something to be determined by the extent of the officials' striving. Consequently, when a philosopher argues that substantial degrees of compliance with the Fullerian principles are necessary for the achievement of sundry ends – either benevolent or malevolent – he or she is not propounding some ridiculously boring thesis akin to the claim that those sundry ends will never be achieved unless the operations of a legal system (or of any system of governance) occur within space and time. That is, the philosopher's arguments are not focusing on a thoroughly unavoidable property; they are not focusing on some property that is insusceptible to being altered by anyone's efforts. They are adverting to some scalar properties that might or might not be present at sufficiently high levels to enable the effects under consideration.

Contrariwise, when proponents of the Authoritativeness Doctrine affirm that the moral authority of any legal regime hinges partly on the strong observational mind-independence of its requirements and authorizations, they are focusing on a nonscalar property. That property of strong observational mind-independence is a given and is therefore not an object of pursuit. Officials' endeavors cannot alter even slightly the extent to which that property is applicable to the norms of their regime, for it is always applicable *tout court* rather than to varying degrees. It is a thoroughly unavoidable feature of any system of governance, just like the property of being located in space and time. Accordingly, although the

Authoritativeness Doctrine is true, it is uninteresting and misleading. We can just as well maintain that the iniquity or the inefficiency or the Islamic character of a legal regime hinges partly on the strong observational mind-independence of the regime's requirements and authorizations. Each of those claims would be true, and each would be uninteresting and highly misleading. Since the norms of a legal regime (or, indeed, of any system of governance) are always strongly mind-independent observationally, any quality of a legal regime whatsoever will hinge partly on the strong observational mind-independence of those norms; no quality of a legal system can be present unless such a system itself exists, and no such system can exist without norms that are strongly mind-independent observationally. Singling out some quality such as moral authoritativeness is arbitrary.

Though the Authoritativeness Doctrine presents itself as an insight into law's moral authority, its only informative message is a regrettably skewed reiteration of my first chapter's conclusions about law's observational mind-independence. In other words, instead of telling us anything that pertains distinctively to the potential moral authority of a legal system, that doctrine – when shorn of its misleadingness – repeats my opening chapter's verdict that laws inevitably partake of strong observational mind-independence. It adds nothing helpful to that verdict.

Seemingly in disagreement with what has been said in the last few paragraphs, many highly sophisticated legal philosophers have articulated views broadly along the lines of the Authoritativeness Doctrine. According to these philosophers, questions about the observational mind-independence of legal norms are indeed of peculiar importance for the potential moral authority of any legal system. Some of these philosophers have elaborated their positions especially with reference to the observational mind-independence of moral principles (which they take to be among the norms of some or all legal systems), but they join their fellow proponents of the Authoritativeness Doctrine in perceiving law's moral authority as distinctively reliant on the observational mind-independence of legal norms. Other eminent legal philosophers, most forcefully Jeremy Waldron, have distanced themselves from the Authoritativeness Doctrine but have marshaled arguments very different from those advanced here. Instead of disparaging the Authoritativeness Doctrine as unilluminating and tendentious (though true), they have submitted that it is false. They believe that its assertion about law's moral authority is important but unsustainable.[1]

Have all these philosophers gone astray? Insofar as any of them regard themselves as locked in a genuinely interesting debate about the connections between law's moral authority and its observational mind-independence, they are indeed laboring under a misapprehension. However, their claims and counterclaims are by no means entirely misguided. On the contrary, they are engaged in a valuable and fruitful dispute – but a dispute over the connections between law's moral authority and objectivity qua determinate correctness, rather than over the connections between law's moral authority and objectivity qua observational mind-independence. While seeming to quarrel about the Authoritativeness Doctrine, they are really quarreling about the need for a high level of determinacy in the law if a legal system is to stand any chance of being morally authoritative. They are disagreeing about the following proposition:

> **Authoritativeness-cum-Determinacy Doctrine**: No legal system can be morally authoritative unless there are determinately correct answers to a huge majority of the questions that arise under its norms.

In other words, instead of training attention on a property (observational mind-independence) that is constant and given, these philosophers are actually training their attention on a scalar property (determinacy) that is susceptible to being augmented or diminished within a system of law by the endeavors of legal officials.[2]

This book cannot recount in any detail the positions of the diverse participants in the debates under discussion. To avoid getting bogged down in matters of exposition and interpretation, my remarks here will paint with quite a broad brush by concentrating on the two principal ways in which someone might deny that legal norms are strongly mind-independent

---

[1] For some of the major contributions to the debates that have been sketched very roughly in this paragraph, see Coleman 1995, 46–47, 60–61; Coleman and Leiter 1995, 244–47; Moore 1982, 1063–71; 1992, 2447–91; Rosati 2004, 309–13; Waldron 1992.

[2] For a valuable discussion of the relationships between law's potential moral authority and its determinacy, see Coleman and Leiter 1995, 228–41. Although my approach to the issues is markedly different from that of Coleman and Leiter, I have profited from their analyses. Their emphasis on the distinction between mind-dependence and most types of indeterminacy is particularly pertinent. I shall discuss their arguments further near the end of this chapter.

observationally. As we shall see, each such denial would be unconducive to any interesting disputes over the links between law's potential moral authority and its observational mind-independence. What appear to be such disputes are really focused on links between law's potential moral authority and its determinacy.

3.3. Weak Observational Mind-Independence?

As has been indicated, the Authoritativeness Doctrine asserts that the strong observational mind-independence of legal norms is necessary for the moral authority of any system of law. One way in which somebody might seek to impugn the strong observational mind-independence of legal norms is to contend that that observational mind-independence is weak rather than strong. Such is the tack pursued by Andrei Marmor, for example, as we have beheld in Chapter 1 (Section 1.2.1). Now, although I have endeavored to demonstrate that Marmor's view of the matter is mistaken, his view is hardly unworthy of serious consideration. It has enticed many sophisticated philosophers, including Marmor himself. At any rate, my present discussion is not aiming to dismiss his position or to rebut it afresh. Rather, what we need to ascertain here is whether any implications for the moral authority of legal regimes would be at stake in a choice between Marmor's position and my own – that is, in a choice between an insistence on the weak observational mind-independence of laws and an insistence on their strong observational mind-independence.

Modified to fit with Marmor's perspective, the Authoritativeness Doctrine would become the following proposition:

> **Weak Authoritativeness Doctrine**: The weak observational mind-independence of legal norms is necessary for the moral authority of any system of law.

Obviously, the modified version of the Authoritativeness Doctrine lays down a condition for law's moral authority that is in some sense less robust than the condition laid down by my own version (which has been stated in the preceding paragraph). However, the question here is not whether the two renderings of that doctrine are equivalent, but whether the contrast between them makes any difference to law's potential moral authority. A negative answer to that latter question is warranted, for, although the contrast between the two renderings is of philosophical importance, it is not of practical significance. Its implications for the status of any particular legal regime – as morally authoritative or not – are nil.

What does have a crucial bearing on the matter of moral authority is the point that is common to my version and Marmor's version of the Authoritativeness Doctrine. Both Marmor and I reject the notion that legal norms are strongly mind-dependent observationally. In other words, both of us reject the notion that the content and implications of each legal norm are perforce what they are taken to be by any observer (namely, by any official or citizen who reflects on the nature of the norm). That shared rejection of strong observational mind-dependence can be conveyed by yet another rendering of the Authoritativeness Doctrine:

> **Hybrid Authoritativeness Doctrine**: No legal system can be morally authoritative unless its mandates and other norms are observationally mind-independent either strongly or weakly.

Were legal norms devoid of observational mind-independence, everyone's views about their contents and implications would be determinative of what those contents and implications are. Such views would be analogous to people's opinions concerning the tastiness of cauliflower, or to a judgment by somebody that he is currently experiencing pain in his left foot. No such weirdly fractionated state of affairs could form the basis for a morally authoritative system of law. Unlike an experience of pain in one's left foot, the contents and implications of legal norms are not radically subjective. Those norms could not satisfactorily perform some of their roles – especially their role in setting authoritative standards for human interaction that serve as justificatory bases for decisions whereby officials resolve disputes or authorize the imposition of penalties – if their contents and implications were determined by each person's beliefs about them. Whether or not some particular legal norm is uniformly applicable in all the ways discussed in Section 1.2.3, the strong observational mind-dependence of its content and implications would effectively undo its capacity to function as a legal norm. Thoroughly undermined would be its capacity to function authoritatively.

We shall presently consider further the proposition that the contents and implications of legal norms are strongly mind-dependent observationally. In particular, we shall explore exactly why the falsity of that proposition has an important bearing on the potential moral authority of legal regimes. For the moment, we should simply note that a repudiation of that proposition is common to Marmor and me. Hence, if there is any morally/politically pregnant dissimilarity between the Weak Authoritativeness Doctrine associated with his account of law's observational mind-independence and the Authoritativeness Doctrine associated with my account, it must pertain to something other than the matter of strong observational mind-dependence. Specifically, it will have to pertain to the difference between strong observational mind-*in*dependence and weak observational mind-independence. Yet, unlike the matter of strong observational mind-dependence, the difference just mentioned is of purely philosophical importance rather than of moral/political importance. It bears crucially on the aim of coming up with a correct philosophical account of the ontological status of legal norms and their contents, but it does not impinge on any regime's actual or potential moral authority.

My discussion of law's observational mind-independence has maintained that legal officials can collectively be in error when they seek to apprehend the contents and implications of the laws which they themselves have collectively brought forth as such. If they do collectively misunderstand any of those contents and implications when arriving at certain decisions, they will unwittingly have departed from the law's prescriptions instead of giving effect thereto. Unless such a collective error is quickly corrected, it will enter into the law and thereby alter what the law has been. An alteration of that sort might be extremely narrow, but, if the precedential force of an erroneous decision or of its rationale is ample in scope, the alteration might encompass a significant part of some area of the law.

Undoubtedly, Marmor tells a different story. He asserts that legal-governmental officials cannot collectively be mistaken when they sincerely expound the contents and implications of the norms in their system of law, and he therefore leaves no room for the unwitting alterations that have just been described. He can of course allow that the officials collectively might on some occasion deliberately distort the law's requirements or authorizations, but he explicitly denies that their honest collective efforts to ferret out the contents and implications of their regime's laws can land them in error. Individual officials can stumble in their interpretations of laws, Marmor concedes, but the officials together as an organized group cannot. Thus, he does not feel any need to explain how the officials' collective mistakes about the meanings and applications of legal norms can become incorporated into the law. In his eyes, there are no such mistakes. If the officials collectively believe that a certain legal norm requires a certain conclusion, then *ipso facto* the norm does indeed require that conclusion.

In sum, the distinction between Marmor's account and mine is centered on situations in which legal officials collectively interpret laws in ways that would be branded as erroneous by my account. Under Marmor's account, those interpretations and the decisions based upon them would be instances of law-application rather than instances of law-alteration. Now, clearly, this divergence between the two accounts is philosophically significant. As has been argued in Section 1.2.1, proper attentiveness to the division between first-order beliefs and second-order beliefs can reveal the untenability of Marmor's position. However, we are addressing ourselves here to moral/political considerations rather than to philosophical significance. Does anything of moral/political weightiness hinge on the competing characterizations of what the officials have done in the circumstances envisaged? Will the difference between those characterizations have any nontrivial bearing on the moral authoritativeness of legal regimes?

A bit of reflection should indicate that the answer to each of these questions is negative. Let us begin by noting two small but not insignificant points. As was avouched in Chapter 1's original discussion of this matter, there are solid grounds for thinking that collective errors of legal interpretation on the part of legal officials will be rare. Although legal officials are not collectively infallible, their knowledgeable familiarity with the products of their own endeavors will help to ensure that they do not often collectively go astray in their interpretations. In easy cases involving straightforwardly classifiable modes of conduct – that is, in the large majority of the cases handled by adjudicative and administrative officials within any functional legal system – the officials will collectively keep one another on track. Only in a subset of hard cases (which, despite their occasional prominence, are far fewer in number than easy cases) will the officials be prone to blunder collectively when they apprehend the contents and implications of the laws of their regime. Furthermore, even on the infrequent occasions when the officials do collectively stumble in matters of legal interpretation, their missteps will not always be for the worse. Since those missteps will occur in difficult cases, their dashing of legitimate expectations will typically be minimal; after all, such cases center on controversial questions that normally thwart the formation of solid expectations by giving rise to many differences of opinion and considerable uncertainty among the sundry people involved. On the substance of the matters in relation to which the officials stumble, at least some of their misinterpretations might enhance the law instead of detracting from it. There is no reason to assume beforehand that their collective misconstruals of the contents and implications of legal norms will invariably worsen the moral tenor of their regime's law.

More important, nothing of moral/political weightiness will turn on the question whether legal officials' collective misinterpretations are to be classified by any jurisprudential theory as misinterpretations or not. As has been stated, the collective misinterpretations will enter into the law of the relevant jurisdiction unless they are quickly perceived as mistaken and are disowned. The fact that they were inaccurate does not necessarily mean that they will ever be queried and dislodged. All the same, they might indeed at some later juncture be reversed. Perhaps their erroneousness will eventually be recognized, but perhaps instead – and more likely – they will be regarded as objectionable on some other grounds. In any case of the latter sort, where what is actually a misunderstanding of some legal norm is regarded as interpretively correct but condemnable on some other ground, the elimination of that misunderstanding from the law will be construed by officials as a deliberate change in the norm that has been misunderstood. In other words, any collective error of interpretation committed by legal officials in the course of their law-applying activities will be subject to reversal even if its nature as an interpretive error goes forever unglimpsed. (Of course, if the legal norm that has been misunderstood is a statute or a constitutional provision, adjudicators and administrators will not be individually or collectively authorized to alter the wording of the formulation of the norm. However, they can appeal to the spirit of the norm in order to up-date the implications of its formulation. Such a tack would not – or would not perforce – involve any recognition of the erroneousness of the way in which the norm has been interpreted in the past.)

Suppose that Marmor were correct in his ascription of collective infallibility to legal officials. Would the susceptibility of officials' decisions to reversal or modification be any different from what has been described in the preceding paragraph? For two reasons, the answer to this question is negative; and therefore the answer to each of the questions in the antepenultimate paragraph above is also negative, since nothing other than this matter of the displaceability of officials' decisions could distinguish my own account of law's observational mind-independence from Marmor's account in a way that bears on the moral authority of legal systems.

In the first place, as has just been remarked, officials' collective determinations can subsequently be dislodged even if they are never perceived as interpretively mistaken. If legal officials collectively arrive at the view that some interpretation of a law should be modified or set aside even though it was correct when it was originally advanced, their abandonment of their past position does not involve any attribution of exegetical incorrectness to that past position. Thus, if Marmor were right about legal officials' collective infallibility, and if the officials themselves shared his belief on that point, they could nonetheless proceed to undo their past understandings of the contents and implications of various legal norms. Departures from those erstwhile understandings would not have to be presented and justified as rectifications of blunders. They could be presented and justified perfectly well as adaptations to new circumstances; the erstwhile understandings could still be perceived as correct for the time when they prevailed, even though the officials might all now accept that that time has passed.

In the second place, even if Marmor were indeed right about officials' collective infallibility, the officials in any particular legal regime might not subscribe to his view of the matter. Judges and other legal officials typically exhibit virtually no interest, and even less proficiency, in philosophical argumentation. Whether or not they are collectively infallible when addressing problems of legal interpretation, their expertise in addressing philosophical problems is decidedly imperfect. Consequently, the likelihood of their aligning themselves with Marmor will be largely unaffected by the truth or falsity of his claims. In any particular legal system, the officials might well be inclined to conclude that some past interpretation of a legal norm was erroneous notwithstanding that that interpretation was collectively upheld at the time by them or their predecessors. Their inclination will withstand any arguments by Marmor or other philosophers who endeavor to show that the officials' interpretive activities cannot in fact go astray. Judges and other legal officials will blithely ignore those arguments, just as they ignore philosophical disputation generally. Although the officials in some regime might ascribe infallibility to themselves collectively in matters of legal interpretation, their doing so will almost certainly derive from grandiose self-importance – or from pseudo-philosophical dogmas – rather than from philosophical acumen. Any such reflexive ascription of collective infallibility on the part of the officials, like a contrary inclination on their part to brand some of their past interpretations as missteps, will generally be reached independently of the competing merits of arguments propounded by full-blown philosophers.

Hence, even if Marmor's arguments were cogent, they would not in themselves provide any grounds for thinking that legal officials will be undisposed to reverse certain past rulings as collective blunders. The philosophical point of contention between Marmor and me is separate from the question whether legal officials will believe themselves to be collectively infallible or not. While the moral authority of a legal system may depend on the readiness of the system's officials to repudiate certain past rulings as mistakes that should be acknowledged and rectified, such readiness can be present irrespective of how the aforementioned philosophical point of contention is resolved. (As has been noted in Chapter 1, incidentally, Marmor cannot coherently account for a situation wherein legal officials do collectively maintain at some time t_2 that they have erred at some earlier juncture t_1. If he insists that they were collectively infallible at t_1, then he will in effect be avowing that they are in error about a matter of legal interpretation at t_2. Contrariwise, if he insists that they are collectively infallible at t_2, he will in effect be avowing that they were in error about a matter of legal interpretation at t_1. Although the general question whether legal officials can collectively go astray in their activities of legal interpretation is a philosophical problem, any specific question about the correctness of a certain interpretation of some law at t_1 and

about the consequent import of that law at t_2 is a matter of legal exegesis –
a matter in regard to which the relevant officials are collectively beyond
error, according to Marmor. He will therefore not be able to dodge the
paradox posed for him by the scenario of the clashing interpretations at
t_1 and t_2.)

In short, as has been stated, the pregnant philosophical difference
between my own account of law's observational mind-independence and
Marmor's account does not impinge in any nontrivial way on the potential moral authority of legal systems. If his account were correct, and if the
Weak Authoritativeness Doctrine associated with his account were consequently to be preferred to the Authoritativeness Doctrine associated with
mine, any apposite judgments about the moral authority of various legal
regimes would remain unaffected. In other words, there is no practical
difference between my Authoritativeness Doctrine – which asserts that no
legal regime can be morally authoritative unless the observational mind-
independence of its norms is strong – and the Hybrid Authoritativeness
Doctrine, which asserts that no legal regime can be morally authoritative
unless its norms are observationally mind-independent either strongly
or weakly. Neither my version nor the hybrid version of the Authoritativeness Doctrine is helpfully illuminating, but each is true.

3.4. Strong Observational Mind-Dependence and Indeterminacy

If we want to find any practical differences, we shall have to look again at
the proposition which Marmor and I are united in rejecting: the proposition that the observational mind-dependence of legal norms is strong.
As has already been indicated, the falsity of that proposition is essential
for the moral authority of any system of law. Strong observational mind-
dependence would be inconsistent with any such authority. However,
when one examines the matter a bit more deeply, one discovers that the
real danger to the moral authority of law is posed by rampant indeterminacy. Only because the strong observational mind-dependence of legal
norms would involve such indeterminacy, should we regard it as problematic on moral/political grounds. By concentrating on mind-dependence

rather than on indeterminacy, the Authoritativeness Doctrine is imprecise and misleading. It does not pinpoint the problem to which it rightly
seeks to draw attention.

As was remarked earlier, the strong observational mind-dependence
of legal norms would consist in a crazily fractionated state of affairs where
everyone's perceptions of the contents and implications of laws would be
dispositive of what those contents and implications are. Consider what
such a bizarrely subjectivist state of affairs could be like. If Jeff believes
that a particular legal norm entails some conclusion X in certain circumstances, then the norm in those circumstances does entail that conclusion
(for him). Simultaneously, if Jane believes that the norm entails a contrary
conclusion Y in the specified circumstances, then the norm in those circumstances does entail that contrary conclusion (for her). And so forth.
When the criterion for the correctness of each person's beliefs about the
contents and implications of laws is satisfied simply by each person's
harboring of those beliefs, the substance of any law can be incoherently
multifarious and fragmented. Although there might be unanimity on the
implications of this or that law in application to certain types of situations, such unanimity will be rare – any sizable society will contain at
least a few daft mavericks – and it is never guaranteed. It always can be
accompanied, and almost always will be accompanied, by disaccord on
countless other points of interpretation. On some of those points, indeed,
the disaccord will take the form of a huge jumble of conflicting opinions.
Hence, the contents of legal norms will not exist univocally. Rather, the
content of each such norm will actually or potentially be divided against
itself, sometimes in a bewilderingly heterogeneous medley of incompatible renderings.

To see that the principal problem under discussion is that of indeterminacy, we should first note how it differs from a lack of transindividual
discernibility, and we should then take account of its potential emergence
notwithstanding the strong observational mind-independence of legal
norms. Like determinacy and unlike observational mind-independence,
transindividual discernibility is a scalar property. The contents and implications of legal norms can be transindividually discernible to varying
degrees, just as they can be determinate to greater or lesser extents. Despite
that important similarity, however, the situation described in the last
paragraph is not equivalent to a situation in which the transindividual

discernibility of the contents and implications of legal norms has disappeared. For one thing, although unanimity in the interpretation of any legal norm is seldom attainable within a sizable society, a very high degree of transindividual discernibility in the interpretation of many aspects of most legal norms is usually present. Most cases in any functional legal system are easy cases. What is necessary for their easiness is not that everyone would agree on the answers to the questions which they pose, but that the large majority of people would agree on those answers. Nothing in the preceding paragraph is meant to suggest that the requisite degree of convergence will generally be missing. Some matters of legal interpretation in any regime are vexingly difficult and controversial, but most such matters are straightforward and even routine. Though *complete* uniformity among people's actual or likely responses to such matters (even routine matters) is typically unrealizable, an ample measure of uniformity among those responses on most issues of legal exegesis is perfectly realistic. When the foregoing paragraph has maintained that the strong observational mind-dependence of legal norms' contents would fragment those contents and deprive them of their univocality, it has not been implying that the fragmentedness would derive from widespread disagreements among people about those contents. The fragmentedness would be ontological rather than epistemic; that is, it would pertain to the character of the contents' existence rather than to the character of people's knowledge. Regardless of the degree of convergence or divergence among people concerning questions of legal interpretation, the contents of legal norms – around which the convergence or divergence occurs – would be radically subjective if their observational mind-dependence were strong. Being relative to the outlook of every observer, each of those contents would have no overarching grip even if most people concurred in specifying what each of those contents is.

Whereas the disjointedness of a situation marked by strong observational mind-dependence is ontological, the disjointedness of a situation marked by a lack of transindividual discernibility is epistemic. We shall return in a moment to the fact that the former type of disjointedness can obtain without the latter. Let us pause briefly to note here that the latter type of disjointedness can likewise obtain without the former. Chapter 1's discussion of transindividual discernibility has, indeed, made precisely this point. Objectivity qua transindividual discernibility resides in the tendency of people to converge in their beliefs and convictions. That tendency can be absent or meager in relation to matters whose observational mind-independence is unquestionably strong. My earlier discussion referred to the problems of cosmology, which focus on phenomena that are paradigmatically endowed with strong observational mind-independence. On many points, the problems of cosmology have elicited far more disagreement than agreement. Epistemically, then, the current state of affairs concerning many of those problems is a state of fragmentedness. Transindividual discernibility is in short supply. Ontologically, however, there is no fragmentedness; the nature of any cosmological phenomenon is certainly not radically subjective.

More important for our present enquiry is that a high level of transindividual discernibility can coexist with the ontological splinteredness that ensues from strong observational mind-dependence. If the contents of legal norms partook of such mind-dependence, they would be thoroughly subjective regardless of whether people might converge in their identifications of those contents or not. Hence, the inconsistency between the strong observational mind-dependence of legal norms and the moral authoritativeness of legal systems does not derive from epistemic considerations. More specifically, it does not derive from any ineluctably negative effect of such mind-dependence on the ability of people to concur with one another in their interpretations of legal norms. On the one hand, a substantial degree of convergence among legal officials and other legal experts in most such interpretations is essential for the functionality of a legal regime; without that degree of convergence, the role of law in guiding and coordinating people's behavior could not be performed. Such interpretive uniformity is therefore obviously essential for the moral authority of any legal regime. A nonfunctional system of law is hardly a morally authoritative system. Thus, if the strong observational mind-dependence of legal norms were incompatible with the requisite degree of interpretive convergence, that incompatibility would itself be sufficient to establish that such mind-dependence is inimical to the moral authority of law. On the other hand, however, there is no such inevitable incompatibility. People's interpretations of just about any legal norm might well converge significantly – at least among the legal officials and other legal experts whose opinions matter – even if the only touchstone for the correctness of each individual's interpretation were the sheer fact that that individual believes it to be true. Consequently, if we wish to pin down why the strong observational mind-dependence of legal norms would undermine the moral authority of every legal regime, we shall have to look elsewhere. Such mind-dependence is not equivalent to, or necessarily promotive of, a dearth of transindividual discernibility. Hence, a concentration on the absence of transindividual discernibility would not enable us to fathom what we are seeking to fathom.

Instead, the inconsistency between the strong observational mind-dependence of laws and the moral authoritativeness of legal systems is due to the indeterminacy that would be entailed by such mind-dependence. That thoroughgoing indeterminacy would be a lack of ontological objectivity rather than a lack of epistemic objectivity (though of course it might be accompanied by a dearth of epistemic objectivity). People's understandings of the content and implications of each legal norm might largely tally with one another, but the content and implications themselves would be devoid of any univocal existence. For each person, there would be no answer – apart from a circularly vacuous answer – to the question how he or she should construe the content and implications of any particular legal norm. Any understanding at which he or she arrives would be correct by dint of his or her having arrived at it. In other words, the content of each law would not serve to constrain at all the range of ways in which somebody could correctly perceive that content. Rather, for each person, the content would be entirely derivative of the way in which he or she perceives it. Because the substance of every legal norm would lack any ontological independence, no construal of the content and implications of any law by any person would ever be better – as a sheer matter of interpretation – than any other construal. No person could ever err by expounding the content and implications of some law in one way rather than another. If a person were to decide that some law carries some implication X in a certain context, then *ipso facto* the law in question would carry that implication in such a context (in relation to that person). If the person were then to change his mind and decide that the law instead carries some contrary implication Y in the specified context, then *ipso facto* the law in question would carry that implication (in relation to that person). Accordingly, the substance of every legal norm would perpetually remain indeterminate. Because no construal of that substance would be exegetically better than any other, no construal would be determinately correct. When there is no such thing as an interpretive misjudgment – when no conceivable interpretive judgment is disallowed as incorrect – there is no such thing as a *determinately* correct interpretation.

In sum, the strong observational mind-dependence of legal norms would render the law completely indeterminate. To say as much, however, is not yet to substantiate my earlier pejorative remarks about the Authoritativeness Doctrine. Nor have we yet seen exactly why the indeterminacy ensuing from the strong observational mind-dependence of legal norms would be fatal to the moral authority of law. Let us take up each of these two points in turn.

3.5. Other Types of Indeterminacy

We should assume for the moment that rampant indeterminacy is indeed incompatible with law's moral authoritativeness. (I will shortly endeavor to show why an assumption along those lines is sound.) Given that we have found that the strong observational mind-dependence of legal norms would involve rampant indeterminacy, my discussion may appear to have vindicated the Authoritativeness Doctrine. All along, however, the truth of the Authoritativeness Doctrine has not been under challenge in any way. Rather, what has been in doubt is the illuminatingness of that doctrine. It is unilluminating chiefly because it is damagingly imprecise. By characterizing the threat to law's moral authority as an absence of observational mind-independence, the Authoritativeness Doctrine tends to obscure the fact that the real danger is posed by an absence of determinacy (or a severe paucity of determinacy). Of course, as we have seen, an absence of observational mind-independence entails an absence of determinacy. If the contents and implications of legal norms were strongly mind-dependent observationally, then there would be no determinately correct answers to any substantive questions about the ways in which those norms should be construed. Nonetheless, although strong observational mind-dependence does entail thorough indeterminacy, there is no entailment in the other direction. Indeterminacy can be rampant even though the observational mind-independence of legal norms is strong; and the indeterminacy is no less problematic than it would be if it were due to the strong observational mind-dependence of laws.

Suppose that a regime has violated Fuller's third principle of legality, the principle of perspicuity, to such an extent as to render indeterminate the contents and implications of all or nearly all the regime's norms. The formulations of those norms are unintelligibly obscure gobbledygook. Of course, given what has been argued in Chapter 2, we can know that these large-scale contraventions of the principle of perspicuity will deprive the regime of its status as a legal regime. *A fortiori*, then, they will exclude it from being a morally authoritative legal regime. Still, the principal point at the moment is simply to apprehend the fundamental affinity between the indeterminacy that is present in this situation and the indeterminacy that would be present if legal norms were strongly mind-dependent observationally.

In one respect, there is a difference between the two situations of indeterminacy; however, that difference will turn out to be unimportant, at least in connection with the moral authority of law. If legal norms were strongly mind-dependent observationally, then the condition for the correctness of any interpretation of a legal norm would be the sheer fact that somebody has arrived at that interpretation. By contrast, in a situation of indeterminacy occasioned by a regime's comprehensive violations of the Fullerian principle of perspicuity, there is no criterion for the correctness of any interpretations of the regime's norms. Conversely, there is no criterion for the *in*correctness of any such interpretations. Purely as an exegetical matter, every construal of any of the regime's norms in such a situation would be no better and no worse than any other construal. Every interpretation would be correct in the sense of not being incorrect. In other words, the upshot of such a situation would be the same as that of a situation marked by the strong observational mind-dependence of legal norms. Notwithstanding that the latter state of affairs would involve a radically subjective criterion for correctness whereas the former state of affairs would involve no criterion for correctness or incorrectness at all, the result in each case would be the absence of any grounds for deeming anyone's construals of a regime's norms to be incorrect. That is, the result would be the thoroughgoing exegetical parity of all interpretations of those norms. No interpretation could ever be disallowed as inaccurate or expositorily inferior, since there would be no basis for any such disallowance.

At the practical level where interpretations of norms are to be assessed and adopted, then, the indeterminacy owing to the strong observational mind-dependence of legal norms and the indeterminacy owing to the utter unclarity of legal norms are indistinguishably corrosive. Each type of blanket indeterminacy consists in interpretive indiscriminateness; each type elides the distinction between sound and unsound understandings of norms. Exactly because of that key affinity between the two types of indeterminacy, each of them is inimical to the moral authority of a legal regime. Consequently, by concentrating solely on the matter of mind-dependence, the Authoritativeness Doctrine obfuscates the nature of the problem which it addresses.

The shortcomings of the Authoritativeness Doctrine become further evident when we take account of another type of sweeping indeterminacy that could afflict and subvert a legal system: the sweeping indeterminacy induced by a regime's wide-ranging violations of the fifth Fullerian principle of legality, which proscribes contradictoriness (and also conflict-ingness). As was discussed in Chapter 2, pervasive contradictions within the normative matrix of some system of governance would rack the system with indeterminacy. To every question whether any particular mode of conduct is permissible or impermissible, there would be no determinately correct answer. A reply affirming the permissibility of the specified mode of conduct would – as an exposition of the law – be no worse and no better than a reply denying the conduct's permissibility. Similarly, to every question whether some particular course of action is efficacious or inefficacious as an exercise of a certain legal power, there would be no determinately correct answer. No worse and no better than a reply affirming the efficacy of the course of action as an exercise of the specified power would be a reply gainsaying its efficacy. Neither "yes" nor "no" in response to any such question would be incorrect, and therefore neither of those answers would be determinately correct.

This latest type of indeterminacy is different in one notable respect from the other two types that have been recounted here. Each of those other types has stemmed from the lack of any objective standards for distinguishing between accurate and inaccurate interpretations of legal norms. When indeterminacy has been engendered by rampant contradictions within the authoritative materials of a system of governance, the content of each norm in itself is not unsettled. Within that system, a norm that confers a liberty to do X is straightforwardly determinate in its content and implications, as is a norm that imposes a duty to abstain from doing X. Indeterminacy arises from the coexistence of those two norms and from the coexistence of countless other pairs of contradictory norms. That is, the indeterminacy pertains not to the implications of each contradictory norm taken by itself, but to the implications of each pair of contradictory norms taken together. Because the hypothesized system of governance comprises a myriad of such pairs, and because the contradictoriness of each pair precludes any determinately correct answer to the question addressed by each norm within the pair, the system yields no determinately correct outcomes. It generates no determinately correct answers to questions about the ways in which its norms bear on any concrete circumstances. To every such question an affirmative answer is no better and no worse than a negative answer, for each of those answers is prescribed by a law in contradictory coexistence with a law that prescribes the other answer.

Once again, however, the divergences between different kinds of indeterminacy are greatly exceeded in importance by the affinities between them. Although pervasive contradictions within a legal system's normative matrix do not result in interpretive indeterminacy, they do result in wholesale indeterminacy at the level of outcomes. Yet that level is also where the other types of indeterminacy wreak their devastating effects. Exactly because interpretive indeterminacy entails indeterminacy at the level of outcomes – the level at which a legal system manifests itself in the world beyond the system's own workings – it is subversive of the moral authority and the very existence of a legal regime. We shall miss this point if we follow the Authoritativeness Doctrine in focusing solely on the indeterminacy that would ensue from the strong observational mind-dependence of legal norms. Instead of adopting that focus, we should concentrate on what is common to the three types of indeterminacy that have been broached here. Common to them, and at the heart of their shared perniciousness, are their effects on the "bottom line" of concrete decision-making in the operations of an ostensible legal system.

They do not prevent the reaching of decisions, of course, but they prevent the reaching of decisions that are genuinely and univocally justifiable by reference to the system's norms.

3.6. Why Is Rampant Indeterminacy Destructive of Moral Authority?

We now need to ponder more closely why arrant indeterminacy – whatever its source – would indeed undermine any legal regime's moral authoritativeness. One obvious point, of course, is that such indeterminacy negates the status of a legal regime as such. If there is no legal system in existence within some territory, then patently there is no morally authoritative legal system within that territory. Such an observation is only the starting point of an adequate analysis, however. What should be pinned down (or, for the most part, recalled from Chapter 2) are the exact respects in which wholesale indeterminacy is at odds with the existence of a legal regime. We shall then be in a position to grasp the destructive impact of such indeterminacy on law's moral authority.

As was emphasized throughout Chapter 2, the central function of law is to direct and coordinate the behavior of countless individuals and groups. The first main respect in which rampant indeterminacy is pernicious, then, is that it tends to thwart the performance of that cardinal function. Here we need to differentiate between the indeterminacy due to strong observational mind-dependence and the other two types of indeterminacy. Suppose for a moment that the observational mind-dependence of legal norms were strong. Those norms' contents and implications would therefore be entirely determined by the interpretive judgments of each person who construes them. Even so, those judgments among various people might very well exhibit an extremely high degree of convergence, in most contexts. (As will be recalled, objectivity qua transindividual discernibility can prevail in the absence of objectivity qua mind-independence and in the absence of objectivity qua determinate correctness.) Moreover, the people who interpret the norms might not be attuned at all to the norms' strong observational mind-dependence. They might very well take themselves to be ascertaining, rather than determining, the contents and implications of the norms.

Each person in most contexts would expect others similarly to view the processes of legal interpretation as an enterprise of discovery rather than of creation. In these circumstances, the guiding and coordinating role of a legal system would not be going unfulfilled. Such circumstances, furthermore, are perfectly credible (if one temporarily accepts, for the sake of argument, the incredible notion that legal norms lack any observational mind-independence). Hence, there are no cogent grounds for thinking that the strong observational mind-dependence of legal norms would be likely to impair the performance of the guiding and coordinating role just mentioned. Consequently, if we train our attention solely on the indeterminacy arising from such mind-dependence, we shall miss the full import of indeterminacy as a general phenomenon. One of the many shortcomings of the Authoritativeness Doctrine is that it encourages just such a narrow focus.

Indeterminacy arising from pervasive unintelligibility and indeterminacy arising from profuse contradictions are much more damaging to the paramount function of law. To be sure, because of the distinction between indeterminacy and unpredictability, there is no absolutely inevitable inconsistency between either of those types of indeterminacy and the ability of authoritative norms to direct people's behavior. In particular, as was remarked in my discussion of the matter in Chapter 2, the tendencies of governmental officials to select between contradictory norms may be sufficiently conspicuous and patterned to be amply predictable. In that event, the sweeping indeterminacy occasioned by contradictions that permeate the normative structure of some system of governance will not preclude the system from guiding and channeling people's conduct along certain paths. Still, although such a state of affairs is manifestly possible, it is not probable. Far more likely is that the system's normative structure will bewilder people and leave them groping for appropriate courses of conduct. Even more plainly at odds with the directing function of law would be a system of governance with norms that are all opaquely incomprehensible. People can scarcely receive guidance from norms if they and the experts who advise them do not know what any of those norms mean.

In short, the pervasive obscurity or incoherence of the norms established by some system of governance would almost certainly frustrate the fulfillment of the central role of law. Accordingly, the indeterminacy bred by the wide-ranging obscurity or incoherence would almost certainly be fatal to the operativeness of a legal system as such. It would therefore be fatal to the attainment of the desiderata that cannot be adequately realized in the absence of such a system. Given that the capacity of a legal system to secure those desiderata is a necessary condition for the system's moral authority, the indeterminacy just mentioned is inimical to such authority. Although the indeterminacy associated with the strong observational mind-dependence of legal norms would not in itself threaten the capacity of law to guide people's doings, the other types of indeterminacy under consideration here would indeed produce such an effect. Thus, instead of championing the Authoritativeness Doctrine, one should champion an otherwise similar thesis – the Authoritativeness-cum-Determinacy Doctrine – that is focused on indeterminacy in all its forms rather than just on strong mind-dependence.

A second pernicious aspect of wholesale indeterminacy is even more important, because it extends to all three types of indeterminacy. When legal norms are determinate in their substance and implications, they can serve as bases for the justification of decisions that are reached by reference to them. They can accurately be invoked as standards of conduct that univocally require those decisions. To be sure, the capacity of legal norms to serve as justificatory touchstones does not per se suffice for their possession of any moral authority. If the substance of some law L is iniquitous, and if the decisions required under the terms of L are correspondingly heinous, then L is devoid of moral authority – regardless of the fact that it obtains as a legally dispositive standard of conduct which determinately calls for particular outcomes in any number of circumstances. Still, although the operativeness of a legal norm as a basis for officials' decisions is by no means a sufficient condition for the moral authority of the norm, it is a necessary condition. If a legal norm is engulfed by indeterminacy and is consequently unable to justify any outcomes legally, it will not be able to justify any outcomes morally. If a system of governance teems with such norms, it will not partake of any affirmative moral leverage. (Of course, when indeterminacy is due to a contradiction between legal norms, one of the norms in any contradictory pair might be a benevolent standard that clashes with a malign standard. For example, a law that imposes a duty on each person to abstain from murdering his or her fellow human beings might be contradicted by a law that bestows a liberty on each person to commit murders. In such a case, the benevolent law *BL* coincides in content with a correct principle of morality. That moral principle is, of course, able to justify outcomes morally. However, *BL* itself, despite its admirable content, is not similarly possessed of moral justificatory power. After all, it is contradicted by another law, which countenances murder; yet *BL* as a legal norm is morally authoritative only if its legally determinative force is not completely offset by another legal norm that calls decisively for outcomes contradictory to those required under the terms of *BL*. A commendable legal norm derives its moral authority – insofar as it possesses moral authority – not only from its content but also from its dispositive sway in the system of law to which it belongs. If its sway is locked in a contradiction with the sway of another law, then its dispositiveness is lost, and its moral authority is therefore vitiated.)

Given that no legal norm can be morally authoritative if it cannot operate as a justificatory basis for officials' decisions, we need to investigate whether any such norm can operate as a justificatory basis if it is encompassed by arrant indeterminacy. As should be evident, the answer to this question – for each of the three types of indeterminacy – will prove to be negative. Let us start with the indeterminacy that would ensue from the strong observational mind-dependence of legal norms. As we have seen, such indeterminacy would consist in the radical subjectivity of the contents and implications of those norms. Each person's understanding of a law's bearing on any particular situation would be correct (for that person) simply by dint of being his or her understanding of the matter. As a consequence, no law could ever serve as an independent justificatory basis for any official decisions. Until an official reaches a judgment about the application of some legal norm to any set of facts, the norm itself would have no bearing on those facts (for that official). If the official decides that the norm in question requires a verdict in one direction, then *ipso facto* the norm would indeed require just such a verdict. If the official decides instead that the norm requires a verdict in the opposite direction, then the norm would indeed require an outcome in that opposite direction. If contrariwise the official deems the norm to be wholly irrelevant to the set of facts which he is pondering, then the norm would indeed be beside the point. In short, instead of serving as the justificatory basis for the official's judgment, the content of any legal norm invoked by the official would be a product of that judgment. The formulation of the norm would simply be the phrasing with which the official expresses himself; it would not convey any independent prescriptive content that could serve to undergird his decision.

Hence, if legal norms were bereft of observational mind-independence, the distinction between the rule of law and the rule of men would not withstand the slightest scrutiny. Legal norms would be empty shells whose contents would be filled entirely by individuals' opinions. Moreover, since those opinions would almost certainly differ among individuals – among a few refractory individuals in clear-cut cases, and among many more individuals in difficult cases – the legal norms would almost inevitably get applied against people for whom the norms would require favorable results. In any such case, a law L would require one result from the officials who implement it and a contrary result in relation to the person(s) against whom L is implemented. Such an upshot would reflect the weirdly disjointed existence of legal norms that would follow from the radically subjective character of their contents. What should be emphasized here is the destructive effect of that disjointed existence on the moral authority of law. Since no legal norm would possess any overarching substance that transcends the opinions of each individual, no such norm could ever bindingly be applied against someone whose interpretation of its terms would not authorize such an application.

In sum, the indeterminacy associated with the strong observational mind-dependence of laws would doubly foil the moral authority of every legal system. It would prevent legal norms from ever genuinely serving as justificatory grounds for officials' adjudicative and administrative decisions, since it would render the contents of those norms entirely derivative of the decisions. Given such mind-dependence, in other words, the operations of a legal system would proceed through coercive assertions of officials' opinions rather than through applications of norms whose contents antecede and govern those assertions. In addition, the strong observational mind-dependence would strip away all moral authority from any invocation of a law against someone who dissents from the interpretation that has led to that law's being invoked against him.

The evils just recounted are not unique to the indeterminacy that would be associated with the strong observational mind-dependence of legal norms. They would likewise afflict any system of governance in which every norm or nearly every norm is bafflingly opaque (even to experts), and any system of governance in which every norm or nearly every norm is contradicted by an antithetical norm. In a regime with thoroughly unintelligible norms, the objective fact of the matter would be that those norms lack any independently meaningful contents. Because each norm would be without any such content, its substance would have to be filled in by the creative understanding of each interpreter. Since each norm itself (devoid of substance) would place no constraint on anyone's understanding, no interpretation could ever genuinely be justified by reference to it. As a matter of exegesis, each interpretation would be no worse and no better than any other. Consequently lacking in moral authority would be any application of an incomprehensible norm against somebody who disagrees with the construal of the norm that underpins the application. Although such an application might carry independent moral authority as the effectuation of a correct principle of morality, it would not carry any such authority in its status as an application of an impenetrably unclear law. Thus, without crediting in any way the notion that laws are strongly mind-dependent observationally, we find that the problems of justification arising from strong observational mind-dependence are associated as well with the comprehensive opacity of a regime's norms. In regard to those problems, the indeterminacy ensuing from the mind-dependence and the indeterminacy ensuing from the opacity are at one.

Somewhat different though essentially similar is the indeterminacy ensuing from pervasive contradictions in the normative structure of a system of governance. Here the problems of justification do not arise from the absence of any independent content in each norm of the system. Each norm is endowed with a determinate content. Rather, the problems of justification arise from the arbitrariness of any choice between each norm and the contradictory norm with which it is paired. Though the choice may be straightforward as a matter of morality – a heinous law can be in contradiction with a benign law – it is wholly arbitrary as a matter of applying the norms that are recognized as such within the system of governance. *Ex hypothesi*, each such norm N is accompanied by a norm with a content that negates N's content. Each of those norms belongs to the system as one of its purportedly dispositive standards of conduct. Thus, there is no basis within the system itself for favoring one of those norms over the other. Because of that indeterminacy, neither norm can genuinely serve as a justificatory basis for any concrete decisions. Each norm by itself calls for specific outcomes in any number of situations, but each norm as an element of a contradiction is generative of logical incoherence that does not call for any specific outcomes to the exclusion of others. Within the sway of that incoherence, every decision is as defensible as any other, and therefore no decision is determinately justifiable by reference to the norms of the system in which it is reached. Hence, by a somewhat different route, we here encounter problems of justification essentially similar to those associated with the other types of indeterminacy. Any ostensible legal system with a normative structure that is permeated by contradictions will not be able to justify any decisions determinately.

Having shifted from the Authoritativeness Doctrine's focus on observational mind-dependence to a focus on indeterminacy (including, of course, the indeterminacy entailed by the strong observational mind-dependence of legal norms), we have found that blanket indeterminacy is incompatible with the moral authority of any legal system. Indeed, it is incompatible with the very existence of a legal system. No regime with a normative structure suffused by any of the three types of indeterminacy can supply genuine legal justifications for any concrete decisions. In circumstances of pervasive indeterminacy, then, the question never arises whether the legal justifications provided by a regime are also morally authoritative justifications; there cannot be any morally authoritative legal justifications if there are no legal justifications.

3.7. Some Apparently Competing Views

My conclusions may seem at odds with those espoused by some of the other philosophers who have written on these topics. In light of the apparent clashes, this discussion will close by briefly considering whether those other philosophers have adopted any positions that really conflict with what has been said here. We shall glance first at an essay by Brian Leiter and Jules Coleman and then at an essay by Jeremy Waldron.

3.7.1. Coleman and Leiter on Indeterminacy

In a sophisticated and enlightening account of legal objectivity and determinacy, Leiter and Coleman proclaim that "[w]e have found no deep commitment of liberalism that requires determinacy." They summarize the upshot of their arguments as follows: "Liberal political theory is committed to a variety of ideals that can be confused with a commitment to determinacy. In fact, however, liberalism is not committed to determinacy in the sense of uniquely warranted outcomes. The existence of indeterminacy in adjudication, therefore, poses no substantial threat to the possibility of legitimate governance by law" (Coleman and Leiter 1995, 240–41). These pronouncements seem at first sight to be strikingly at variance with my own claims about indeterminacy. In fact, however, the inconsistencies vanish upon closer inspection.

My discussion has concentrated on situations of comprehensive indeterminacy. The indeterminacy associated with the strong observational mind-dependence of legal norms would necessarily be comprehensive, since that mind-dependence would obtain across the board if it obtained at all. Were legal norms characterized by strong observational mind-dependence, the necessary and sufficient condition for the correctness of any particular interpretation of each such norm would be the sheer fact that somebody subscribes to that interpretation. Such a criterion for correctness would govern every interpretation of every legal norm if it governed any. Hence, the indeterminacy deriving from the sway of that criterion would engulf every decision that might flow from any such interpretation. That indeterminacy is a nonscalar property; it applies in an all-or-nothing fashion. By contrast, the other two types of indeterminacy that have been under consideration here – indeterminacy due to unintelligibility and indeterminacy due to contradictions – are scalar properties. Each of them can be present in legal systems to many differing degrees. My discussion in this chapter has focused on situations in which indeterminacy of either of those scalar types is all-encompassing or nearly all-encompassing. When all or most of the norms in an ostensible legal system are indeed in the grip of indeterminacy, the system is not a genuine regime of law, and it does not partake of any moral authority.

A situation marked by indeterminacy on a much more modest scale is far less problematic. Though contradictions in the normative matrix of a legal system are always regrettable, the presence of a few contradictions in a vast array of formulated norms will not perceptibly detract from the moral stature of the regime which comprises that array. Much the same can be said about opaquely incomprehensible legal norms. A few such norms in a large legal system will not derogate from the system's moral authority to more than a trivial extent. Of course, insofar as the contradictoriness or obscurity affects more and more norms within a legal system, its impairment of the system's moral stature will become more and more significant. If the contradictoriness or obscurity becomes wide-ranging, then it will threaten the very sustainability of the system as a regime of law. Still, those severe effects will not materialize when the contradictoriness or obscurity is more narrowly confined.

Indeterminacy on a minor scale is not very problematic, whereas on a large scale it is crippling. My discussion has concentrated on the large scale not because rampant indeterminacy is a common problem, but because such a focus enables us to descry the parallels among the three kinds of indeterminacy that have been probed here. Since the indeterminacy associated with the strong observational mind-dependence of legal norms would be all-encompassing, and since the authority-subverting effects of that indeterminacy would be due to its obtaining ubiquitously rather than restrictedly, any illuminating comparison between it and the other two kinds of indeterminacy has to ponder them on a sweeping scale rather than on a modest scale. When we do consider each of those other types of indeterminacy as an unrestricted phenomenon, we discover that each of them is just as destructive of law's moral authority as is the indeterminacy associated with the strong observational mind-dependence of legal norms. This crucial homology among the three kinds of indeterminacy is not strictly denied by the Authoritativeness Doctrine, of course, but it tends to get pushed out of sight by that doctrine's preoccupation with mind-dependence. In order to highlight the aforementioned homology and in order to show that the danger posed to law's moral authority by strong observational mind-dependence is only one variety of a broader menace, my discussion has proceeded in the manner indicated.

Coleman and Leiter, by contrast, are not referring to indeterminacy as an unrestricted phenomenon. Instead of considering a fanciful scenario in which indeterminacy besets every decision or virtually every decision that is to be reached by the officials in a peculiar system of governance, they are considering the realistic hypothesis that indeterminacy will beset some of the decisions (a small proportion thereof) that are to be reached by the officials in any legal system. Though they appear to believe that the degree of indeterminacy in an ordinary legal system is more extensive

than I myself would contend, they firmly reject the skepticism of the
Critical Legal Scholars. They announce, for example, that "the arguments for indeterminacy, as usually presented, are often unconvincing
and typically overstate its scope" (Coleman and Leiter 1995, 218). Hence,
when Coleman and Leiter declare that indeterminacy does not jeopar-
dize the moral authority of a legal regime, they are not asserting anything
that is irreconcilable with my own claims about indeterminacy. The phenomenon of indeterminacy on a modest scale is indeed compatible with
the functionality and moral authority of a legal system.

Incidentally, when one seeks to understand why indeterminacy on
a modest scale is largely untroubling, one can usefully advert to the
preceding chapter's discussion of the legal validity of unenforced legal
mandates. As was noted there, persistently unenforced mandates such as
jaywalking ordinances can retain their legal validity because they exist
alongside the far more numerous legal mandates that are given effect
quite regularly. A broadly parallel point is applicable here. When most
but not quite all of the decisions to be reached by the officials within some
morally worthy legal system are determinately justifiable by reference to
the norms of the system, the overall justificatory leverage of those norms
can bestow moral bindingness on the relatively few decisions that are perforce arbitrary. Because the system does supply determinate justificatory
bases for most of its decisions, and because the presence of some degree
of indeterminacy is inevitable in any regime of law, officials' decisions
in the occasional areas of indeterminacy can partake of moral authority. Those arbitrary decisions are necessary for the sustainment of the
legal system's regulatory and policing and dispute-resolving functions
in circumstances where arbitrariness is unavoidable. Those decisions fill
in the areas of unsettledness left by the system's matrix of norms, and
they thus enable the system's morally authoritative operations to handle
matters that should not be left unaddressed. Those matters are better
handled through arbitrary decisions than not handled at all. Given that
such conundrums form only a small proportion of the problems that
confront the legal system in question, and given that no regime of law
can avoid indeterminacy altogether, the officials of the system act in a
morally legitimate and authoritative manner when they deal dispositively
with those conundrums. The general authoritativeness of their regime,
which depends crucially on the fact that most of the outcomes reached

therein are determinately justifiable by reference to the regime's norms, carries over to the officials' good-faith grappling with questions to which no answers can be determinately justified in that fashion. Indeterminacy which if pervasive would destroy a legal system's moral authority is something that can be absorbed into the system's morally authoritative workings when it is exceptional.

Also of some importance for squaring the position of Coleman and Leiter with the position taken in this chapter is that their remarks about the innocuousness of indeterminacy are focused on a species of indeterminacy different from the three that have been investigated here. That fourth type of indeterminacy is in fact the type that was principally explored in my opening chapter's discussion of determinate correctness. What Leiter and Coleman have in mind are situations in which determinately correct answers to pivotal legal questions are altogether absent because of incommensurability or vagueness or evenly balanced countervailing considerations. Now, on the one hand, if the indeterminacy due to any of those factors were to pervade a legal system, it would be nearly as problematic as the other three kinds of indeterminacy that have been highlighted in this chapter. If no questions or hardly any questions about the legal consequences of people's conduct within some jurisdiction were determinately answerable, then the resultant arbitrariness would deprive the jurisdiction's regime of any moral authority. Were the adjudicative and administrative rulings by the jurisdiction's officials always or almost always arbitrary rather than just occasionally so, their regime would lack any reserve of justificatory leverage that could redeem occasional arbitrariness. On the other hand, despite this affinity between the fourth type of indeterminacy and the other types, there is an important disanalogy. Because of that disanalogous feature, this fourth kind of indeterminacy is less troubling than the others.

As Leiter and Coleman point out, the indeterminacy arising from vagueness or incommensurability or evenly counterpoised considerations does not exclude the existence of factors that can be invoked in support of a decision (Coleman and Leiter 1995, 238–40). Although any judgment within such an area of indeterminacy will be arbitrary, it need not and should not be unreasoned. Notwithstanding that the considerations which substantiate the judgment are evenly or incommensurably offset by considerations that cut in the other direction, they are present and perhaps weighty. They are available to be invoked. Competently conscientious legal officials will indeed adduce those considerations in explanation of their decisions. There is plenty for them to say, even though there are equally or incommensurably pertinent things to be said on the other side of the matter.

In this respect, the indeterminacy to which Coleman and Leiter devote most of their attention is quite different from the other varieties of indeterminacy which we have examined. Most strikingly in contrast with it are the indeterminacy arising from legal norms' strong observational mind-dependence and the indeterminacy arising from legal norms' unintelligible opacity. Were legal norms strongly mind-dependent observationally, there would not genuinely be anything internal to those norms that would militate in favor of their being construed in any particular ways as opposed to others. There might typically be independent considerations such as moral principles that would dictate in favor of certain interpretations and against others, but the legal norms themselves would not yield or constitute any grounds for selecting among interpretations. Because the contents of those norms would *ex hypothesi* be entirely derivative of people's perceptions of them, they could never genuinely constrain or influence those perceptions. To invoke a legal norm in support of some way of construing it would be to engage in a misconceivedly circular enterprise. Such a sorry situation is plainly more disconcerting than the situations of indeterminacy envisaged by Coleman and Leiter. In the contexts which they envisage, the indeterminacy is not due to the radically subjective hollowness of legal norms. Rather, in each such context, it is due to the existence of counterbalanced considerations that tell respectively for and against the applicability of some legal norm to some set of facts. The content of the legal norm at issue is hardly vacuous; instead of being misconceivedly circular, an invocation of the formulation of that norm is an essential part of any argument for deeming the norm applicable or inapplicable to the specified set of facts. In short, in the situations of indeterminacy contemplated by Coleman and Leiter, justificatory argumentation focused on the contents of legal norms is entirely apposite even though no conclusive justifications are available. In a world marked by the strong observational mind-dependence of legal norms, contrariwise, justificatory argumentation focused on the contents of those norms would be deluded or fraudulent. In an important respect, then, the indeterminacy discussed by Leiter and Coleman is less problematic than the indeterminacy entailed by the aforementioned mind-dependence. We should therefore not be surprised by their relaxed attitude toward the prospect of indeterminacy (though, again, such an attitude would be unwarranted if it were not for the fact that the indeterminacy is quite rare).

A similar contrast can be drawn in connection with the indeterminacy that stems from the impenetrable obscurity of legal norms. Whereas reasoned disputation focused on the contents of legal norms is genuinely possible when indeterminacy results from vagueness or incommensurability or equipollently countervailing justifications, it is not similarly possible when indeterminacy results from the incomprehensible opacity of legal norms. If the formulations of those norms are meaningless gobbledygook (even in the eyes of legal experts), then efforts to justify adjudicative or administrative decisions by reference to the contents of those norms are either mendacious or naively misguided. Given that those contents are irretrievably nonexistent, invocations of them will not genuinely go the slightest way toward explaining any decisions. Indeterminacy of this kind, then, is considerably more troublesome than the type of indeterminacy on which Coleman and Leiter concentrate. We should also note that, whereas some indeterminacy of the latter type is inevitable, indeterminacy due to the unintelligibility of formulations of legal norms is perfectly avoidable. Articulating such norms in reasonably comprehensible terms – terms comprehensible to lawyers and other legal experts, at any rate – is not such a formidably difficult feat as to lie beyond the wit of legal officials.

Like the indeterminacy due to the unintelligibility of legal norms, the indeterminacy due to contradictions in the authoritative materials of a legal system is avoidable. Likewise, it too is more nettlesome than the indeterminacy pondered by Leiter and Coleman. When a choice has to be made between two contradictory legal norms, an invocation of either norm in itself will not do anything to vindicate the neglect of the other norm. Any such choice will therefore have to be based entirely on extralegal factors. The situation is quite different from that which obtains when the applicability of an ordinary (noncontradictory) law to some set of facts is in dispute. In the latter situation, a disputant can pertinently appeal to both the wording and the purpose of the legal norm in question.

Even though there may be equally or incommensurably powerful considerations on the other side of the controversy, a disputant who germanely appeals to the formulation and purpose of the norm will be adverting to factors that genuinely tell in favor of his or her interpretation. By contrast, when two laws are in contradiction, an invocation of the wording and purpose of either law will not per se contribute to explaining why the other law (with its own wording and purpose) is being set aside. A choice between the two may be straightforward on moral grounds or other extralegal grounds, but there will be no legal basis for selecting one law over the other. When somebody argues for the applicability or inapplicability of some ordinary law to a set of circumstances, and when he points to features of the specified law that cut in one direction or the other, he is adducing legal factors that genuinely count in favor of his position. No such opportunities for adducing strictly legal factors – factors of applicability and relevance – are present when somebody is confronted with two contradictory laws. The relevance of either of those laws to any set of facts is as great or as meager as the relevance of the other; each of them bears on those facts to precisely the same extent as the other, even though the conclusions to which they point are diametrically opposed. For example, if a law that forbids Joe to walk his dog in the park will have a manifest bearing on some instance of his conduct, then so too will a law that permits Joe to walk his dog in the park. Hence, when a legal official has to explain a choice between implementing one of those laws and implementing the other, he will not get anywhere by showing that one or the other of them is plainly applicable to some specified set of facts. If either of them is plainly applicable, then both of them are. (Likewise, if either of them is plainly inapplicable, then both of them are.) Reasoned disputation concerning the selection of one contradictory law over another will have to eschew legal considerations of relevance or applicability, and will have to concentrate instead on extralegal matters such as the moral merits of the two laws. In this respect, the indeterminacy that ensues from contradictions in a legal system's normative matrix is more vexing than the indeterminacy that ensues from vagueness or from incommensurability or from evenly balanced arrays of competing considerations. Although any outcome reached in the presence of the less vexing indeterminacy is ultimately arbitrary, it lends itself to being advocated and controverted through legal argumentation. No such argumentation is apt in the presence of indeterminacy owing to contradictions.

In sum, Coleman's and Leiter's reassuring remarks about indeterminacy are not in tension with my more gloomy remarks. Crucially, their remarks – unlike mine – pertain to indeterminacy as a marginal phenomenon rather than as something that permeates the norms and workings of a system of governance. What would be devastating on a sweeping scale is not nearly so harmful on a minor scale. Moreover, the indeterminacy on which Coleman and Leiter train their attention is less debilitating than the kinds of indeterminacy on which my own analyses in this chapter have chiefly focused. Thus, when the dissimilarities between their discussion and mine are carefully noted, the compatibility between our respective pronouncements on indeterminacy becomes apparent.

3.7.2. *Waldron on Disagreement and Determinacy*

We should now turn to the powerful line of reasoning that lies behind Waldron's opposition to the Authoritativeness Doctrine. His arguments concentrate largely on the objectivity of morality rather than on the objectivity of law, but Waldron himself maintains that moral standards sometimes serve as legal norms (Waldron 1992, 160). Although that claim about moral standards would be challenged by some legal positivists – known as "Exclusive Legal Positivists" – I join most other theorists in accepting it (Kramer 2004a, 17–140). Furthermore, even the Exclusive Legal Positivists allow that moral judgments are sometimes prominently necessary in the adjudicative and administrative activities of legal officials. Still more important, Waldron's arguments can be extended to all legal norms by somebody who is so inclined. Hence, if his arguments were sound and were at odds with my own worries about indeterminacy, they would indicate that those worries should be rethought.

A central theme in much of Waldron's work is the salience of disagreement in political and legal decision-making. His emphasis on that theme informs his approach to the question whether the objectivity of morality (or law) makes any difference to the moral authority of the decisions that are reached by legal officials on controversial matters. Waldron frames most of his discussion with reference to objectivity qua mind-independence, and therefore he can rightly be classified as a foe of the Authoritativeness Doctrine. Nonetheless, he helps to reveal that any worthwhile version of that doctrine will really be concerned with objectivity qua determinate correctness. For him, the issue of the moral authority of legal officials' decisions on contentious matters is an issue relating to the arbitrariness of such decisions. In other words, the question which he is primarily addressing is whether the presence of determinately correct answers to difficult legal problems will bear on the moral legitimacy and authoritativeness of legal officials' endeavors to deal with those problems. His response to that question is resoundingly negative. He submits that, once we take due account of disagreements about the aforementioned legal problems among officials and among citizens – that is, once we take due account of the scantiness of transindividual discernibility in the juridical domain – we should recognize that the existence of determinately correct solutions to those problems is no safeguard against arbitrariness. Regardless of how perceptive and well-intentioned the officials in a legal regime may be, there is something profoundly arbitrary in the fact that their views on highly controversial matters prevail over other people's views. Legal officials do not enjoy any privileged epistemic access to determinately correct resolutions of those matters, even if there are such resolutions. At any rate, they certainly do not enjoy any special epistemic access that can be demonstrated as such to the satisfaction of all or most of their compatriots. Why, then, should these unelected officials have a decisive say in shaping a society's efforts to come to grips with vexed issues that affect people's vital interests? Such is the challenge which Waldron mounts. Because his challenge can rely solely on the epistemic limitations of legal officials (and other people), he does not need to impugn the notion that there are determinately correct answers to the knotty legal questions that face judges and administrators. Whether or not there are such answers, the judges and administrators will be on dubious ground when they stand ready to wield the coercive mechanisms of governmental institutions to enforce their own beliefs about those answers.

Waldron, in short, takes the view that the presence or absence of indeterminacy in the law does not affect the moral authority of legal institutions and legal decision-making. At least upon initial inspection, then, his view is starkly contrary to my own. Before we probe that evident inconsistency more closely, we should consider why his arguments are best construed as being focused on indeterminacy. After all, as has been stated, Waldron himself talks mostly about mind-independence and transindividual discernibility. Nevertheless, for three reasons, his arguments are best understood along the lines suggested above.

In the first place, as we have seen, the strong observational mind-dependence of legal norms would consist in their radical subjectivity and their consequent indeterminacy. Until each person has settled what the content of any particular legal norm is, that norm would have no content (for that person). Hence, given that Waldron denies the practical importance of questions about observational mind-independence, he is in effect denying the practical importance of questions about the presence of the indeterminacy just mentioned. Yet, if he is in effect denying the practical importance of those questions, he is also in effect denying the practical importance of questions about the presence of the other kinds of indeterminacy that have been explored in this chapter. His arguments about the epistemic limitations of legal officials would be no less pertinent in application to situations that might be marked by those other kinds of indeterminacy. For example, whether or not the countervailing considerations in a difficult case are arrayed in such a way as to make one outcome uniquely correct, people will almost certainly disagree intractably in their views of how the case should be handled. As has been stressed in my earlier chapters, the determinate correctness of this or that outcome does not entail its demonstrable correctness. Thus, regardless of the type of indeterminacy that might be involved, its presence or absence in any contentious case will not affect the very high likelihood of significant divergences of opinion among people. If those divergences of opinion themselves render doubtful the legitimacy and authority of the decision-making role of legal officials in hard cases, that corrosive effect will not be averted through the existence of determinately correct solutions. Waldron's line of argument accordingly leads to the conclusion that neither the sway nor the absence of indeterminacy in any of those hard cases will bear at all on the moral character of the workings of legal institutions.

Second, Waldron himself in the closing section of his essay synopsizes his reasoning with explicit reference to determinate correctness. He claims that, if the moral principles in legal decision-making are mind-independent, "then there is a right answer to whatever questions of principle the judge puts to herself. We are apt to think of this as some sort of comfort: the right answer is there, so the judge is constrained after all." He then seeks to puncture the sense of comfort which he has evoked:

> That there is a right answer . . . certainly means that a judge is not making a fool of herself when she goes out ponderously in search of it. But its existence doesn't drive her to pursue it, let alone determine that she will reach it. Different judges will reach different results even when they all take themselves to be pursuing the right answer, and nothing about the ontology of the right answer gives any of them a reason for thinking her own view is any more correct than any other. (Waldron 1992, 183–84)

Third, Waldron in fact goes too far in implying that the observational mind-independence of legal norms will ensure the existence of a uniquely correct answer to every pivotal legal question. On the contrary, if legal norms are observationally mind-independent, and if there are occasional questions about the contents or implications or existence of legal norms to which there are no determinately correct answers – as Chapter 1 has argued – then the absence of a determinately correct answer to each of those infrequent questions is a mind-independent fact.[3] Hence, if, as the closing portion of his essay tends to indicate, Waldron is really concerned to establish that the presence or absence of a determinately correct answer to any controversial legal question is of no practical importance, then he should be concentrating on that matter rather than on the matter of mind-independence. To concentrate on the latter matter is to focus on a dimension of objectivity that is sometimes associated with indeterminacy. Consequently, a theorist who wants to make a point about the practical unimportance of determinacy should not think that that issue can be taken as interchangeable with the issue of the practical unimportance of mind-independence.

Let us now return to the incompatibility between Waldron's position and my own. This chapter has highlighted the destructive effects of indeterminacy on law's moral authority, whereas Waldron has argued that the

---

[3] For technical reasons that lie beyond the scope of this book, an acknowledgment of occasional indeterminacy is not easily squared with an embrace of the minimalist account of truth that has been championed in my first chapter. However, the complicated task of reconciling the two is feasible. For an admirably lucid discussion of the problem and a fine effort to resolve it, see Holton 2000. (I endorse Holton's solution in most respects, though not in a few matters of detail.)

presence of indeterminacy is of no practical importance. To see how these antithetical positions are partly reconcilable – though only superficially so – we should note that Waldron trains his attention on controversial cases in which legal officials differ fiercely among themselves and with many citizens. Only because of these vigorous disagreements does the moral authority of the officials' decisions come into doubt. Yet the legal questions that do elicit widespread and intense controversy are only a very small proportion of the questions addressed by any functional legal system. As has been remarked at several junctures in this book, the ordinary workings of a legal system are routine. Countless decisions by adjudicative and administrative officials are utterly uncontroversial and are therefore largely unnoticed by legal scholars who quite naturally prefer to study more exciting occurrences. Deeply contentious decisions – most of which attract far more interest from academics and journalists – are much rarer. Some of them are of great importance, but they are hardly representative of a legal regime's day-to-day operations. They are unusual rather than typical. Precisely for this reason, the presence of genuine indeterminacy in some of those contentious cases does not impair the moral authority of the legal system in which they arise. As has been argued already in this chapter, indeterminacy in a narrow range of cases is only minimally problematic for the functionality and moral stature of a legal regime. That moral stature does not hinge on whether an especially difficult case is marked by indeterminacy or merely by uncertainty.

We may thus seem to have arrived at the same result as Waldron. Like him, my discussion here has just maintained that the presence or absence of any determinately correct answer(s) to the pivotal question(s) in a vexingly controversial case does not affect the moral authority of the regime that handles the case. That presence or absence does not make a practical difference. However, the superficial resemblance between my conclusion and Waldron's pronouncements is overshadowed by a major dissimilarity between them. According to Waldron, the practical unimportance of indeterminacy in heatedly contested cases is attributable to the fact that the role of legal officials in deciding such cases is morally dubious irrespective of the existence or inexistence of determinately correct answers to the questions raised therein. In my discussions, the practical unimportance of indeterminacy in some heatedly contested cases is attributable to the fact that such cases are truly exceptional and are hence not a danger to the moral authority of a benign legal system's operations. What Waldron aims to impugn, I aim to vindicate.

Furthermore, my whole emphasis is fundamentally different from Waldron's. His principal concern is with the absence of transindividual discernibility and with the consequent shakiness of any basis for non-democratic means of resolving disagreements. Because Waldron is pre-occupied with controversy, he addresses himself only to cases in which the matters to be decided are hotly disputed. He does not express any view about cases that are routine – the vast majority of the cases in any functional legal system. Specifically, he does not state whether the presence of indeterminacy in those uncontentiously humdrum cases would be problematic. However, the drift of his argument appears to indicate that he would not be troubled by such indeterminacy. If virtually everyone agrees on the answer to some legal question in a benign scheme of governance, then the illegitimacy of nondemocratic procedures for resolving that question will not become an issue; legal officials will not be imposing their favored solution in the face of widespread and intractable dissent. Thus, although Waldron does not himself raise the matter and therefore does not take an explicit stance on it, he seems to have no grounds for deeming the presence of indeterminacy in uncontroversial cases to be worrisome.

By contrast, my principal concerns have been twofold: the sustainability of law's function in guiding and coordinating human conduct, and the role of legal norms as justificatory bases for the decisions of legal officials. Although rampant indeterminacy due to the strong observational mind-dependence of legal norms could be consistent with the fulfillment of law's guiding function, it would be inconsistent with the role of legal norms as justificatory bases for decisions. (Rampant indeterminacy of any other type would usually be incompatible with law's guiding function and would always be incompatible with the role of legal norms as justificatory bases.) Hence, if legal norms were indeed strongly mind-dependent observationally, the moral authority of every legal regime would be undermined. Although citizens and officials might not be aware of the strong observational mind-dependence, and although they might accordingly treat the contents of legal norms as independent sources of direction and as binding grounds for decisions, their beliefs about those contents would be illusory. Justifications advanced by officials in support of their decisions within any legal system would in fact amount to ersatz justifications, however benevolent in substance the decisions and the system might be. Those putative justifications would not accurately reflect the status of the contents of the laws which they invoke. Consequently, if the workings of a benign legal regime are to consist in genuine interpretations and justifications rather than in collective delusions, legal norms must be possessed of observational mind-independence. Such mind-independence is prerequisite to the moral authority of law.

In sum, whereas Waldron's line of argument supplies no reasons for thinking that pervasive indeterminacy is of any practical significance, my accounts of the effects of indeterminacy on law's moral authority have provided just such reasons. Of huge practical importance is the difference between highly cabined indeterminacy and ubiquitous indeterminacy. Whereas indeterminacy that occurs in a very small proportion of the circumstances confronting a legal system is compatible with the system's functionality and moral authority, rampant indeterminacy is not. Rampant indeterminacy is always fatal to a legal regime. It will usually be fatal to the directing function of such a regime, and it will always be fatal to the regime's justificatory role. Legal norms can hardly serve to justify decisions, if no determinate implications follow from those norms prior to each decision. Whether the wholesale lack of determinate implications is ascribable to the absence of any independent content in each such norm, or whether it is instead ascribable to contradictions or other factors, it is destructive of law's capacity to justify concrete outcomes. Since that capacity is a necessary (though insufficient) condition for the moral authority of any system of governance, pervasive indeterminacy is of the utmost practical importance. Like the other five dimensions of legal objectivity, objectivity qua determinate correctness is something without which neither law nor morally authoritative governance can exist.

3.8. Conclusion

Although the relationships between objectivity and the rule of law (and between objectivity and the Rule of Law) have been explored throughout this book, the current chapter has sought to enquire more deeply into a few of those relationships. We have concentrated especially on observational mind-independence, on determinate correctness, and – to a somewhat lesser extent – on transindividual discernibility. Of course, the chapter's focus on those dimensions of legal objectivity has not been meant to imply that the other dimensions thereof are less weighty or less deserving of investigation. On the contrary, the main reason for my paying less attention here to objectivity qua impartiality and objectivity qua uniform applicability is that they have been probed quite extensively in each of the preceding chapters.

As for semantic objectivity – objectivity qua truth-aptitude – the paramount reason for my neglect of it here is that Chapter 1's minimalist account of truth has effectively elided the distinction between the determinate correctness and the truth of meaningful declarative answers to legal questions. On the one hand, determinate correctness and truth are not equivalent. Determinacy is an ontological property that pertains to the settledness of legal facts, whereas the evaluability of legal statements as true or false is a semantic property that pertains to the relationships between those statements and legal facts. On the other hand, my minimalist accounts of truth and facts (and my deflationary version of the correspondence theory of truth) allow us to say that, if any meaningful declarative legal statement is determinately correct, it is true. Only if no legal statements were ever meaningful and declarative would the transition from determinate correctness to truth be untenable. However, the notion that no legal statements are ever meaningful and declarative is preposterous; that notion would be firmly rejected even by most theorists who contend that the principal role of such statements is to express certain prescriptive attitudes. Thus, with regard to the countless legal statements that are indeed meaningful and declarative, their determinate correctness amounts to their truth, and their determinate incorrectness amounts to their falsity. Accordingly, this chapter's focus on determinacy has implicitly also been a focus on the conditions under which legal statements can be true or false.

Taken together with the previous portions of this book, then, the present chapter has endeavored to show that every dimension of legal objectivity is indispensable for the rule of law and the Rule of Law. Indeed, each of the Fullerian principles of legality is inextricably bound up with one or more of the dimensions of legal objectivity. For instance, several of the principles – promulgation, prospectivity, perspicuity, noncontradictoriness, constancy – are manifestly promotive of the transindividual discernibility of legal requirements. Of course, at least one type of legal objectivity (namely, the strong observational mind-independence of legal norms) obtains willy-nilly in a blanket fashion whenever a legal regime exists, whereas other types (such as the transindividual discernibility of legal norms) are scalar properties that obtain to varying degrees across legal regimes. That difference obviously bears on the extent to which the attainment of a given dimension of legal objectivity is a matter of deliberately focused striving, but it does not bear on the question whether each such dimension is essential for the rule of law and the Rule of Law. To that latter question, the answer is unequivocally affirmative. Objectivity, in each of the six chief varieties expounded throughout this book, is integral to every system of legal governance.

Bibliographic Notes

I here refer readers to some of the countless important works on objectivity or the rule of law that have not hitherto been cited in this book. Although several of the essays in Brian Leiter (ed.), *Objectivity in Law and Morals* (Cambridge: Cambridge University Press, 2001) have indeed been cited already, the volume as a whole should be mentioned here as an admirably stimulating point of departure for anyone who wants to explore further the complexities of legal objectivity. Also constituting a fine point of departure is Brian Leiter, "Law and Objectivity," in Jules Coleman and Scott Shapiro (eds.), *Oxford Handbook of Jurisprudence & Philosophy of Law* (Oxford: Oxford University Press, 2002), 969–89. My own views differ significantly from Leiter's on a number of points, but his limpid and vigorous prose is especially helpful for people who are quite new to the subject. Much the same can be said about Jeremy Waldron, "On the Objectivity of Morals," 80 *California Law Review* 1361 (1992). Likewise commendably clear is David Brink, "Legal Theory, Legal Interpretation, and Judicial Review," 17 *Philosophy and Public Affairs* 105 (1988). Less readable, but worthy of perusal, is Nicos Stavropoulos, *Objectivity in Law* (Oxford: Oxford University Press, 1996).

As is mentioned near the outset of Chapter 1, several aspects of objectivity have been explored more searchingly in moral philosophy than in legal philosophy. Relevant works are far too numerous to be listed exhaustively. A very good collection of essays, some of which have been cited in this book, is Ted Honderich (ed.), *Morality and Objectivity* (London: Routledge & Kegan Paul, 1985). A few other important collections are David Copp and David Zimmerman (eds.), *Morality, Reason, and Truth* (Totowa, NJ: Rowman & Allanheld, 1985); Geoffrey Sayre-McCord (ed.), *Essays in Moral Realism* (Ithaca, NY: Cornell University Press, 1988); Walter Sinnott-Armstrong and Mark Timmons (eds.), *Moral Knowledge?* (Oxford: Oxford University Press, 1996); and Ellen Frankel Paul, Fred Miller, and Jeffrey Paul (eds.), *Moral Knowledge* (Cambridge: Cambridge University Press, 2001). For an interesting and highly lucid exchange, see Gilbert Harman and Judith Jarvis Thomson, *Moral Relativism and Moral Objectivity* (Oxford: Blackwell, 1996). Much of the work of Thomas Nagel on objectivity is particularly insightful and piquant. See, for example, his *The View from Nowhere* (Oxford: Oxford University Press, 1986).

Among the innumerable perceptive studies of the rule of law or the Rule of Law that have not been cited heretofore in this book are T. R. S. Allan, *Constitutional Justice: A Liberal Theory of the Rule of Law* (Oxford: Oxford University Press, 2001); John Finnis, *Natural Law and Natural Rights* (Oxford: Clarendon Press, 1980), 260–96; F. A. Hayek, *The Constitution of Liberty* (Chicago: University of Chicago Press, 1960); Mark Murphy, *Natural Law in Jurisprudence and Politics* (Cambridge: Cambridge University Press, 2006); John Rawls, *A Theory of Justice* (Oxford: Oxford University Press, 1999) (rev. ed.), 206–13; and Joseph Raz, "The Rule of Law and Its Virtue," in *The Authority of Law* (Oxford: Clarendon Press, 1979), 210–29. A few of the many important collections of essays on the topic are Richard Bellamy (ed.), *The Rule of Law and the Separation of Powers* (Aldershot: Ashgate Publishing, 2005); David Dyzenhaus (ed.), *Recrafting the Rule of Law* (Oxford: Hart Publishing, 1999); Jose Maria Maravall and Adam Przeworski (eds.), *Democracy and the Rule of Law* (Cambridge: Cambridge University Press, 2003); and Ian Shapiro (ed.), *The Rule of Law* (New York: NYU Press, 1994).

From time to time in this book, I have looked askance at the Critical Legal Studies movement. For some more detailed rejoinders to the Critical Legal Scholars, see Andrew Altman, *Critical Legal Studies: A Liberal Critique* (Princeton:

Princeton University Press, 1990); John Finnis, "On 'The Critical Legal Studies Movement,'" 30 *American Journal of Jurisprudence* 21 (1985); Kenneth Kress, "Legal Indeterminacy," 77 *California Law Review* 283 (1989); and Lawrence Solum, "On the Indeterminacy Crisis: Critiquing Critical Dogma," 54 *University of Chicago Law Review* 462 (1987).

References

Bix, Brian. 2005. "Cautions and Caveats for the Application of Wittgenstein to Legal Theory." In Joseph Keim Campbell, Michael O'Rourke, and David Shier (eds.), *Law and Social Justice* (Cambridge, MA: MIT Press), 217–28.

Blackburn, Simon. 1993. *Essays in Quasi-Realism*. Oxford: Oxford University Press.

Coleman, Jules. 1995. "Truth and Objectivity in Law." 1 *Legal Theory* 33–68.

Coleman, Jules, and Leiter, Brian. 1995. "Determinacy, Objectivity, and Authority." In Andrei Marmor (ed.), *Law and Interpretation* (Oxford: Clarendon Press), 203–78.

Craig, Paul. 1997. "Formal and Substantive Conceptions of the Rule of Law: An Analytical Framework." *Public Law* 467–87.

Duxbury, Neil. 1999. *Random Justice*. Oxford: Oxford University Press.

Dworkin, Ronald. 1965. "Philosophy, Morality and Law – Observations Prompted by Professor Fuller's Novel Claim." 113 *University of Pennsylvania Law Review* 668–90.

Dworkin, Ronald. 1977. "No Right Answer?" In Peter Hacker and Joseph Raz (eds.), *Law, Morality, and Society* (Oxford: Clarendon Press), 58–84.

Dworkin, Ronald. 1978. *Taking Rights Seriously*. Cambridge, MA: Harvard University Press.

Dworkin, Ronald. 1985. *A Matter of Principle.* Cambridge, MA: Harvard University Press.

Dworkin, Ronald. 1986. *Law's Empire.* London: Fontana Press.

Dworkin, Ronald. 1991. "On Gaps in the Law." In Paul Amselek and Neil Mac-Cormick (eds.), *Controversies about Law's Ontology* (Edinburgh: Edinburgh University Press).

Dworkin, Ronald. 1996. "Objectivity and Truth: You'd Better Believe It." 25 *Philosophy and Public Affairs* 87–139.

Endicott, Timothy. 2000. *Vagueness in Law.* Oxford: Oxford University Press.

Fine, Kit. 2001. "The Question of Realism." 1 *Philosophers' Imprint* 1–30.

Freeman, Michael. 2001. *Lloyd's Introduction to Jurisprudence.* London: Sweet & Maxwell.

Fuller, Lon. 1969. *The Morality of Law.* New Haven, CT: Yale University Press. Revised edition.

Green, Michael. 2003. "Dworkin's Fallacy, or What the Philosophy of Language Can't Teach Us about the Law." 89 *Virginia Law Review* 1897–1952.

Greenawalt, Kent. 1992. *Law and Objectivity.* New York: Oxford University Press.

Hare, R. M. 1963. *Freedom and Reason.* Oxford: Oxford University Press.

Hare, R. M. 1981. *Moral Thinking.* Oxford: Clarendon Press.

Hare, R. M. 1989. "Principles." In *Essays in Ethical Theory* (Oxford: Oxford University Press), 49–65.

Harris, J. W. 1997. *Legal Philosophies.* London: Butterworths. Second edition.

Hart, H. L. A. 1961. *The Concept of Law.* Oxford: Clarendon Press.

Hart, H. L. A. 1983. "Lon L. Fuller, *The Morality of Law.*" In *Essays in Jurisprudence and Philosophy* (Oxford: Clarendon Press), 343–64.

Hills, Alison. 2004. "Is Ethics Rationally Required?" 47 *Inquiry* 1–19.

Holton, Richard. 2000. "Minimalism and Truth-Value Gaps." 97 *Philosophical Studies* 137–68.

Horwich, Paul. 1998. *Truth.* Oxford: Oxford University Press. Second edition.

Kramer, Matthew. 1998. "Rights without Trimmings." In Matthew H. Kramer, N. E. Simmonds, and Hillel Steiner, *A Debate over Rights* (Oxford: Oxford University Press), 7–111.

Kramer, Matthew. 1999a. *In Defense of Legal Positivism.* Oxford: Oxford University Press.

Kramer, Matthew. 1999b. *In the Realm of Legal and Moral Philosophy.* Basingstoke: Macmillan Press.

Kramer, Matthew. 2001. "Getting Rights Right." In Matthew H. Kramer (ed.), *Rights, Wrongs, and Responsibilities* (Basingstoke: Palgrave Macmillan), 28–95.

Kramer, Matthew. 2004a. *Where Law and Morality Meet.* Oxford: Oxford University Press.

Kramer, Matthew. 2004b. "The Big Bad Wolf: Legal Positivism and Its Detractors." 49 *American Journal of Jurisprudence* 1–10.

Kramer, Matthew. 2005. "Moral Rights and the Limits of the Ought-Implies-Can Principle: Why Impeccable Precautions Are No Excuse." 48 *Inquiry* 307–55.

Landers, Scott. 1990. "Wittgenstein, Realism, and CLS: Undermining Rule Skepticism." 9 *Law and Philosophy* 177–203.

Leiter, Brian. 2001. "Introduction." In Brian Leiter (ed.), *Objectivity in Law and Morals* (Cambridge: Cambridge University Press, 2001), 1–11.

Locke, John. 1975 [1689]. *An Essay Concerning Human Understanding.* Oxford: Clarendon Press. Edited by Peter Nidditch.

Lucy, William. 2005. "The Possibility of Impartiality." 25 *Oxford Journal of Legal Studies* 3–31.

Madison, James. 1961 [1788]. "Federalist Paper No. 10." In Alexander Hamilton, James Madison, and John Jay, *The Federalist Papers* (New York: New American Library), 77–84. Edited by Clinton Rossiter.

Marmor, Andrei. 2001. *Positive Law and Objective Values.* Oxford: Oxford University Press.

McDowell, John. 1985. "Values and Secondary Qualities." In Ted Honderich (ed.), *Objectivity and Morality* (London: Routledge & Kegan Paul), 110–29.

Moore, Michael. 1982. "Moral Reality." 1982 *Wisconsin Law Review* 1061–1156.

Moore, Michael. 1992. "Moral Reality Revisited." 90 *Michigan Law Review* 2424–2533.

Nozick, Robert. 2001. *Invariances: The Structure of the Objective World.* Cambridge, MA: Harvard University Press.

Paske, Gerald. 1989. "Rationality, Reasonableness, and Morality." 10 *Logos: Philosophic Issues in Christian Perspective* 73–88.

Patterson, Dennis. 2006. "Wittgenstein on Understanding and Interpretation." 29 *Philosophical Investigations* 129–39.

Pettit, Philip. 2001. "Embracing Objectivity in Ethics." In Brian Leiter (ed.), *Objectivity in Law and Morals* (Cambridge: Cambridge University Press), 234–86.

Postema, Gerald. 2001. "Objectivity Fit for Law." In Brian Leiter (ed.), *Objectivity in Law and Morals* (Cambridge: Cambridge University Press), 99–143.

Raz, Joseph. 1996. "Intention in Interpretation." In Robert George (ed.), *The Autonomy of Law* (Oxford: Clarendon Press), 249–86.

Raz, Joseph. 2001. "Notes on Value and Objectivity." In Brian Leiter (ed.), *Objectivity in Law and Morals* (Cambridge: Cambridge University Press), 193–233.

Reiff, Mark. 2005. *Punishment, Compensation, and Law: A Theory of Enforceability* (Cambridge: Cambridge University Press).

Rosati, Connie. 2004. "Some Puzzles about the Objectivity of Law." 23 *Law and Philosophy* 273–323.

Sainsbury, R. M. 1988. *Paradoxes*. Cambridge: Cambridge University Press.

Schauer, Frederick. 1991. *Playing by the Rules*. Oxford: Oxford University Press.

Simmonds, N. E. 2004. "Straightforwardly False: The Collapse of Kramer's Positivism." 63 *Cambridge Law Journal* 98–131.

Sosa, David. 2001. "Pathetic Ethics." In Brian Leiter (ed.), *Objectivity in Law and Morals* (Cambridge: Cambridge University Press), 287–329.

Stavropoulos, Nicos. 2005. "Objectivity." In Martin Golding and William Edmundson (eds.), *The Blackwell Guide to the Philosophy of Law and Legal Theory* (Oxford: Blackwell), 315–23.

Stroud, Barry. 1977. *Hume*. London: Routledge & Kegan Paul.

Summers, Robert. 1993. "A Formal Theory of the Rule of Law." 6 *Ratio Juris* 127–42.

Svavarsdóttir, Sigrún. 2001. "Objective Values: Does Metaethics Rest on a Mistake?" In Brian Leiter (ed.), *Objectivity in Law and Morals* (Cambridge: Cambridge University Press, 2001), 144–93.

Tamanaha, Brian. 2004. *On the Rule of Law*. Cambridge: Cambridge University Press.

Waldron, Jeremy. 1992. "The Irrelevance of Moral Objectivity." In Robert George (ed.), *Natural Law Theory* (Oxford: Clarendon Press), 158–87.

Wiggins, David. 1998. *Values, Needs, Truth*. Oxford: Oxford University Press. Third edition.

Williams, Bernard. 1985. "Ethics and the Fabric of the World." In Ted Honderich (ed.), *Morality and Objectivity* (London: Routledge & Kegan Paul), 203–14.

Williams, Bernard. 2001. "From Freedom to Liberty: The Construction of a Political Value." 30 *Philosophy and Public Affairs* 3–26.

Williams, Glanville. 1956. "The Concept of Legal Liberty." 56 *Columbia Law Review* 1129–50.

Index